Praise for
RAZOR WIRE WILDERNESS

"That was before..." Before things go badly for Krystal Riordan, an inmate at a Correctional Facility in N.J., and for Lucy, her prison friend, and for Stephanie, the author herself. Before and after are different in this powerful, riveting, wise, detailed, and heartbreaking book. The past is never distant and affects every decision in this compassionate, well-paced book where the three women's lives, as well as the juxtaposition of several others, are intertwined. Dickinson's writing is lyrical and emotionally charged. Who is the victim and who is the perpetrator? Is there a wrong time and place? Or are events the cumulation of history or fate? This is a visceral book of wounds and choices. As the author says, "We cannot fully abandon our former selves, but we can go beyond them."

—**Laurie Blauner**, author of *The Solace of Monsters* and *I Was One of My Memories* (forthcoming from *PANK*)

"Stephanie Dickinson confronts readers with the harrowing existence of inmates locked in the literal razor wire confinement of a women's prison—the deprivations, the indignities, the violence. But beyond that reality, she challenges readers with the moral razor wire we face when measuring ourselves against those convicted of violent crimes. Are we different kinds of people or just fortunate to have been able to lead different kinds of lives? It's not an easy distinction."

—**Walter Cummins**, author of *Local Music*

"This raw, real, and captivating book, in all its grit and glory, is a refreshing read. What could have become a distasteful rehashing of prison life is made softer by Stephanie Dickinson's always luxurious prose. Hold your breath and dig in. You'll come away braver and wiser after reading this book of hope."

—**Chila Woychik**, author of *Singing the Land: A Rural Chronology*

Part memoir, part true crime, and part meditation on the resilience of the human spirit, *Razor Wire Wilderness* is penned with precision and grace. Due to Stephanie Dickinson's unique ability to identify and magnify the personal details that are often unknowingly or willingly overlooked, this book transforms the way we see not only the complexities of a tragic crime but also the way violence becomes embedded in our lives and collective social systems. At its core, this is a story about friendship, but it is also about survival, what happens to us, and what we get to decide during our brief existence. It is about the way we live when we are caged, be that literally or figuratively, and the beckoning light of genuine human connection."

—**Jen Knox**, author of *After the Gazebo* and *Resolutions: A Family in Stories*

"Despite the haunting beauty of Dickinson's language, naked is possibly the best way to describe her prose. Naked emotion. Naked observation. The warts and the pimples of living presented with the same intensity and honesty as the finely curved hips and thick auburn hair that give life its pleasure. No one writes like Stephanie Dickinson, except maybe God."

—**Alice Jurish**

"In the '*Razor Wire Wilderness*' of Stephanie Dickinson's exquisitely lyrical portrayal of female incarceration — intimately researched by becoming pen pals with many inmates over many years — she reveals her own dark attraction and identification with Krystal Riordan. ... It is not, 'There but for the grace of God go I,' but because of Dickinson's grace and amazing god-given talent that she is able to take us into the heart, mind, memory and imagination of Krystal, passive accomplice to a nightmarish crime. In prison where there is no weather, Dickinson manages to encompass the great Outside; her rendering of Maximum Compound is the opposite of a claustrophobic read. Like Hamlet, bound in a nutshell, Dickinson is king of Infinite space, Infinite empathy, and the Infinite beauty of bad dreams."

—**Jill Hoffman**, *Mudfish* editor and author of "*Black Diaries*," "*The Gates of Pearl*," and "*Jilted*"

"Stephanie Dickinson writes with the beauty of a wounded angel. The protagonists in these eleven stories are achingly real, so natural that they craft their own lives. Most, but not all, are women; most, but not all, are young. Each has met humanity's dark underbelly—through war, predation, neglect, the crueler vagaries of family—and felt the jagged elbows of alienation. And yet, like the 'Flashlight Girls Run' of the title, they power on with a particular awkward grace that makes these stories hard to put down, and impossible to forget. Gorgeous, heartbreaking, empowering stuff!"

—**Susan O'Neill**, on *"Flashlight Girls Run"*
author of *"Don't Mean Nothing: Short Stories of Vietnam"*

Books by Stephanie Dickinson

Blue Swan, Black Swan: The Trakl Diaries

Girl Behind the Door

Port Authority Orchids

Love Highway

Heat: An Interview with Jean Seberg

Big-Headed Anna Imagines Herself

Road of Five Churches: Stories

Flashlight Girls Run

Corn Goddess

Half Girl

RAZOR WIRE
WILDERNESS

LEGAL NOTE

This work is not authorized or approved by the New Jersey Department of Corrections or any other law enforcement organization. The views and positions expressed by the author do not reflect the views or positions of anyone other than the author. The author's descriptions of any legal proceedings, circumstances and events relating to crimes charged are drawn solely from the court record, other publicly available information, and her own research.

RAZOR WIRE WILDERNESS

by

Stephanie Dickinson

Kallisto Gaia Press

for Jill

In the Company of Bad Girls

I'm sorry to ask but if possible can you send me a little money?
We order on Sunday. And after this Commissary we don't order
for 3 weeks.
I need to stock up on my hygiene products.
—Krystal Riordan, Inmate #661387

Our first communication is a letter, and we write for months. Krystal does not ask for money, and then she does.

I am glad when she asks. I am a debtor and I owe her. I've modeled a fictional character on some part of her and I've begun writing about her life in prison. She is my material. There is something terrifyingly transactional in that. So I'm off to the post office to buy the first money order. In the two years before JPay opens digital money transfers, before email and Global Tel Link, her fellow inmates see little value in friendship between someone on the outside and someone on the inside without favors and money orders.

The ground rule is Do Not Judge Me. Krystal has been judged, ad infinitum, as an adopted child, an Élan student-resident, in court by the judge, by the victim's family and her own, by the general public, and by prison officers.

And yet there is always another presence haunting us both. Jennifer Moore.

Underlying my friendship with Krystal and my commitment to her are the dark woods where a murdered girl wanders. There is a hidden truth—an erasure on an old-time blackboard. Like holding paper up to the light, the paper that lies under the actual paper written upon. The pen's indentations become almost words, almost sentences, revelations where secrets expose themselves and the mystery of The Girl Who Watched is uncovered. I feared for my life. I was sure I would be next.

All these years and I have never directly asked. Why, when Jennifer was screaming, did you turn the sound of the TV up? Nor have I directly asked Why didn't you try to help Jennifer?

And who am I? Why have I committed myself to Krystal Riordan?

I am old enough to be Krystal's mother. I am a child of the farm. Foursquare religion. The girl whose widowed mother teaches junior high English. I am the youngest with two older brothers. The girl who still wanders the ditches and fields, all the while yearning for the crazy-rough side of colored lights. The girl who waits for the mail truck's coming at 11 a.m. then talks to herself through the long afternoon that lasts a century. I am on my own.

I am the 18-year-old girl leaping without looking, the girl who hitchhiked to North Carolina from Iowa, telling no one. I am the girl meeting Michael, a 19-year-old boy with long black hair, a boy who says our eyes match—their dark milk running through our fates. We are setting off to a Thanksgiving party. I know unluckiness, Jupiter aligning with Mars, a male perpetrator. That kind of willfulness and bad luck in unequal measures. I will always be Thanksgiving night, when the girl born the healthiest of my mother's three children is rebirthed, this time maimed. I am the girl who said goodbye to her left arm in a bathroom. Who doesn't know when she takes her last bath, eats her last meal, and brushes her teeth for the last time with two working arms. I am the hitchhiking girl who opened her legs to rapists and one-night stands. The girl who is forever and only the shot girl, girl with a paralyzed arm.

I am the girl who threw her life away on Thanksgiving Day, November 25, 1971. A forever mistake.

4

MUGSHOTS OF TIRAMISU AND RAZOR WIRE
EMCF   Clinton, New Jersey

New Jersey's most dangerous women can be found in a four-traffic-light town not reachable by public transportation. From Newark, take Interstate 78 to Clinton, turn left at the traffic light. Across from the WalMart Plaza lies the entrance to the Edna Mahan Correctional Facility. EMCF is a two-hour trip by car from Manhattan, but for those visitors without vehicles there's a prison bus that leaves from Midtown on Friday evening and arrives eight hours later. All must prepare to be searched and to stow their possessions in a locker before visiting an inmate. No water, no sodas, nothing but your flesh covered appropriately, i.e., no halter tops or bustiers.

Seen from the air, the prison appears like a wheel-shaped medieval city, its modular units the beige color of the inmates' uniforms surrounding the century-old Warden's Hall. Instead of a moat guarding the fortified walls, double strands of razor wire coil between watchtowers to isolate the beings inside. The violent offenders. Murderers and kidnappers. The crazy. EMCF's website lists notable inmates. Amy Rose Locane, the actress who starred in the first season of Melrose Place, served three years in Maximum Compound for vehicular homicide. She tops the list.

Inmate Krystal Riordan, known to true crime bloggers as the Jen-Slay Hooker, is not listed as a notable.

&

Maximum Compound revolves around the sun but the air is darker and more confined. Upon arrival prisoners are housed temporarily in the reception area, then divided according to the length of their sentence and the severity of their case. EMCF assigns those convicted of violent and more serious crimes to Maximum Compound where the day is rigidly structured with four headcounts a day. Those convicted of drug offenses, which carry shorter sentences, are assigned to Minimum Compound where rules are more relaxed.

Understand, these aren't the femme fatales and sex-selling dahlias, not the thieves and drug dealers, not the welfare cheats or DUI violators; these women are the violent offenders. They don't pull up in a Porsche; they're transported under armed guard. They're young, they're ghetto, white trash, a few are middle-aged college graduates, some will get their GED here and take college classes, others will become senior citizens, and some will die here. They'll arrive pregnant, psychotic, post-traumatically stressed; they'll deliver their baby here, or have a hysterectomy. They've got dreads, and natural blond locks, they're tattooed like a graphic novel and wearing the last address of their baby daddy inked on their wrist. Many of these women have killed or kidnapped an employer, neighbor, husband, child, or a stranger.

Maximum Compound women arrive encumbered with their crimes and the weight of their sentences. They arrive put-upon and willing to use anyone.

&

It's a rule-bound world, a world where dance competitions and making birthday chili and rice for your girlfriend co-exist with fight blood on the floor. Although time is filled with a job, a routine, a Mess Hall schedule, real time stales. It doesn't flow; it pools around you, goes stagnant. Each day is similar from the view of a locked world, a day hard and long to get through, and the years flying away. There are no hickories or maples or quaking aspen, no huge-eyed deer. No smell of burning pretzel dough. No strolling into a Starbucks for a coffee tall. No dressing to go out looking edible as tiramisu. The outside world stands still, remembered. The inmates in Maximum Compound number their absence from the outside in decades. Television and electronic tablets are their windows. Rules, rules. Yet life teems here—new inmates arrive, new friendships, new loves, and new hates.

I've been a friend to this prison planet, this Maximum

Compound where the most dangerous women in New Jersey live, the ones the media portray as topping the depravity index. Women like Krystal.

&

There are online galleries of the earliest nineteenth-century mugshots that portray women with their crimes scrawled across the bottom of the image. Theft of shoes, bed sheets, onions, poultry. The stench of poverty. Jane Farrell, a cleft-chinned 12-year-old girl, her dark eyes unfathomable, her frayed jacket and skirt thin as potato sacks, arrested for stealing two boots and sentenced to ten days' hard labor. Ann Sterling filched a gold watch, 17-year-old Isabella was caught thieving a waistcoat, and 60-year-old Alize carried off a chicken. Rebecca Feinberg's mugshot is labeled A Jewish Prostitute, her specialty: "Whilst the man is in bed, the bullies rifle through his clothes."

I lose myself in the women, seated with their hands flat against the abdomen, fingers splayed. Hands examined for missing fingers. Life was rawer then—women boiled soaps from bones and lye; they butchered and chopped—fingers and thumbs lost to the ax, the knife, the grist stone. Women sentenced to hard labor for skinning or stealing the clothes off the back of a child, for ringing the change or shortchanging customers.

There is Krystal's EMCF mugshot, the softest among the many bruised and battered faces. A schoolgirl has wandered into an alternate universe, a demonic one, an American beauty in an American nightmare. Krystal is a beauty; her height 5'9", her skin, the plush pale of an eighteenth-century baroness whose face never sees sun. Incarcerated for over a decade, Krystal has moved beyond the headlines that once depicted her as a monster. In a later picture I find online, Krystal stands, in the sneakers, white knee-length shorts, and short-sleeved T-shirt inmates wear in warm weather. Summers in the New Jersey heat there's no air conditioning to cool inmates in Maximum Compound, as only the administrators can control their climate. Winters, Krystal wears gray sweats, an undershirt, a hooded sweatshirt, and tie-up boots.

A photographer comes on visiting day and the inmates can purchase pictures with their State pay. Everything runs through Commissary: the real food, the fun food, the legal pads and birthday cards, the vented hair brushes, panty liners, and foam ear plugs, dental floss and toothbrushes, shampoo and bar soap, sneakers and shower shoes, thermal tops and sweatpants.

I'm really struggling. I have 1 bar of soap to my name.
Is there any way you can send me $30 by next Wednesday so I can
order? I feel like a bum.
—Krystal Riordan, Inmate #661387

Once you've befriended an inmate, the Maximum Compound of requests comes at you, things that only someone on the outside can finesse. Please help me buy a toy for my daughter's birthday from Kmart or Toys R Us. Some type of fashion design kit of lip glosses or a cute purse from Hey Kitty. You, who can make duplicates of court documents, who can google and download welfare applications, who can xerox copies in full color of the nameless photographs that come in stacks. The photographs are so old, especially those of the outside: photos of three girls sticking out their pierced tongues, arms thrown around each other; girls in indigo-blue robes graduating, choir girls singing; girls in slinky club clothes blowing lipsticked kisses.

Some photos are taped so they stick to the glass of the Xerox machine and you feel the heft of something precious in your hands. Many are of children—brown-eyed boys and girls ages 2 to 7, infants in flannel footsie pajamas; many of the children's photos are old and those pictured have grown and left behind the selves they are here, but to their mothers, the children are fixed; they do not change.

The newest inmates have Facebook pages and you can print pictures from their photo gallery, but no gang signs or middle fingers allowed, unless you color out hand signs with a marker. The recent photographs are from the inside of Maximum Compound—a parade of women in pairs standing before colorful wall paintings (as if an altar) wearing winter's gray sweats or summer's T-shirts. They are lovers, friends, and bunkies. Many smile with lips pressed together. Not quite the blankness or shock of a mugshot, but hiding something all the same.

Anything with glitter is great. The girls go crazy over that.
We use it for make-up and art so when you see a card with glitter,
send it.
—Krystal Riordan, Inmate #661387

Krystal lives in the locked land of EMCF, where she has a cell to herself and works on the grounds detail. She mows lawns, paints, waxes floors, takes out the trash, and moves people from maximum to minimum security units. Generally, she's a people-pleaser and the inmates and guards like her, but that can change in an instant. A slight. A perceived insult. Last winter, a new inmate punched Krystal in the face in Mess Hall. She could avoid punishment only by letting herself be hit. It's almost impossible to let yourself be attacked, to feel the fist in your face, as if whoever is clocking you will do it again and again, the fist forcing you into facing left while the rest of your body twists right. A corkscrew. Krystal punched back and officers punished both women.

Depending on their offense, women are assigned to North Hall, South Hall, Hillcrest, or Stowe I and II. It's North Hall's individual cell where Krystal is first assigned because of the seriousness of her crime, her kidnapping and accessory after the fact to homicide. She likes moving from unit to unit in her job, the way she used to love rush-hour traffic. South Hall also houses in cells those convicted of murder, aggravated assault, and kidnapping, those with behavioral problems. Hillcrest is a semi-dorm for 60 inmates, those here for robbery and drug convictions, those who've earned low points with good behavior. Write-ups by officers for breaking one of the infinite rules result in high points. Like fruit flies, the rules. Stowe I and II house 200 inmates in semi-dorm conditions, those whose sentences are measured in years rather than decades.

&

Nights at EMCF, Krystal struggles to sleep, which is almost impossible without headphones. Lights go out at 10 p.m., but quiet never reigns. The shouting between cells in North Hall shatters the stillness. The youngest inmates stay up all night and the chatter never stops. Nights, with foam ear plugs in, she lies on her bunk remembering movies she's seen. In one, a jet opens the sky with its tail of mist. Terrorists on a plane. The clouds herding like elephants. An explosion brewing. Panning shots of caves, temple ruins, islands—chunks of burning meat over the sea's fire. If you talk like that with the street pimps, their eyes roll back. She starts making up her own movies.

The Mess Hall food trays disgust her. Nights, she dines in the best restaurant in Acapulco, and on her plate, a pyramid of shrimp enchiladas. Yummy. She casts herself as the Marriott maid who cleans the room of Tristan Wilds, a hot black actor from The Wire. Soon they're sprawled in the loungers; the remains of breakfast, scrambled eggs and muffins, spilling everywhere. Raspberry jam and butter for lube. She wears a long, billowing white robe. The robe spreads across the aquamarine pool's surface like a napkin. The blue color of her eyes, she dives in. This is the movie—the one in which she escapes Draymond and her own fate.

&

Nights, Krystal is bitten by spiders and her elbow and forearm swell up. When the redness starts to fade, a lesion appears on her arm, then another on her leg. Krystal goes to Medical and is told that the spider's venom has caused a blood infection. The poison is oozing out through those spots. The spots are like weeping red eyes that open on her torso. Where the poison seeps out, it eats away at her flesh, leaving deep and painful wounds. The inflamed sore on her leg makes it impossible to walk and then the soaring

10

fever sets in. Antibiotics and Motrin are at last prescribed. I wonder if Dray is finally leaving her body. Pour rum over yourself
and strike a match—ultimate flambé. His dark poison, his love.

THE LUNAR SURFACE OF NOSTALGIA
EMCF Clinton, New Jersey

I was the girl that all my friends' mothers wanted them to be like.
I want to be like that again.
—Krystal Riordan, Inmate #661387

"Yes, I was a jock girl," Krystal Riordan says, recalling her school years when she was still a role model to her friends. That was before the running away, the staying out all night, before telling her adoptive parents, you're not my real mother and father. Well before Élan, the residential school for troubled youths, before turning 18 and meeting Draymond Coleman, before the prostitution and the escort services.

"Basketball and softball were my sports." A first-string basketball star light-years before group therapy, before rupture and reconciliation with her adoptive parents, before the murder and guilty plea, before the headline Ex-Orange Woman Sentenced to 30 Years, before becoming Inmate #661387. She grows tall and believes basketball will be her life, dribbling and shooting baskets. Called a natural by her coach, she's already being scouted.

Her success on the court pleases her parents. In a photo I've downloaded she's wearing a maroon St. Mary-St. Michael's letter jacket and holds a basketball. The solemn oval of her unsmiling face is lit by blue sapphire eyes (or are they gray) that stare at the camera and soft, expressive lips. It would take an evil clairvoyant to conjure this eighth-grade girl's Maximum Compound future. She exists in the past and Krystal longs for her.

&

Days in Maximum Compound begin at 5:45 a.m., when the lights blast on like a firing squad. Krystal lunges up and runs to the bathroom, hoping to beat ten other women vying to get inside to use the one toilet, one sink, and one shower before the guard comes for the Count between 6:00 and 6:10 a.m. Krystal brushes her teeth in the sink, while another inmate uses the toilet, while a third jumps in the shower. She lines up for Count, and when it's cleared, the officers call breakfast.

&

Krystal marches to Mess Hall and the inmate workers serve up a breakfast fit for prisoners—a cup of grim decaf coffee, sausage gravy, two boiled eggs, three pieces of bread, and a spoon of margarine. Fifteen minutes allotted for breakfast. She's accustomed to eating fast, no date taking her to a leisurely dinner for calamari and pan-seared salmon baptized in white wine and shallots. Inmates carry bowls to save food to eat later. She's spreading margarine on her second piece of bread when the officers tell her to get moving. Maximum Compound seems all about the undertow of the hurry-up routine yanking your feet out from under you. Krystal rushes, hoping she'll be seen in the Medical Unit this morning for the weird episodes that have started again. She's still hungry and looking forward to the real food later, not what is served in Mess Hall. Real food is Commissary food purchased at reduced rates, like Frosted Flakes, a 12-ounce bag for $2.88 or Ramen noodles at 24 cents each. Krystal has learned to cut cheese and sausage with her ID card. From her earnings, a net $28 a month, she's able to order taco bowls and hot sauce, her hygiene products, pound cake, and mac n cheese. Her new work assignment in the Medical Unit will pay more, almost double what she's getting now.

She never fails to check off Maxwell House instant coffee on her Commissary form. Coffee is a medium of exchange here; two tablespoons in an envelope given to the inmate on the laundry detail gets your clothes folded, rather than all jumbled together. All the real food is drenched in preservatives, sodium, and sugar. Krystal thinks of chili-in-the-pouch as comfort food. Inside the woman who grows a year older on January 24th is the 4-year-old in bed with her two sisters, all three crying from hunger.

&

By 7:30 a.m. Krystal is in full uniform with her ID badge on display, heading down the moldy hall that leads to the Medical Unit. Because of all the buckets set out to collect water leaking from the ceiling, she figures it rained last night. Even the air hates being here, air breathed in and out of so many bodies it's turned into silt and soil to be tamped down with stones and electric wire. The air carries stagnant time; it clings to the nostrils.

There's exhaustion in the noisy units, as well as laughter and chatter. There are the endless Counts. No names, only numbers. Count the concrete blocks. Count the lights under their wire baskets. Easy to forget how the outside feels, your legs and arms swaying like trees, light sifting through the green and splash of traffic, sunrise after an all night up.

"Isn't it funny," Krystal writes, "I dream about birds. A sparrow I saw trying to spear a bagel with its beak and drag it away." Like trying to drag away a 30-year sentence, a 40-year sentence, 75 years. People don't believe her when she tells them she'd rather be in Maximum Compound than Élan School.

&

The Medical Unit charges inmates $5 for every appointment and $2 for each prescription. You can't carry anything into the unit and there's no soap at any of the sinks. When Krystal reaches her destination, the Chief Medical Officer tells her there's no one here to take a look at her. "Go lean against the wall, Riordan, and wait—or else come back tomorrow. By the way, I heard you might be working down here."

She waits. At one time she might have been able to look out the window, but the glass has been painted over. An inmate stretcher crew pushes two empty wheelchairs into a broom closet.

"Riordan, it's not going to be today. Go back to your unit."

&

It's hard moving through the days, standing for the three half-hour Counts, dreading especially the 11–11:30 a.m. one. You don't talk during restricted times and no one makes a peep during Counts or when in lines of any kind. There's no list-of-rules orientation given to incoming prisoners, nothing but to learn by trial and error.

The strange smells have begun again, those weird episodes where she blanks out. Krystal has told her mother, who suggests she get therapy, but she has tried telling the officers, putting in request after request for a medical consultation, and been ignored. Perhaps she's hoping her mother will call the Administration Office and speak on her behalf. Her mother never volunteers. Krystal tells her that the spells come without warning and the air changes color, as if all the lights have dimmed. Sometimes there's the odor of musty bedding or an overturned laundry basket spilling near her face with sleeves tickling her nose. She's trying to breathe through her mouth, trying not to inhale.

I don't remember my birth parents really doing much of anything to help. We didn't bathe. When Child Services took us they said we were all so dirty. I don't know who taught me how to talk.
—Krystal Riordan, Inmate #661387

The odors may come from her childhood; little Krystal sending signals from the past where she was abandoned. The sheets unwashed, three girls in the same bed, pee stains left to dry. Little pee girls. Stair steps. Their smells. And he's part of the smells, the one who calls himself Uncle. Uncle has a huge stomach, but it's not a belly, he tells her, only his sack for Christmas presents, what she'll get if she's a good girl. It's her first home she keeps returning to: the bed with three girls radiant in their hunger, Tiffany on one side and Nicole on the other. The night comes and the sisters huddle in darkness until sleep separates them. The electronic clock watches over them, the red church bell tolls three times. Moonlight shines in.

Her uncle shines too. Sitting next to the bed, he is a human fish; his tiny scales shimmer. His hand is a forked tail as it

15

swims toward her. She rolls against Nicole, hugs her sister, who is a warm pool of milk the color of moonlight wearing its mustache of milk. He'll tickle her until she screams. He'll pick her up; he'll move her hand over him. She snuggles deeper against her sister, her cold feet touching Nicole's warm toes, like peanuts, salty, nutty. Nicole, Nicole, she nudges her, let's go to the bathroom, please. Since they know how to lock the door, the sisters must escape to the bathroom. And on the worst night of her life it's dawn when Draymond's bare hands clamp Jennifer's neck. Krystal escapes to the bathroom and stays inside a long time.

&

To quiet herself, she works harder on her tattoo art. Krystal's body is marked (or marred) by the hieroglyphics of prison. Still time. Frantic time with Counts, line-up minutes, idle hours. She's learned the art of tattooing, practicing first on her own flesh, then on inmates. Indigo sunrises on her calves; Dray and Tiana and Rikii, a litany of names, as if Hail Marys are inked on her forearms; single lightning bolts on her knuckles.

Tattooing is part and parcel of the underground economy. Krystal has a reputation as EMCF's most talented tattoo artist. "Prison tats are a mixed bag of bad art, infections, and horrible morning-after-the-tattoo hangovers. Krystal has had zero infections. Zero that didn't take. Zero regrettable," says her inmate friend Lucy. Krystal draws the design on the inmate's skin, and then uses a sewing needle, a nail file, and pencil lead shaved to powder mixed with VO5 shampoo to make a gel. The gel is painstakingly poured into the skin, i.e., the rivulet made by the file.

It's a slow process and it keeps her mind occupied.

IN THE BLINK OF A BRAKE LIGHT
Weehawken, New Jersey

Hi Stephanie,
I'm a Research Producer at Sirens Media. From my research I
know you wrote a novel Love Highway loosely based on the Jen-
nifer Moore murder and Krystal Riordan's participation in it. I also
know you have corresponded with her. I'm interested in speaking
with you about your experience interacting with Krystal.
—Marlene McCurtis

The day has been overcast and now the dim light is dying in the
sky. I am riding in a Lyft car from Midtown Manhattan toward
New Jersey. Thursday, 5:10 p.m., and rush-hour traffic is madly
heading into the Lincoln Tunnel. Cars, trucks, and buses swarm-
ing out of the City. Soon the river will flow around us and the
orange taillights of the interstate's four lanes will, like the autumn season shrinking into winter, reduce itself into two lanes.
The leaves will change color and fall in a week; trees reveal their
black trunks. The driver struggles to maneuver the car through
the tunnel; moving, creeping, and then moving again. My heart
pulses in my throat at each blink of a brake-light. I'm feeling the
claustrophobic nearness of walls, the vehicles before, behind,
and beside. Is this what prison feels like? Is this how the room
you are about to be murdered in closes around you?

Sirens Media has paid for the car taking me to the Em-
bassy Suites in Secaucus for the interview that I've been warned
lasts at least three hours. I'll meet the production team hired
by TV One's For My Man series. They are filming an episode
about Krystal Riordan, and through an interview with her public defender have learned that her family will not talk to anyone
from the media. Ostracized by friends and business clients since
the news of their adopted daughter's involvement in the Moore

murder became known over a decade ago, they dread publicity. I've never seen nor heard of the L.A.-based show, which features crimes committed by women for the men in their lives.

During a telephone interview with Marlene McCurtis, she asked whether I would consider being filmed speaking on Krystal's behalf. In the course of her research McCurtis had found a number of on-line articles I had written about Krystal and there seemed to be no one else willing to speak for her.

&

She Let Her Die, the New York Post's July 25, 2006, headline read. Killer's girlfriend saw it all but did nothing to save Jennifer. Krystal Riordan's arrest mugshot was splashed across the New York Daily News' cover. Hooker Watched Boyfriend Kill Teen.

I was electrified by those five words. The bottomlessness of them. Almost unfathomable, especially after seeing the prostitute's face—her lips caught mid-quiver, her wide eyes, and her terrified expression. Two days prior, the face of Jennifer Moore, an 18-year-old girl from Harrington Park, New Jersey, had occupied the same space. Teen Missing After Night of Underage Drinking.

For a day, no one knew the whereabouts of Jennifer, who had been partying at a Chelsea club with a girlfriend. In the photo, Jennifer's fine straight hair brushes her shoulders and parts on the side; the part made deep so the hair falls like a sheer curtain across her right eye. She appears born underwater of a half-fish, half-human species, dreamily sloe-eyed, as if she's looking over your shoulder. Her half-smile mysterious like the Mona Lisa's. The next day, Jennifer's body was found inside a suitcase left in a Weehawken dumpster.

&

The Lyft car inches forward; in front of us, more brake-lights spark endlessly on and off. Highway fireflies. I take in Weehawken's antiquated power lines that trestle and stretch between poles. I've never seen lines that sag like these jump ropes for giants. Perhaps they're weighed down by the exodus of a vanquished people and

18

their canceled futures, by the misbegotten stranded in this place of poverty, grit, sex, and drugs. High priests of ruin. Other streets lead to wealthy Weehawken neighborhoods but not here where Jennifer's last hours were spent. I imagine the fear she must have felt, her nerve endings like birds eerily out of place. Fear distilled into the panic of a pigeon flock at a hawk materializing out of nowhere.

&

Jennifer, her friend Talia, and another friend had come in from Harrington Park for dinner in the Meatpacking District. Perhaps their waiter remembered Jennifer and her smile—teeth like small pearls. Talia and Jennifer drove the third girl home and then cruised back to Manhattan. They were the bolder girls—daredevils, mermaids in heat—and the lure of the City was powerful. They parked their car in a No Standing zone. Jennifer left her bag locked in the trunk and slipped her cell phone into the pocket of her mini. Whether both girls had fake IDs or bouncers waved them inside on their good looks alone, I don't know.

In a now-defunct Chelsea club they ordered drinks, and then free drinks kept coming. When the girls left the club, it was well after midnight. and they discovered that the car had been towed. They trekked to the 11th Avenue Pier 76 Impound, where workers refused to release the car to the visibly drunk young women. Jennifer's friend was so drunk she passed out. Workers called an ambulance to transport Talia to a nearby hospital.

&

Fearing arrest, Jennifer walked into the 4:00 a.m. darkness. Alone, lost, drunk, and carrying only her cell phone, her footsteps echoed on the almost-deserted streets near the West Side Highway. She was far from the towers of Midtown, far from Times Square's canyon of glass, where the beautiful people captured in billboards looked down from on high, their navels and bare shoulders polished by so many eyes. She was far from Harrington Park; far from her soccer field; and her father, sure to be disappointed if he learned she had lied to him. Walking behind her but growing closer and larger with each step, the ex-con and small-time pimp Draymond Coleman. Trolling the last dregs of a Monday already Tuesday, he spotted the slender girl in a white mini and black halter top.

Did he take her for a prostitute? Was he thinking he needed to get her to where he controlled the space? The sky, dim and starless between buildings. He offered his help, a knight, but surely not one in shining armor. "Let me help get you a cab."

&

It seems fitting I should be traveling through the geographical heart of this story. I shiver looking at Weehawken from a safe distance, not the up-close July hotel room of broken walls and sperm-encrusted mattresses. I am envisioning the room, breathing and tasting it, and collecting my thoughts.

The Park Avenue Hotel sat on a pot-holed Weehawken street in a tangle of power lines, as if even the electricity had to be kidnapped. A brick five-story structure with mustard-yellow trim, a 24-hour hot-sheet hotel or a seedy rent-by-the-week with desk clerks negotiating room prices for sex workers. Budget-minded tourists visiting New York City sometimes booked rooms and forever regretted it. Mice and chicken bones under beds, filthy sheets, fist holes in the doors. No closets.

Here, Draymond Coleman, age 34, brought Jennifer. Brawny at 6'1" and 275 lbs., he coaxed the 100-lb. teen up the outside stairs. His girlfriend, 20-year-old Krystal Riordan, met them on the landing. Angry at him for bringing the girl here, she threw words like, "I'm going to leave you," in Draymond's face. He ordered Krystal to go pay the taxi driver and maybe she again mumbled that she intended to leave him, before plunging down the stairs with the money for the driver. He had lied to Jennifer, claiming there was a charger for her cell phone inside, and so she entered the repulsive room. Draymond, with the goatee and ox-like shoulders, followed, closing the door behind them.

After Krystal paid the taxi driver she climbed the stairs and returned to Number 37. The room was already hot and airless, even before sun—the flaming orange of a stone crab—started peering into the window. Soon the beatings would begin, until, according to police, every bone in Jennifer's face was broken.

&

On Weehawken Heights there's a rock ledge where Alexander Hamilton's son Philip, age 19, was shot in a duel. A few years later, Hamilton himself died from a bullet wound he received dueling Aaron Burr on the same rock ledge. Another kind of duel was played out in the hotel room between that rage-fueled attacker and a petite soccer player fighting for her life. Teen left in trash bin, ex-con, hooker held. The ménage à trois ended with one girl dead, the other girl charged as an accomplice, and her boyfriend confessing to kidnapping, murder, and rape.

After four years in custody and facing the death penalty, Draymond accepted a plea bargain that required him to implicate Krystal. He testified that both he and Krystal had sex with Jennifer before he strangled her.

Others say Draymond alone raped Jennifer in front of Krystal. Prostitute Saw Whole Thing. An anonymous person emailed me to claim there was a jealous woman in that room named Krystal and she was responsible for Jennifer's murder. That Krystal did not let Jennifer die, but instead willed it.

Did Krystal let Jennifer die?

Everything hinges on the word "let."

I followed the case closely, so closely it bordered on obsession. Is it because of the bloodlust coded into our DNA that we are fascinated by the horrific? Not since the Manson Family murders of my childhood had a true crime caught my attention and held it. Yet those ghastly murders didn't transfix me as this one did. There was no girl who watched.

&

One had been a Girl Scout, another a church choir singer, and one a homecoming princess. Their heads tossed back, saucy, a nonchalant cockiness in the way they carried themselves, they looked amused at the proceedings, giggling while facing the

21

death penalty. They were stars of the homicide realm, a jaunty trio, holding hands. Patricia Krenwinkel, Susan Atkins, and Leslie van Houten. They were Charlie's girls.

In photos shot from a distance, they looked like white girls did in 1969, long dark hair parted in the middle, short skirts, pale skin, bare legs. But up close, in head shots or mugshots, each pair of dark eyes was mesmerizing, a well you could throw yourself into and not drown. Those eyes held death and sex, they were murderers' eyes. I could not stop looking.

I was an Iowa girl who had never gone anywhere, raised on a farm in a Presbyterian home by a widowed mother who did not allow television in the house. I was in junior high when I started cutting the Manson girls' pictures out of the Cedar Rapids Gazette, the daily newspaper of eastern Iowa.

All that year, I cut and kept every new photo of them—the shaved-head girls, their foreheads carved with swastikas, the gamin girls, their hair beginning to grow out. What was the fascination? I was a weed, living in a world of prayers before meals and bedtime Bible readings, taught little else.

These Manson Girls had thrown their futures onto the pyre for this man with rabid eyes, this charismatic ex-con who hijacked their souls. He had created a Family of castoff girls, foster care girls, lost girls who would sleep with men at his command, and that he could order to murder for him. That they would—that they could—seemed almost unfathomable.

The Tate-LaBianca murders had been committed in August, but Manson and the girls weren't indicted until December. From my cold gray Iowa farm, I studied and saved photos of the girls wearing dresses with puffed sleeves arriving in court, the three swinging hands as if without a care in the world, with the sun shining down on a permanent California summer.

The graphic crime scene photos I pored over were mute witnesses to an unbelievable savagery that seemed a galaxy removed from the trio of laughing girls—as do more recent pictures of wrinkled women penned in a California prison for half a century.

My time for rebellion was still a few years away, but I already felt the restlessness, the yearning for the faraway, for the dramatic. I immersed myself in Truman Capote's *In Cold Blood*, reading it from cover to cover three times under the bedsheets by a flashlight. My school library contained little else in the way of true crime. In high school, I happened upon the 750 page *Andersonville* by MacKinlay Kantor, a Pulitzer Prize winning novel that detailed the horrors of a notorious Civil War prisoner-of-war camp where Union soldiers were starved. I would never forget the passage that told of emaciated prisoners picking kernels of corn from their excrement and eating them.

It may have been the tragedy of my young father's death when I was a 3-year-old that planted the seed of my fascination with the extreme situation and the sufferings of others.

After I was shot and lost the use of my left arm, I read survival literature obsessively. Memoirs written by Auschwitz prisoner-doctors, life stories penned by Russian victims of Stalin's purges and gulags, and diaries of Hiroshima survivors. Their voices sustained me.

It was the sweltering July of 2006 in New York City when a newspaper headline captured my attention. Jennifer Moore, not a media celebrity like Sharon Tate, but a petite 18-year-old, had disappeared. The next day, readers learned Jennifer's body had been found. Within a few more days, the alleged murderer was arrested, along with his prostitute girlfriend.

Now it was her face, plastered across local newspapers, that grabbed my attention. I made these notes as I studied her mugshot: The killer's girlfriend's arrest photo perplexes me. Pale skin, blond hair, perhaps needing a shampoo, bewildered frightened eyes. It's a face like that of a nineteenth century innocent.

The opening sentences in the New York *Daily News*' article read, "Riordan allegedly watched Coleman rape, beat, and kill Moore. She was with him when he was arrested by the NYPD."

Not a Manson girl. She apparently had not taken that final step into the abyss, but she had been to the edge. Those bewildered eyes haunted me. What path had led her to that shabby hotel room, what had turned her into the girl who watched another young woman raped and beaten to death?

&

I followed the news accounts as both Coleman and Riordan made their way through the court system, indicted, tried, and sentenced. My initial fascination with her never faded. On May 8, 2012, I emailed EMCF, trying to ascertain if Krystal Riordan was actually incarcerated there.

That brief email became the first step on my own path into Krystal's life and her story.

&

Weehawken disappears into the geography of cacophony, exits and billboards, green signs sprouting up like trees in a lightning-struck forest.

Hudson County detectives discover surveillance video that shows the couple leaving the hotel, lugging a suitcase that Jennifer's body was purported to have been inside. The detectives who first entered the room recall the unspeakable filth and heat. Almost 90 degrees, the air conditioner on the blink. The crime scene a shambles.

&

Sirens Media has rented a conference room for the filming. Do Not Disturb signs hang from the door, and I hesitate before edging through them. Inside the large darkened space, screens surround two chairs; one chair faces the tripod camera and a spotlight illuminates it, like the unchanging white sun of an interrogation. Krystal's interrogation lasted 16 hours. On the far side of the room there's a table stocked with water carafes and packages of freeze-dried apple puffs. A woman named Christine, who will conduct the interview, introduces herself. I fill a cup with water and look over the photos of Krystal I sent the production team. Snapshots Krystal mailed me, which I'd had blown up

24

into 8 ½" by 11" glossies.

There's Krystal wearing the white T-shirt and shorts, white socks, and white sneakers—the Edna Mahan Correctional Facility summer uniform. A cross dangles from a gold chain around her neck. It's 2010 and her first year in EMCF's maximum detention unit after spending more than three years in Hudson County jail awaiting sentencing. Lost are the pounds the twenty-four-year old gained in county jail. Again she's the slender blonde, a glowing All-American girl. Free of Draymond, her eyes shine.

Much younger here, perhaps a ten-year old, she's hugging a large black dog named Finnegan. She wears the St. Mary's Elementary School uniform, a gray sweater and plaid skirt. Her face turns toward the camera, her eyes somber, and her cheek presses the dog's body as if she loves him more than herself.

In the last photo, Krystal's adoptive parents have come to visit her for the second time in the years she's served. Although both are smiling, her mother, who has had cancer, and her father, recently retired, appear frail. Like sparrows. Krystal has donned her glasses and styled her long hair, which is no longer blond, but light brown. Towering over both, she stands in the middle, an arm around her mother and an arm around her father, as if she could cradle and protect them.

"Who's that?" Christine asks, not recognizing Krystal.

"Krystal. After more than a decade in prison," I answer. Christine introduces the cameraman and the soundman, and I'm shown the chair, where a microphone has been placed. The soundman snaps smaller mikes on my jacket. He tells me that my voice is in the right register. Perfect. What people find easiest to listen to. He doesn't have to adjust the sound. "Think of this as a conversation. Don't look at the camera, only at me. We use the past tense."

Christine seats herself in the chair across from me. "Who is Krystal Riordan?" she asks. "Where is she now?"

&

Krystal Riordan is a 30-year-old female, 5'9", 150-180 pounds, serving a 30-year sentence in Edna Mahan Correctional Facility. I stumble through my answer trying to compress a hundred thoughts. She's the felon I have made a commitment to. I've promised to be there for her. She's the daughter of a French prostitute and an Irish drug dealer. A 4-year old, her skin pink as a rabbit's eye, she's a rabbit, shivering ready to scram and take cover. The child with one older sister and one younger. The girl who is the middle sister with lice, the one molested by her uncle. She's the girl removed from the home and put into foster care, the one adopted by a rich couple. She's the basketball natural. A role model turned adolescent rebel. A truant, an embarrassment to her adoptive parents. She's a graduate of the Élan residential school for troubled teens. An 18-year-old blonde in the Big Apple selling herself on eros.com. The wide-hipped goddess sex worker that all the men love. The girl who an ex-con pimp fought another pimp for. She's merchandise. She's the prostitute lover of Draymond Coleman, the one who is like heat, the one who seethes.

&

She's the 20-year-old having threesomes with her lover, the ex-con she can't live without. She's July 25, 2006. A forever mistake. She's the shabby Weehawken Park Avenue hotel waiting for him to come home. The one who pays for his cab when he returns at dawn with a scantily dressed teenager. Who saw Jennifer's anguish after the door to the room closed. The girl who left the room for a soda while another girl fought for her life. The girl who knows what a room after a murder is like. The air quiets, the downpour abruptly ceases, and the walls uncover their eyes. She is the one who feels for Jennifer's pulse. The tiny wing beating in the wrist gone.

Everything her life could still be depends upon her actions now. The one who watched her lover having sex with Jennifer's cooling body. The girl who carries the horror of that room everywhere.

26

"Jennifer was no match for Dray," Krystal says, as if taking weird pride in her lover's brute strength. Krystal is the one who flipped the mattress over and sold sex in the bed Jennifer died in. She had no choice. She'd traveled to the Kingdom of the Damned.

&

She's a people pleaser. The one with numbness in her head. Weak-minded, and that's why she admits that on the morning of the murder she was angry that Dray hadn't brought weed with him, as she'd given him money and her body was his ATM.

She is the girl, who after the murder of Jennifer Moore, after the disposal of her body, waited alone in a Harlem hot-sheet hotel while Dray went to buy weed. The girl I see on July 27th peering out from the cover of the New York *Daily News*. Her eyes are wells of fear, wide and vulnerable. She is the story I have been telling over and over for years. The girl who frames every anecdote in the language of the victim. Giver of few specifics, she hides herself inside the truncated sentence. Girl who speaks in a throaty Lauren Bacall register, the abridged version of her adolescence. The girl I have never met. The girl I care deeply for. The girl whose soul I think I know.

VISITATION
EMCF   Clinton, New Jersey

Me and Nicole were damaged when we got adopted.
I would always tell them they weren't my parents.
I just wanted to go home, except I didn't know where that was.
—Krystal Riordan, Inmate #661387

Eva, Krystal's birth mother, stares at the camera with anthracite eyes that glitter as if they could withstand a miner's pick. Her black hair, too, gives off a costume gem's gleam. A striking woman on whose olive-colored face I recognize Krystal's petal lips but little else. The birth mother, a short woman, appears chiseled entirely from rock, while her daughter seems soft in comparison. The cream-puff skin and sometimes blue and sometimes hazel eyes. The reasons for Eva's neglect of her children, unknowable. She is a prostitute.

Krystal holds on to little of her early years before she was taken from her birth parents and put into foster care, joining a children's crusade of the blighted. How did she learn language? She remembers there weren't any toys. Eva bequeathed to Krystal her old crack pipes and her daughter would play with them, pretending the pipe stems were bridges over the maroon rivers of spilled wine. When she crossed the river she'd find herself in a forest. Birds whistled and she understood their every word, no matter the pitch. She would smell the dreams of the leaves. Or she would hold Eva's hand mirror under her nose and wade into the ceiling.

As an adult she searched for her real mother and saw her twice. "I'd looked for her and found her," Krystal says. "I wish I hadn't. She stole my money."

28

Disappointment settles between her shoulder blades like her desecrated childhood.

&

Krystal seems to know very little about her biological father and mother, not even the reason she and her sisters were taken from the home. It appears Krystal's father had been arrested for selling drugs, and while he sat in jail the girls were left in an uncle's care, the same uncle who molested his nieces. Where the mother is, not a clue. Child Services removes the girls and the State severs parental rights.

Krystal has a letter Tiffany, her eldest sister, sent her in prison, about the day of rupture—the last day the sisters spent together. The girls hide behind the nubby gray couch while police lights bleed through the window. Officers carry the screaming sisters out to waiting cars, the two younger in one, the oldest in another. They remark on how filthy the girls are. Hardly human. Tiffany regrets that the three of them weren't kept together and believes things would have turned out differently for Krystal and Nicole if their big sis had been there to love and guide them.

Tiffany was my protector. I felt safe with her.
We loved eating hot dogs and SpaghettiOs.
There weren't any good memories with Eva or Charlie.
—Krystal Riordan, Inmate #661387

I only know the haziest of details about Krystal's past. When I asked her who had discovered their neglect, Krystal said, "School."

Like all her answers, they are flat statements without embroidery, and try as you might to wade into them, you'll find no drop-offs into deeper water where the truth lies. I wonder if she has forgotten whole years of her life. Trying to understand her story, I run into her inexplicable nature.

&

In foster care, the little girls are washed up and they shine. Blond and blue-eyed one, the other hazel-eyed. Adults love to touch their hair; how beautiful the girls are to look upon. Porcelain dolls. The girls are adopted.

Inside, the Krystal doll is a host of troubled imaginings. She dreams that the bad man in the white shirt, her birth mother's brother, leans over her bed to wrap his arms around her. It's not his fault but hers that his mind is intoxicated by her little girl-skin. He wants to sauté and bake her; he wants to feast on her. Mouthful after mouthful, he keeps chewing and smacking while she screams and wakes the house. She dreams about being shut inside a closet and left behind. Her adoptive father later remarks upon Krystal's sleep broken by screaming. The child Krystal tries to form words from pictures that convey what she beholds.

How else will we understand the strange girl who watched? Like stone fruits, the peach and nectarine, seeds encased in a skin, the seeds of trouble wait for puberty to scatter.

&

Her adoptive parents are coming to Maximum Compound and Krystal feels electrified. In all the years of her incarceration they have visited once. EMCF makes it difficult with long processing waits and full body searches, in some cases.

They are coming today, these strangers she once so resented being told to call Mother and Father, she now gladly calls Mom and Dad. She doesn't want her tattoos to show and for days has been trying on sweatshirts, long-sleeved and short. Her mother used to be strict, such a perfectionist. In the old days, if a friend asked her to stay for dinner her mother's answer was always no. Krystal's B's failed to impress her compared to Melody's straight A's.

&

She waits for her name to be called. The Riordans, partners in their own accounting firm, will soon walk into Maximum Compound's common room. It's all boring talk and the dull silver gleam of officers' badges as they patrol the family groups, white, black, and brown, or watch from the corner where the vending machines used to be. Because some visitors hid drugs in the coin return and can-retrieval slots, the machines were removed, along with the ashtrays after smoking was outlawed.

She knows her mother used to smoke to calm her nerves but stopped with the first cancer diagnosis. There are whole swaths of her past she's forgotten, but she remembers the wisps of smoke rising from the glass ashtray where her mother's long white cigarette smoldered. Krystal's finger liked to poke and trace the wavy shapes of the wisps. Indoor clouds.

&

Her palms feel clammy. Her heart pounds, and then it feels like it stops altogether. A man and a woman walk toward her and the fourteen years that have passed since she's seen them fall away. Can this be her mother, this tendril of a woman who can't weigh more than 90 pounds, the in-charge brown-eyed blonde, the accountant, the mother who saw everything and whose temper frightened the adolescent Krystal? Her father, younger than her mother by seven years, looks frail. His once thick dark hair is thinning. They are both smiling and crying. Krystal rushes toward them, overjoyed.

&

When people ask Krystal why the Riordans adopted her and her sister she seems unable to give an answer. "I don't know. Maybe they wanted to look good." Krystal can't be certain.

The couple's motives for adopting two girls, ages 5 and 3 1/2, can only be guessed at. Did they want sisters for Melody, their biological child, or were they trying to replace the dead son? Did they want a larger family? Krystal's mother had two sons by an early marriage that had ended in divorce. After she married Krystal's father, one of her sons was killed in an industrial accident. When she received a settlement, which she called blood money, she donated it to Yale-New Haven Children's Hospital.

Her pregnancy with Melody had been difficult, and since she was in her mid-forties, she decided not to get pregnant again.

31

She told friends she was adopting two girls from Catholic Charities. Krystal and Nicole, sisters.

Friends say that she wanted a successful family. She was a Girl Scout troop leader and carpooled Krystal and her friends to basketball practice. She had not really faced the hard truth that enrolling damaged girls in music lessons and sessions with a therapist specializing in children who had been sexually abused might not be enough to ameliorate the harm already done. Neither would summer weekends spent at the beach house and sleepovers. Nicole suffered from ADHD and would become a heroin addict and Krystal, a prostitute. But in the beginning, who could resist the beauty of Krystal and Nicole in tulle skirts and hair ribbons, Krystal and her younger sister clutching hands?

&

They sit. After she proudly introduces them to the officer who passes, Krystal holds her mother's hand and swallows the thickness in her throat. There's so much she'd like to say. *I'm sorry for pushing you away.*

"How are you feeling, Mom?" Krystal asks. "You look good."

Her mom's brown eyes are smiling as the shock of seeing her child in this place, the one who showed such athletic promise, recedes. "Better, honey. The throat scans showed no recurring cancer."

"We were so happy about that, Krystal," her dad says in his gentle voice. Always, always, he had been kindly toward her.

The ashtrays rise up again in Krystal's mind. The one made of blue glass was shaped like a swan and the cigarette, sometimes two, resting between the wings. The smoke drifting upwards toward the ceiling fan like swans riding the breeze. Krystal in hair ribbons. When Krystal was little she liked to stir milk into her blue paint until the color was almost erased.

Her mother smells less smoky, less fiery. Krystal had loved watching her mother drink, loved the shake of her tumbler, the ice chips and limes, the gin and tonic. Best of all was the light glinting through the tall glass, a green pool her tongue wanted to swim in. There is a shyness about the three of them, almost as if they are strangers meeting for the first time.

"I found some of the china teacups from your tea party," her mom says, wistfully. "You probably don't remember your first birthday with us, do you?"

"I do remember," Krystal says.

For her sixth birthday, the year of her adoption, her mother throws a dress-up tea party. Krystal wears a pink party frock with a bow sash. This is her birthday kingdom—china teacups and lace doilies, tarts and tea sandwiches. Her mother wants it to be perfect down to the Victorian parlor games. The strawberry-frosted cake and ice cream.

In another world Krystal's inmate friends are concocting her cookie and candy bar cake in the microwave. In another world a good gift is a pack of batteries.

&

Her father has brought the pictures she asked for and the three of them move closer together, looking. Here is the foster child Krystal entering Pre-k. So pale the teacher can probably see the scribbles of blue veins at her wrists and temples. She hangs back, and then creeps into the good-smelling room where the best thing she learns is that a carton of white milk arrives in the middle of the morning. It's the first time she's used a straw, and one day, instead of white, the milk is chocolate. The chocolate day is so far the best day of her life.

&

Her father shuffles the next photo from the envelope. Here are four tanned, long-legged girls in uniforms, their blond hair tied back in ponytails. The tallest and prettiest is unsmiling Krystal. Number 13. Five feet, nine inches tall. She and her teammates will soon be on their way to Florida for basketball nationals. They're raising money for the trip—selling red velvet cupcakes and brownies. College coaches are already scouting 13-year-old Krystal.

33

"I was very good," she says. Some of the girls in the photo will make the U.S. Olympic Basketball playoffs. A mother of one of Krystal's teammates, her daughter Alysia also a highly ranked player, remembers the adolescent Krystal, the vibrant eyes, the niceness. She stood out among the many friends her daughter had.

&

There are no pictures here of Krystal on the covers of New York's daily newspapers like those that still exist in the digital universe. Photographs underscored by headlines—*Jersey City Prostitute and Murder Suspect Advertised Sex. Felony Murder Charge for Girlfriend of Teen Slay*. She doesn't like to think about her parents' shock at reading those headlines. *Ex-Orange Woman Gets Prison in Teen's Death*. Like acid thrown into their faces. People who her Mom and Dad thought were friends distancing themselves. People in the grocery store staring and pointing. Parents of that monster.

&

Krystal examines the picture of herself as a bridesmaid at her sister Melody's wedding. She marvels at her flushed and radiant face. In the conga line her arm is thrown over the shoulder of a dark-haired boy, who is a head shorter. She wears a pink satin sheath and her blond hair has been styled in an upsweep with a cornucopia of side curls. For a last moment we see the innocent Krystal, the jock in love with dribbling a basketball, and her own racing heart.

"Are you still having those episodes? Those seizures?" her mother asks, concern in her furrowed forehead. "Do they understand what is going on?"

The blinking and disorientation, her pupils dilated, her left larger than the right. Her lips turning blue as her oxygen is hijacked by the heart and lungs. The sleepwalking state. She's running with her sister into a long-ago mall, she's outside a 7-Eleven sipping a cherry Slurpee, she's being stung by a bee. Trying to hold onto others, calling them by her sister's name, stumbling as

34

if drunk. Afterwards she's confused and trembles and has to pee. The regular rhythm of her breathing returns.

"They took me to Saint Francis Hospital for an MRI. I had back-to-back mini-seizures on the way," Krystal explains. "They said I needed more tests to find out the underlying condition."

"Did they give you the EEG test? You mentioned that," her mother asks.

"No, it never happened. Medical just gave me an anti-seizure prescription."

Her father shakes his head and stares into the air.
Her mother asks, "How long have the seizures been going on?"

She explains that they started about three years ago. Before the seizures she will usually see a greenish halo, and breathe something bad from long ago that reminds her of her uncle, an odor that doesn't exist.

Epilepsy? Brain abnormality? Tumor? Her uncle fondling her before she was even four years old? When the smells come to Krystal she enters the jagged dark of her uncle's touching. A rock, a place of cold, her uncle's cigarette dropping its icy ash, flakes of snow, large five-pointed stars freezing her flesh. One of the doctors told Krystal that her symptoms suggest a very uncommon seizure that only happens in women. Rett Syndrome. The syndrome manifests itself in childhood with loss of muscle tone and diminished crawling and walking. This in a girl, an all-star basketball player, seems wildly off the mark.

Her father asks her about the college classes she had mentioned.

She's proud to tell them she has enrolled in English Lit and Philosophy. The for-credit college classes are taught by professors who are paid, and come with syllabuses and lengthy reading assignments. Krystal is one of the high test scorers. Her poetry class will be taught by a Princeton PhD whose *Paris Review* and *Los Angeles Review of Books* essays are brilliant.

The time rushes by and visiting hours are almost at an

end. *I love you*, Krystal thinks, *I love you both.* She wants to hang onto them for dear life.

&

Back on her bunk she drinks her sugar coffee and studies a picture in which she and Alysia are curling each other's hair and making up each other's faces. On the cusp of teenagehood, soon leaving behind this kind of silliness, but for now they are laughing, modeling the foundation bronzing their cheeks, the sable and jade eye shadow shimmering their lids, the fudgy lipstick ready for hand kisses. Wipe it all off and they start again with kohl eyeliner and clouds of white face powder. They become geisha girls. They are body and eyes, and happy in their pubertal beauty, like photographs floating in the air. Buttocks and muscled flanks ready to gallop. Krystal, the palomino, all silk and butter and heart.

&

"Krystal, would you like to stay for dinner?" Alysia's mother asks. The tall, bright-eyed Krystal, used to being fed hot dogs at home, accepts gladly.

When the mother asks, "Did you let your mother know?" she nods.

She likes her friend's mother and wonders if God mixed her own mother's hawk eyes with vinegar before he put them in her face. Her friend has two sisters too, but they get along and share a camaraderie with their mother. She likes being here where it feels like the sun is shining, even at night. The girls help set the table, the mother carries in a wooden bowl of fresh tossed salad, and from the oven comes ravioli swimming in mushrooms and cheeses. Krystal loves ravioli and stretching the strings of mozzarella from her fork and then twirling them.

She's hardly chewed and swallowed her first ravioli, when there is a loud knocking on the door. Krystal stiffens. The door opens to Krystal's angry mother in a rage.

"Krystal! Liar. Liar." Krystal falls back, her face pales with fear. Liar! The word crawls like a stinkbug. "You're a liar. No one

36

gave you permission to eat here," her mother says, glaring at her friend's mother. "Get in the car."

Liar, thing of yellow feelers. A charcoal husk. Her mother's breath rattles—a fortune cookie caught in the blades of a fan.

&

Krystal returns to the day when everything changed. She's 14, and some cute older guys show up at the basketball court where she and her friend Alysia shoot baskets. Little cypress stump, her basketball girlfriend's only 5 feet, two inches, but she's fast and good.

"Show us what you can do," one of the guys calls out. Krystal hooks the thumb of her left hand in her cutoffs pocket and in her right hand she balances the basketball. She jumps, heaving the ball up and sinking it through the net.

The guys clap. "Pretty good. A one-handed shot."

They ask the girls if they can shoot a few baskets too. Isn't life fresh and green when you're 14? Still far from the gardenia rot of the Weehawken July and its gouged-out murderous neighborhood.

&

Lying on her bunk she pictures the two guys from the basketball court who invited themselves over to visit her. The house empty except for Krystal, who is playing sick to stay home. Her sisters in school and her parents busy at their accounting practice. The bed with white ruffled spread unmade because she's lying in its nest of sheets. White wicker furniture, chairs and bedside table. A girl's white room.

The guys from the basketball court show up with weed. The older one has blond hair that gives off sparks when she touches it. The younger one has a sturdy build, and although he's short, there's something rakish about the shape of his face and the devil's cloven trademark—his cleft chin. They're seniors in the public high school and she goes to a private Catholic school. A basketball girl embarking on a journey to an unfamiliar shore that begins in her white bedroom. She shivers with the teenage thrill of the forbidden. Her mother's house has become hers.

The boy's chest pressing against her skin feels fine as an eyelid. Music volume goes up. The weed is already rolled, but Krystal hesitates, knowing better than to light the joint.

&

Sometimes she thinks it really happened, what the townspeople spread about her and the boys. Three smoky mouths, three naked bodies that youth makes beautiful. Krystal's hair raining over the pillow, the part in her hair so clean and white and her pelvic bones lifting through her skin. The boys take turns inside her and sucking her breasts. Hickeys bloom. They light the joint and giggle as Orange, Connecticut, goes about its day. They have sex until they become a syrupy tangle. In the white room they're laughing and a light blinks in Krystal's head as she pulls her foot back and kicks the sheet off the bed. The tunes and the laughing, the moaning and crying out, muffle the sound of her mother's car driving up.

That's what gossips still say happened, but that's their fantasy. The boys have come over, they're smoking, and they're listening to music. That's all. The front door is opening and closing, her mother hears the boys' voices. She opens the bedroom door. Krystal clutches herself in the blizzard of howling. "Get out. Get out or I'll call the police."

The boys grab their jackets and flee.

&

Krystal has crossed the line and her mother is reeling. The hellish family her daughter was born into must be claiming their own. Is Krystal's genetic inheritance bubbling to the surface? Her mother rips the sheets from the bed and takes them into the yard and, dousing them in lighter fluid, burns them.

After trying so hard, her mother wants to drop to her knees and weep; instead she consults the top psychologist in the field of disturbed adolescents. He recommends sending Krystal to Élan, a residential school in Maine for troubled teens.

ÉLAN
Poland Springs, Maine

I always said that I would rather be here in EMCF than at Élan. When I try to explain it to people they think I'm lying. I was there for three years. If I'd never been sent there I might have had a full Basketball scholarship. They broke me down but I never got built back up.
— Krystal Riordan, Inmate #661387

On the drive north from Connecticut into Maine, Krystal notices the white pines, the fissured gray trunks so still, as though pretending to stand in one place but ready to move. She sees the back of her mother's head. The blond hair with the tight curls just below her ears, the ears that hear everything.

"White pines," her father says, "they're so stately. Tall like you, honey. You'll be taking hikes through them." They've been told the Élan residential school's program includes hiking, camping, and outdoor sports.

"Dogwoods and swamp birch and horse chestnuts," her mother chimes in, reading from a brochure they picked up from a Maine Visitor's Center. "I envy you. Krystal, you're going to live here. It's like a park. You always liked to climb trees when you were younger."

Krystal studies the pines. She wants to wrap herself in their bluish-green needles and gather their cones. She sees dogwoods with their explosion of white blossoms. She hasn't seen any towns for miles. How much farther until Élan? This is nowhere. Will she be able to run away?

Child Services calls the boarding school they're taking her to THE LAST STOP.

&

The Directors and Founder are the Great Horned Owls of these forests, turning their heads 270 degrees, their keen hearing and eyesight overseeing their isolated Élan empire. But for her parents, the Directors are only people. They greet her parents politely, but do not offer to show them the grounds. The school costs $50,000 a year. Either Krystal's parents have written a check, in full, or the State of Connecticut has paid.

The Founder tells them he was once a heroin addict and it was through this therapy that the addict in him was eradicated. In the bright light, Krystal can see the gleam on his hard teeth and his thin hair and bushy eyebrows.

Her parents can't get away fast enough.

The Founder tells her she must write a letter of confession to her parents. She is told to write that she does drugs, drinks, and that she is a whore. Three lies. The pen trembles in her hand. She's thirsty and wants a glass of water but fears asking.

Outside, the residents have gathered, at least a hundred kids sitting in a circle. The trees are close, and she can hear water flowing in the leaves. Stand up, tell them your name, and sing Mary Had a Little Lamb. The lump in her throat keeps growing, her mouth is dry, and her tongue feels like wood. No words come out. She stares at her sneakers, at the terry cuff of her white gym socks. Already the kids are snickering and someone yells that she is fat. Worthless, stupid, a waste of protoplasm.

&

Looking out a window is forbidden at Élan. Forest surrounds the school and guards are posted in the trees to stop anyone trying to escape. Krystal wants to glance out at the landscape the facility has chosen—the Maine wilderness. Afternoon clouds billow into the shape of America, you can smell the fir and black spruce and cedar, and hear the rustle of quaking aspen.

Although she looks older, Krystal is 14 years old. An Expeditor, the Strength student who stands with a clipboard watching and writing down infractions, has her eye on Krystal, who is tall and lovely with tendrils of blond hair damp against her neck like bloodied cornsilk.

There are only two types of people, she is told: Strength and Non-Strength. She knows instinctively which she is.

Krystal hasn't yet learned that as a Non-strength she isn't allowed to talk to another Non-strength, only to a Strength. There is a cesspool of do-nots. Talking too loudly. Talking too quietly. Slouching. Negative body language. Taking longer than 3 minutes to shower. Looking at the floor. Smiling without permission. Being tired. Sleeping too long.

Each is what Élan calls a Guilt and is punishable.

&

It's already dark when actual school classes begin after dinner. At 7 p.m. Krystal sits at a rickety desk where a book already open has been placed in front of her. It is an algebra book with marks made by others erased, and she wonders if any message has been left for her by the ones who came before. She can trace the not-quite-invisible river the pen made, its indentation.

The teacher, a bearded, slope-shouldered man, chalks something on the blackboard, the kind Krystal's never seen before—not a green board, but an actual black one. The teacher tells them to copy a page from the book and hand it in. No exams. No homework.

After the Algebra teacher leaves, the history teacher shuffles in. Short, her small face lost in black frame glasses, she says hello to the class and seems to smile at Krystal, singling her out. She dares not smile back at the teacher because one of her classmates might tell.

When classes end at 11 p.m. she files out of the room and walks down the thin halls. The teacher's smile lingers. "You're beautiful," she imagines the teacher whispering.

&

Krystal learns that the residents run everything. Those who have proved themselves worthy act as night monitors, keeping watch over the sleeping residents.

The nights stretch endlessly; sleep comes, then the flashlight shines over her body. Every ten minutes until the sun comes up the monitor lifts the blanket for the shirt-sheet check, making sure her feet are bare and not planning to run or enter the woods. That she wears only one shirt and not two.

Can they see the blue of the moon in her fingertips? Has she been looking out the window? She has been warned about Ding-ball, a cougar living in the woods. The end of Ding-ball's tail is ball-shaped and hairless; he craves human flesh and sings with a human voice to lure you into the woods, then splits your skull with that ball tail.

The trees come to Krystal when she closes her eyes. You are never allowed to be alone here, yet she is filled with the loneliness of animals abandoned by their mothers. You go outside only during gym class once a week.

At night, under her lids, she can open doors that are always locked, she can go outdoors and walk in the maples, red and orange leaves crunching. She can breathe any weather, clothe herself in a hot summer afternoon. At night when her empty stomach rumbles, the girl in the bunk below hers giggles. Krystal closes her eyes and sees herself eating shrimp heaped on a bed of yellow rice, fluffier than the one she lies on. The shrimp are slippery and light, one after another they swim into her mouth.

&

She's told not to look directly at a member of the opposite sex. Punishment for looking at a boy might be washing a toilet with her bare hands. Flirty behavior would be worse.

Krystal has to train herself to use the bathroom the Élan way. You're allowed three bathroom passes: morning, noon, and midnight. She learns that a support person must go into the bathroom with her, and she is not allowed to close the stall door. The Directors discover her fear of the dark. They blindfold her and stand her beside a tall tree where they tell her an owl roosts. The Great Horned Owl with tufted ears and yellow eyes like a cat. She listens for the batting velvety fringes of his wings, waits for the owl to seize her with its talons and crush her skull.

&

Krystal has not eaten fast enough in the eight minutes she's allowed; plus, her scrubbing of floors is deemed lackluster, and her waxing suspect.

Her parents refuse to believe her when she describes the conditions. Why should they believe the daughter whom they gifted with their name, fed, and loved, only to be lied to and sparred with?

During her phone call home, her voice shakes and she tries to tell her father to come get her.

Her Support Person cuts the call in mid-sentence.

I was one of the last people to get a 'ring.'
I fought two huge girls and a boy for one minute each.
It may not seem like a long time but when it's happening it is.
—Krystal Riordan, inmate #661387

The Ring is the crown jewel in Élan's brainwashing wizardry. Monitors escort Krystal to isolation, where she's given boxing gloves. The three residents she'll face are already shadowboxing. She watches the huge girl, tall like Krystal but built like a refrigerator with bologna arms and legs, stuff her hands into a pair of gloves.

A Strength tosses boxing gloves at Krystal and tells her to put them on fast. Show us how tough you are, Non-Strength flirty nobody, show us.

He pushes her into the room's center. She fights one, then another, then another.

I was sent to the corner if I didn't want to get up in front of the house and sing. If I didn't get on my hands and knees and properly scrub their floors. If I didn't want to participate in groups when I was supposed to yell and curse someone out.
— Krystal Riordan, Inmate #661387

Once again she's facing the corner.

43

Krystal keeps her eyes open, must keep them open and stare straight ahead. Her face must line up with that corner crack, no looking up or around, no slouching, her hands on her knees always where the watcher can see them. Her ears are still hers and the quaking aspen takes her. She follows the bits of light sparking through holes in the leaves, a private speech.

This time her eyes are being punished. She's looked at a member of the opposite gender. Did she spend four minutes instead of the mandated three minutes taking a shower thinking of him? Her temples throb, yet she feels a calm spreading through her cells.

All the hours with little food and no sleep. Her head could be bread dough, her body, soggy toilet paper. The wall blanches into the paleness of a migraine. The wall has become a window. The sun keeps coming, hitting the window. She asks the Strength person if she can use the bathroom to pee.

Not yet, she has to wait. Hours.

Some residents spend weeks in the corner. In the old days of the 1970s she heard you had to use a bucket to pee and sometimes the bucket was poured over you.

In the hurricane eye of her migraine she can see blue sky and stars. She's rising out of herself and shedding her Élan-issue shapeless T-shirt and jeans.

&

On weekends in the spring the residents are allowed to go outside. They are surrounded by security watching, always watching, for split-risks. In the forest where they can't go the rare plants and herbs are growing. Named like ingredients for a witch to cast love spells with. Unicorn root and grape ferns. Moonwort and foxglove.

&

Krystal wakes up excited, today is one of those rare days, they are going swimming in the lake. No bikinis, no crop top swimsuits, nothing that shows stomach. She puts on the one-piece swimsuit and shorts. The appropriate swimwear.

44

"They don't want us looking like whores," she says to her bunky.

Weren't they all whores, all the girls here? Isn't what they all had to write in the Guilt Letter home, their first act after the shower and the handing over of their clothes, jewelry, whatever they came with? There are girls here who stabbed themselves in the stomach, a girl who broke a jar of maple syrup over her rapist stepfather's head. Another slashed on black eyeliner, shoulder bag bulging with clean underwear, retainer and inhaler, and slammed out the front door wearing only her skin into a frigid winter night. All of them deemed persons in need of supervision, all kidnapped to Élan.

&

Krystal follows the resident in front of her, single file down the rocky path. No matter the mile they have to walk between brush and rubble to the lake, the sun beats warm on her face. They are careful for they are still being watched, each sneaker crunch on the gravel, every shuffle and kick at the gravel, someone has logged.

No messing up, no talking too quietly or too loudly. No looking at the opposite gender. Wind steals a few strands of her hair, blowing them into birds, but before they fly away, she grabs them back.

&

Water weeds tremble on the shore of the lake. She loves to swim, she loves to dive, her body slicing the surface, the first cold awakening, the escape underwater. She can breathe on her own. No bunk beds to make up with hospital corners. Life is opening into something bigger, freer here. Free of time and space, she can sense fish when they flutter against her, the quiver of the water, movement, her hair rippling.

Everything stops. A Non-strength of the opposite gender, a guy, has committed a Guilt, not just looking at a girl but actual physical contact in the water, splashing and touching.

Krystal wants to keep swimming, doesn't want to leave

the lake, but they are ordered out of the water. The Dealing Crew tells them that for punishment, every one of them must gulp a mouthful of lake water and carry it in their mouths up the rocky path, and for the whole mile walk back to Élan.

It's harder going up. The pebbles scatter. The heat of the dirt burns through the soles of her sneakers and her thirst grows. The tufts of dry grass and gray spruce needles look thirsty too. She wants to swallow even the stale lake water in her mouth. The sticky air licks her.

Once they reach the school's grounds, they are told to spit out the water. If they no longer have the water in their mouth they will be punished.

&

Élan enters Krystal's sleep. In her dream someone has given her an apple but she's forbidden to have it. The clipboards are coming toward her. She must hide the apple, she presses her lips to it, kisses the red peel. The apple whispers to her. Save me.

She doesn't want to dream the other dream, the one that often comes. A woman is weeping with the invisible crying sounds a fish makes pulled from the water. The mouth of the woman makes the O shape, gulping. Krystal inches toward the fish woman, calling out Mommy, Mommy and reaching for her.

We went to class in a trailer.
Honestly I don't really remember too much about classes.
There was one teacher who was very nice and his name was Mr. Moss or Foss. School only lasted about 3 or 4 hours. We went all year-round.
—Krystal Riordan, Inmate #661387

After being in group therapy and shouting and confessing most of the day, after the 8 minutes allotted to eat dinner where she knows better than to chew after Meal Blows or Stop Eating is called, it's time to go to school. 7 p.m. to 11 p.m.

When Krystal first tells me she went to school at night

year-round I was shocked. Classes begin when residents file into the room and pick up a textbook. The textbooks are old, out of date. Age groups aren't differentiated, like in old-time one-room schools.

The teachers are not in on the secret of Elan, its sadistic heart and mind. Some of the teachers are actually nice. There are no tests here, you grade your own papers, you return your book to the pile. There is no music or art, no group projects, no fieldtrips, no audio-visual equipment, no homework assignments—just three hours of instruction in the basics and an hour of study hall where students copy pages from the textbooks.

When parents learn their child is passing with B's after consistently flunking, they believe Élan has performed a minor miracle.

&

When I read of Élan's perfunctory school and heard from Krystal about the night sessions, I thought about my own high school. There were 42 farm kids in my graduating class. Our teachers included the bedroom-slipper-wearing Algebra teacher Mr. Shedletsky, who whispered when he taught. His class was the only math offered, period.

Madame Reeve, past 70, taught French, the only foreign language available for 30 miles. I can still see the black hairs nesting in the wrinkles around her mouth, as accentuated by the comment *allez-vous* tightening her lips.

My own high school career was not inspiring. But I had books to escape into, along with a certain amount of privacy. It felt like my high school curriculum had been created in the principal's sleep. No conscious person could have imagined that the course offerings prepared our student body for college.

Likewise, Élan's program of study seemed an afterthought, a hastily manufactured one, which shortchanged the college-bound. Being robbed of an education, I think, has to be added to crimes Élan committed against Krystal.

&

With schoolwork confined to a few hours in the evening, the days are free for the group therapy sessions and the dreaded General Meetings.

Krystal attends the smaller therapy encounter group, where she dredges up her past and listens to others do the same. The moderator, who has no formal training, is a former Élan resident who has graduated.

Of all the therapy groups these are the ones she dreads the least. Although Krystal will be shouted at during the session, it is usually only one resident who screams and not the whole group. When she's brought before the four-member Dealing Crew, residents who have climbed the Élan hierarchy, she knows she is about to be punished for some Guilt. If a resident has committed an actual infraction, not just a Guilt, a General Meeting is called.

The "GM" has a noxious reputation among Élan graduates. The one who has been found guilty stands alone to face a screaming mob of 50 to 100 residents, goaded on by staff. Residents learn to scream for seven minutes, because if the watchers see you not screaming they write your name on the clipboard and a General Meeting will be called on you. Former residents of Élan speak about how they learned to take a breather after three minutes of screaming or shouting to rest their voices, and then start again to avoid strain or even permanently damaging their vocal cords.

&

In one General Meeting Krystal recalls, a waifish girl who looked about 12 years old faced the mob. She had confessed to having an abortion before coming to Élan.

The moderator gives the order. "GET YOUR FEELINGS OFF!"

The residents surged toward her, shouting and screaming, "You're a whore." "We wish you were dead." "You lying bitch." "You worthless piece of protoplasm." "Baby-killing bitch." "Slut." The girl broke away, running across the dining room and diving

48

into the plate glass window. The reinforced glass remained intact, while she fell onto her back, unconscious.

The room went deadly still.

After a few minutes, she regained consciousness and stood up—and the moderator immediately directed the shouting to begin again.

&

I first heard of Élan in the 1998 book Murder in Greenwich, written by Mark Fuhrman about the Martha Moxley murder. Michael Skakel, Ethel Kennedy's nephew as well as Moxley's neighbor in the exclusive Belle Haven enclave, was a prime suspect in the still-unsolved 1975 murder.

Skakel had been sent to Élan in 1978 and spent two years there. When Skakel was first brought to trial in 2002, it was on the basis of an alleged confession he made at Élan. The defense attorneys put the school and its behavior modification program under a spotlight. Former Élan residents testified that Skakel had been put in a ring and forced to box other residents; each time he denied having killed Moxley he was hit again. He was made to wear a sign that read ASK ME WHY I KILLED MARTHA MOXLEY. He stood up in a General Meeting before a hundred residents cursing and screaming at him to confess.

Skakel said he began to think that maybe he did do the thing they accused him of.

&

Later, Krystal would repeat to me those words almost verbatim. She no longer knew whether or not she had done all those things they accused her of, all the things she had confessed to.

&

I had followed Skakel's trial, absorbing testimony about the infamous school where attack therapy and humiliation were the prime therapeutic tools. When Krystal asked me to print out information on Élan so she could show her inmate friends, I began some deeper research into the residential year-round school. I watched videos, read newspaper articles, perused Joe Nobody's graphic novel Joe vs. Élan School, which is not only visual but remarkably explanatory.

I watched a number of videos with actual footage of Élan and the screaming and shouting chilled me to the marrow. I had to mute the sound. The residents themselves had been "weaponized."

An acquaintance of Krystal posted on the Public Élan Facebook page, "There are things about my fellow classmates I am still trying to scrub from my brain. Lots of times people made shit up or exaggerated shit just to be congratulated and feel that 'Élan embrace.'"

Krystal's close friend Tamara posted as well on the Facebook page. She wrote, "Krystal was my best friend in Élan. We know way more than what was reported in the news about Krystal's formative years and what she went through. We all know too much. I mean, it was forced down our throats to know each other."

A spokesman for the Illinois Department of Children and Family Services told the Associated Press that the department's evaluation team had "never seen anything quite so bizarre and degrading. The whole concept of this program seems to be a brainwashing technique."

&

The internet has drawn Élan survivors together. I was shocked at the sheer volume of testimony I found, a crescendo of voices, page after page. There was the Public Élan Documentary Facebook group, YouTube videos, and The Last Stop documentary. The Reddit thread I WAS AN ÉLAN CULT SURVIVOR yielded reams.

I printed out over 70 pages of testimony from various men and women who, in their words, had survived hell on earth. I made two sets and sent one to Krystal.

&

After forty-one years of operation Élan closed in 2011. Reports continue circulating on the internet—stories of student humiliation, deprivation, and abuse, alongside almost unbelievable corruption. Tuition of $42,000 to $56,000 a year purchased a student-to-teacher ratio of forty to one. In my research, I found no reliable numbers on student outcomes, but anecdotes abound, of students who committed suicide, went to prison, or subsided into lives more quietly damaged.

Many of those who were sent to Élan refer to themselves not as alumni, but survivors.

&

It becomes clear to Krystal that unless she moves up the power ladder she will be unable to graduate. So she learns. She learns to avoid punishment by stepping aside, by joining in when required. By shutting down.

After two years, Krystal becomes a Strength; after three years, a Coordinator, but she climbs no higher. As a Strength, once a week she receives two packs of gum, watermelon or strawberry Bubblicious. Now on Friday nights she eats a slice of pizza and drinks a can of soda with the other Strengths.

After she graduates, she signs herself out.

STAR
New York City

I worked on Craigslist and did escort services sometimes. I walked the streets when I first started. It was scary because there are rules you have to go by. The pimps would chase me down and corner me. If I made eye contact with one I was considered out-of-pocket and he could take my money.
—Krystal Riordan, Inmate #661387

In the beginning it's easy. She and Keri-Ann, a friend from Élan, go shopping for real labels, not knockoff brands. Or she walks alone through Times Square to the hotel where she sometimes meets men. She stretches her wings, she stops for a pretzel slathered in mustard. She stops again for a piña colada pineapple smoothie. Three years in Élan, lunch and breakfast the same tasteless glop, dinner three minutes to eat before MEAL KICKS is called. STOP EATING. If you're lifting a forkful of food to your mouth, drop your fork.

Having money is freedom; she's generous and loves to buy gifts. Krystal pierces her nose; she sings to herself among the towers of lights: the Gap Jeans girl's flowing hair is a forest. MoneyGram. Second Stage Theater. Bread Factory. Disney. B.B. King's. She is her own celebrity. When the taxi she's waiting on pulls up, she vanishes, leaving behind the puddles of overripe perfume.

Eighty dollars for a blowjob seems a high price but James, her friend's pimp (and now hers) says you're eighteen, and men like teenage tongue.

Her adoptive parents have offered to pay for college, but after four years of Attack Therapy, college sounds like a thicket of restrictions, rules, and humiliations. The only condition for living in the nice apartment she shares with Keri-Ann and James, her boyfriend/pimp, is that she work for him, too.

After Élan, where screaming residents attacked her for complaining about the food and made her wear a diaper over her jeans for a week, wearing a sign around her neck that read *Feed me pureed puke, I am a Baby,* it's easy to sit on the edge of a bed and wait for the man in the fake leather jacket to unzip. Easy to lick it like it's the sweetest, best-est ice cream.

They list her with Eros.com and Escorts.com as "Lisa," and the men love her. "I was 18, blond, and decent-looking. So calls were coming in," says Krystal.

&

James initiates Krystal into the life of a working girl. In the army this would be termed boot camp; the sex world calls this breaking a girl in. James, known for being a little rough, takes her to a rent-by-the-hour hotel. The neighborhood is dangerous. Prostitutes, addicts, gangs. They have sex on the bed for what feels like hours. Afterwards, her hair hangs in tangles and she's drenched. There's no air in the room. His chest shines like a street wet with rain.

She sees his hand, and the huge thing he has in it, like a flashlight. A dildo. "Get up," he orders, pushing her against the wall. He sodomizes her, jamming the monstrosity in her. Something tears. Lightning flashes, although she hears no thunder.

I remember all the wetness dripping down my leg. I was confused.
When he was done I looked down and I was covered in blood.
There was a chunk of my insides on the floor.
There is still a spot in me that hurts to this day.
—Krystal Riordan, Inmate #661387

She's torn, but at her age physical injuries will mostly heal.

Krystal, tall and blond, so new to the city, to the selling of her flesh. She's free, and she's as beautiful as the model with sable eyelashes walking her doggy stroller past a man with his pants at half-mast, relieving himself. She is still a long way from rent-by-the-week hotels and windows patched with black electrical tape, lobbies with the musty odor of a rabbit hutch that a slow-moving fan stirs.

&

James takes her to a hotel, where three other men and a camera are waiting. He hands her baby-doll pajamas and knee-high stockings to put on, white knee-highs.

They are going to make a video and she'll be the star. She's frightened and the men like that. Soon the room is vibrating. It's the worst thing that has ever happened to her. Ejaculations in repulsive blasts that scatter like buckshot. Through it all, she wears her white knee-highs. Perhaps *White Knee-Highs* will be the name of the video.

The guys were mostly okay. There were a few jerks. Cops mostly.
I had a gun put to my head and a knife to my throat.
They demanded free sex, usually weird stuff.
—Krystal Riordan, Inmate #661387

The off-duty cops show up in unmarked cars and work as a team to rape the girls. This cop already has his zipper down and a thumb hooked in her mouth. Work it. His pinkish meat threaded with blue veins like those movie rivers she'd always wanted to visit, like the Mekong, the Volga, and the Seine.

She pictures herself one of the floating flower sellers. A long-haired girl oaring her canoe, carrying a white sea of orchids.

&

Freedom's End drops by one evening in the form of one of Keri-Ann's friends.

Draymond Coleman is fourteen years older than Krystal, tall, muscular, and seething with the righteous anger of an unwanted foster care child. Krystal perceives him as a gentle giant, funny and attentive, as they share their damaged pasts. His height, his body mass pumped up into the physique of a wrestler,

54

make him, in Krystal's eyes, dangerously handsome.

Perhaps Krystal saw Draymond, his anger and posses-siveness, as love. He raised her from the living death of Élan. A mother/father figure, a jealous god.

He made her laugh as they stood outside to smoke a cig-arette. All the light of the city blots out the night sky, hiding the stars, but the moon is a cool, pale green lake above Madame Xu's Chinese Food and Pedicure. A moon of slow-moving water that Dray tells her he's going to give her; she's worth it. The moon, the shape of his head, his thick mustache, his strength.

She'll learn soon that Dray is like the heat. He seethes at you rather than talks. He must be molten inside and, at his core, mercury crusted over with charm.

WORK DETAIL:
SIX RED MOUTHS THE BULLETS MADE
EMCF, Clinton, New Jersey

*At first I thought Lucy acted like she knew everything
and talked like a book. There was a girl here who tried to punch
me more than once, and I'd heard Lucy was her buddy.*
—Krystal Riordan, Inmate #661387

It's happening again. The lights blasting on and officers shouting, once again she rises and gets herself to the sink. Running the hot water until it's scalding, she fills her mug, then adds a heaping tablespoon of Maxwell House instant coffee and 13 sugars: Maximum Compound's speedball. She likes holding the hot mug between her palms and cooling the coffee with her breath, then slurping.

One day she'll ride a horse into the foothills she's seen on TV, and there will be no one within miles to order her around. No more officers barking. *Get up, Riordan. Line up for Count.* The coffee burns her tongue the way she likes it. She hears the horse's tail swishing in the dry grasses. Her long legs wrap around the mare's flanks (snuggly, perfectly). They stop in a grove of fruit trees, and she reaches up for a ripe peach.

&

In Mess Hall, as always, she hurries through the line. Little changes in Maximum Compound, as if it is always the same day. Today it's a sausage patty, a half cup of cottage fries, one tablespoon margarine, a biscuit, two sugar packets, and a cup of decaf brown swill that few inmates drink. There's a knot in her stomach and she eats only the cottage fries and pockets the sugars. She misses real fruit; her mouth waters for apricots, nectarines, plums. An orange, an apple, not orange-colored water. It's been nine years since she's eaten blueberries or honeydew or any of the above.

&

Krystal walks between two female officers down another long hall where the dirt no longer shines like it once did. There are the same buckets in the corner waiting for the next strong rainfall. She's a bit shaky about meeting her workmate. Her new assignment in Medical means she'll have more money for Commissary, yet she'll be partially responsible for a severely disabled inmate, or at least that's the rumor she's heard. The chunky officer tells her to relax; no one's going to execute her. It must be the Maxwell House caffeine and sugar. Just her luck that the sweet black syrup she loves so much is making her skin clammy.

&

At the nurses' station the tech who likes to call herself a nurse sits overlooking her realm. Supposedly she worked as counter clerk in a pharmacy and knows the arcane details of all the drug interactions. How if you drink your blood pressure medicine with grapefruit juice your left ventricle might explode. Customers loved her, but she'd been fired for stopping up the break room toilet, causing it to overflow. She returned with her boyfriend and held the place up.

"That's Krystal Riordan," the tech says to the dark-haired inmate already waiting beside the nurses' station, pointing to the tall girl being marched in between officers. "You'll be working with her."

&

Krystal immediately sees that they are an odd coupling, and for once she's glad she's almost six feet tall. She towers over Lucy. Krystal's high hips and thick ash-blond hair don't go unnoticed by Lucy. They're looking each other over intensely, their eyes taking small bites—morsel by morsel—all the while pretending to notice nothing at all. Lucy is big-breasted and full-figured, and her dark Italian eyes match the dark hair that sweeps the small of her back. Krystal has heard the scuttlebutt about Lucy, who is said to be friendly with a nutty C-Cottage inmate.

57

&

Neither has an inkling that their friendship will someday be legendary in Max. A thing of wonder, making some inmates jealous, and others feel awe. There will be envious inmates who try to break them apart, but the officers will give respect to the unusual and long-lasting friendship. Radiating from the darkness, a friendship rare as a diamond in Maximum Compound. Neither can see that they will tattoo each other's initials on their wrists and shed fight-blood for the other; that whenever Krystal hears Lucy yelling she'll come running ready to fight, and Lucy will back Krystal up absolutely because everyone knows they're a package deal. That when Lucy's transferred to a halfway house and struggling with the overwhelming task of reestablishing her life outside, Krystal will still be serving time in Max, taking a poetry class and watching the mail for letters that, though fewer than she'd like, always recall the bond.

Lucy, days from release, will be cataloging her losses: nine teeth, her uterus (hysterectomy), broken nose, left foot surgery undone in a fight, hair thinned from stress. Always on the gains side of the ledger, her friendship with Krystal.

Those days are years away.

&

Another inmate tech who once took a class in medical proofreading enters the unit. "Zarina Macaya suffers from multiple sclerosis and she can only use her right arm. You're responsible for her."

Both techs advise their trainees to listen hard because they'll give this in-service training only once. Lucy rolls her eyes and mutters under her breath. They are rushed through instructions on how to change a catheter bag or a diaper, and sponge-bathe an immobile body. The Hoya Lift isn't mentioned as the go-to equipment for transferring patients from bed to wheelchair. Just the kidney dish and gloves.

"Are you in Hillcrest?" Krystal asks her new workmate in her low husky voice. A phone-sex voice. She pulls on the plastic gloves and tosses another pair to Lucy.

"Yes," Lucy answers, snapping on her gloves. "And you?" When Krystal answers, "North Hall," Lucy knows that her work partner's crime was serious. Inmates convicted of violent crimes live in the cells of North Hall, not the semi-dorms of Hillcrest.

We spent 8 hours a day, 7 days a week together, working. I admired Krystal for her strength. I never asked her anything about her crime for a very long time. I just wanted to get to know her for my experience of her.
—Lucy Weems, Inmate #922870C

The tech escorts Krystal and Lucy into Room #1, a single cell where a plump older Hispanic woman lies in the bed. It might be easy to miss the lost prettiness of her fine features. Her beige-gowned body lies inert like a weird planet whose language they can't speak. A non-motorized wheelchair faces the corner.

"Did they tell you I'm innocent? I was sentenced to 40 years for shooting my husband. Justifiable homicide. The judge doesn't like Puerto Ricans." She lifts her right hand and brushes back the shift, her immobile legs are beige too. Those of a plus-size mannequin.

&

Trial photos of Zarina's face suggest a drowned beauty that the tide has forgotten to wash out. Her eyes are ghosts of her younger self; they glance up at an armed guard. Graying hair pulled into a bun matches the severe twist of her lips as if biting down on the judgment about to be made. Her lawyer argues that because she suffers from multiple sclerosis and requires around-the-clock care, Zarina should be exempt from a prison sentence, or else serve her time in a nursing home. The 47-year-old has pled not guilty to killing her husband. At 3 a.m. Zarina gets out of her recliner and uses her walker to hobble into the master bedroom. Having snugged the gun inside the waist of her stretch pants, she confronts her husband. He menaces her and she points the gun and squeezes the trigger. Six shots.

&

The chunky officer strolls in. Zarina tries to raise herself up on an elbow. "At trial I had a reclining motorized wheelchair. I don't know why I couldn't bring my own in. 40 years and that thing in the corner's too small."

Sometimes inmates speak about their trial as if it were their wedding day or their sweet sixteen party, a day in which they starred. The officer chuckles that 40 years of Zarina is no gift. Lucy and Krystal wonder how Zarina managed to get to her feet, let alone kill anyone.

"He emptied my bank account of the money won in a personal injury lawsuit. The stupid DA accused me of the single most dastardly act he'd ever prosecuted—shooting a defenseless man while his kids were asleep on the other side of the bedroom wall. They were my kids too. At 6'2" he weighed 340 pounds. A glutton. Do you call that defenseless?" Unlike another inmate who stabbed her husband 62 times, Zarina allows herself just those six shots.

For five hours she waits, watching the man she married, whose children she bore, begin his journey. In the yellow dawn he looks like he's kissing the floorboards with the six wet red mouths the bullets have made. The eldest daughter testifies against her own mother.

"Can you bring me some water?" Zarina asks Krystal.

If you ask Krystal, she will tell you she did not like me from the start because some crazy girl named Cocoa told Krystal that I was her best friend and so that made Krystal question my sanity (the girl Cocoa is nuts).
—Lucy Weens, Inmate #922870C

Zarina's definitely a mess with her fat everywhere and now her flesh belongs to them—the unmoving left arm, the tree trunk legs. A blob with a mouth, an anus, a vagina, and one working starfish hand. Krystal and Lucy immediately like her.

Lucy exercises Zarina's leg by lifting it and bending the knee. "You know state law forbids inmate to inmate contact. Any inspection of EMCF's Medical Unit that found us dressing, feeding, and bathrooming a severely disabled inmate would result in fines or censure," she says.

"You sound like a book," Krystal says. "How about the stretcher crews? Aren't those inmates touching other inmates when they're picking them up for medical emergencies?"

"Rules bend when it's a prisoner population being served. There's no adequate record-keeping here, nor is it computerized, which leads to flu shots being administered twice to the same inmate like happened to me."

"Do you always talk like this?" Krystal has never heard anyone use the words nor or censure. "So how come you're here? Are you innocent like everyone else?"

Lucy smiles. "I'm guilty as hell but it was a drug dealer I robbed, and I didn't think it mattered."

Krystal laughs in her low-throated way, a good laugh, not a fake one.

&

When it comes to draining the leg bag, they take turns playing nurse. Get the pitcher and empty the urine into it. Close the valve, screw in the new hose. Zarina's nice and funny but she never shuts up about Carl. Killing him once wasn't enough. They change the older woman's diaper and sponge-bathe her. Zarina wonders if there is any way to return to herself, to the time when she belonged in the world. When she got sick with MS, she repulsed him. That she can't forgive. The walker, the cane, the wheelchair. Her trembling hands and unsteady gait. Her sickroom scent. Old lady Opium gone rancid.

By 8 a.m. he's bled out like a grizzly pig brought down. At 8:01 a.m. she calls 911. "I think I killed my husband." No mercy, the judge decides, her disease did not stop her from committing murder. But he murdered me, she thinks. The children are being raised by her husband's mother. "Is there any way we can get him back?" one of Zarina's twins asks.

&

The days pass and Krystal doesn't mind as much Lucy talking like a book or always knowing everything; they're together eight hours a day, seven days a week and handling bodily wastes. It's funny that Lucy, who can recite whole Wikipedia entries, has a kittenish, cute voice as if she's a 15-year-old teenager, not a thirty-something felon. Krystal holds the empty pitcher that they'll drain Zarina's leg bag into.

"That girl Cocoa told me you're her best friend," Krystal says, watching Lucy's solemn expression change from eyebrows drawn together as she unplugs the hose to a burst of laughter. It's nice how a belly laugh, not a smarmy or snide one, which isn't a laugh at all in Krystal's eyes, causes that horse she likes imagining to canter toward her with the sun shining through its mane.

"In her dreams," Lucy says, rolling her eyes. "Maybe she wishes I was her best friend. Doesn't Zarina's leg bag look like a loaf of pee bread?"

They chuckle again and Zarina joins in. It feels good, the three of them sharing a moment, three bad girls. It feels like those times her adopted father took her to the stables and let her ride a horse, telling her not to pull on the reins or look down, but keep her eyes straight ahead. The roan so gentle. Her father didn't have to tell her not to squeeze the flanks between her long legs, she already knew how to be at ease. It was like basketball; she was a natural.

&

"How do you like Hillcrest?" Krystal asks, as she wrings out a washcloth and starts to bathe Zarina, telling her to close her eyes. "It's good. You should try to get moved there," Lucy says, picking up Zarina's immobile hand, turning it over, and examining the palm. "Zarina, you have a water hand. Your palm is long and oval and you have long skinny fingers."

"What does that mean? A water hand?" Zarina asks. "Are

you a palm reader? Carl used to get his fat hand and his lady friend's read and put it on the charge card."

"You're a highly imaginative bad girl. You operate on feelings. I'm looking at your heart line now," Lucy says, tracing the line at the top of Zarina's palm. "It looks like love is in store for you. A man."

Krystal bursts out laughing "What bull crap! A man!" She pats the damp cloth over Zarina's eyelids, which look like eggshells made of skin.

"Did I tell you my husband took his new lady to New Orleans? The bastard spent the money I saved for the mortgage." Zarina can't stop her mouth and both Krystal and Lucy wonder if being immobile in your body causes your mouth to run like a faucet.

"Yup, you did, Zarina, and more than once," Lucy says with a chuckle. "Forget Carl, lady. There's love out there."

"I didn't tell you he treated me to pictures on Facebook— close-ups of the gorger, his lady friend, and my eldest daughter eating lobster, oysters Rockefeller, stuffing themselves on fried clams, cheesecake and washing it down with red wine. The pig was dabbing his fingers in his water glass."

"Zarina, we practically know the menu. Shut up or we'll pour Ensure down your throat." This time Lucy doesn't chuckle, and Krystal wonders if she means it.

"Where in New Jersey are you girls from?" Zarina asks.

"Orange, Connecticut," Krystal answers.

Lucy empties the pitcher of urine into the stainless steel toilet and flushes it. "Wow! I'm from Sheffield, Connecticut."

"Do you have any kids?" Zarina asks. "I have my traitor eldest daughter and I have my twins. They look like a boy and girl, but they're really angels."

The room goes quiet.

"I have two beautiful girls, Hope and Faith." Lucy says, a wave of guilt sweeping over her. Krystal knows how her work partner hungers for her young daughters, thirsts to hold them.

Krystal's thinking about her own daughter, Tiana, the name she chose, a tween now, who Draymond, her lover and pimp, forced her to give up for adoption. Tiana might not be her name; her new parents could have erased it. How will Zarina's twins grow up without parents, who will raise Lucy's girls? They change Zarina's diaper and Krystal remembers those few days of changing her daughter—the sweet smell of baby skin like breeze and vanilla.

&

Yet there is another mother here, as there always will be. Candida Moore, whose daughter, Jennifer, was raped and strangled by Draymond Coleman in front of Krystal. The grieving mother read a statement at Krystal's sentencing: "Not a day or night goes by without us reliving the horrors our daughter suffered—the fear, pain, and agony she experienced at the hands of these two strangers."

It's a devastating statement and probably influences the judge who metes out his draconian sentence of 30 years to Krystal. Jennifer's family watched the hotel video, which recorded the hallway's dense shadows in those early morning hours. They saw Krystal leave the room twice—once to go to the bathroom and once to visit the lobby.

Krystal dreams of the filthy hotel room, which has become tiny as a bathroom in a Greyhound bus. In the metal mirror her hair is a mess of dirty string, her lips welted with pinpricks. The tiny steel sink drains into a bucket of blood. She wants to wake from her sleep. She swims to the surface of her dream but can't pull herself up onto land. The red bucket keeps splashing, spilling.

&

The silence doesn't lift until Zarina suggests they go into her Commissary trunk and get the stuff to make brownies. "Let's make the goodies before the officer does her rounds," Lucy says. Yesterday they cooked the rice and beans from Zarina's Commissary trunk; all the real world food comes in pouches salty and preserved to last until judgment day. All three women like the

64

saltiness that makes their hearts beat faster.

Krystal crushes the whole pack of chocolate cream cookies with the bottom of a mayonnaise jar. Lucy nukes the milk saved from lunch and melts in the no-name chocolate bar. Two minutes in the microwave and they attack the semi-sludge with spoons. Bravo!

&

"Lady, what are you doing?" Lucy asks, when it's time to turn their charge from side to side to prevent bed sores, and sponge the chocolate goo from her chin. With her one working hand Zarina begins washing her private parts including some inappropriate personal touching.

Krystal chimes in. "Zarina, you're molesting our eyes." They can't see into the future when Zarina will add a man to her visitor's list, a brother of a high school girlfriend who had always admired her from afar. He will visit and write her love letters. Months into their relationship he'll kiss her, and in another month use the tip of his tongue.

&

When Krystal mentions the new girl she's been assigned to work with, my ears perk up. Her work partner's name is Lucy and she, like Krystal, grew up in Connecticut. The two women share so much besides being Connecticut natives. Both have been convicted of kidnapping, both know the parking lots and side streets where the sex work goes on. They've both been trapped in the rear view mirrors their dates employ to decide if they're fuckable. Krystal tells me they are becoming inseparable. During their microwave cooking sessions and marathon dance contests, they giggle themselves sick, pretty much forgetting they're in prison. They make up dance steps, one is a pantomime to a prison fight. Lucy pretend-twists one of Krystal's arms, then Krystal fake-elbows Lucy. Good one! Lucy pins Krystal on the floor, half-sits on her stomach.

"Get off, fool!" Krystal manages to choke out the words, her laughter turning to hiccups.

&

I'm surprised when I receive a letter from Lucy, the first of many fat envelopes decorated with long-stemmed roses, watercolor petals, some turquoise, others blush-pink. Inside, the handwriting that I will come to know well fills page after page of stationery. Her folded paper art spills out—origami cranes and swans and dogs.

At first, I hesitate in replying. Her letters feel a bit pushy and seem to intrude upon my relationship with Krystal. I've chosen Krystal, not any other inmate, and I can't be bribed by folded paper no matter how artful.

&

It doesn't take long before I appreciate Lucy's intelligence and open-handedness as well as her head for business, evidenced by her art enterprise flourishing on the underground prison economy. We become friends, and good ones.

I come to understand more of the cooperative nature of the inmate subculture. You share with your friends, and your friend becomes your friend's friend. Most assume it's dog-eat-dog in prison and every inmate for herself. You're prepared to deal with inmates a bit hungrier and more dangerous than individuals on the outside, but not with their surprising generosity.

&

While Krystal often speaks in abbreviated sentences without giving specifics, Lucy is effusive, almost her friend's polar opposite, as she thrives in a world of particulars and delicious anecdotes. She tells me how a cigarette had been planted in her trunk between some Goya beans, ramen, and powdered milk. The officer, a fat ass made even bigger by her uniform, orders Lucy to spread her legs, feet apart. Shake out your hair. Lean forward. Put your head back, let me see up your nose.

Lucy sticks out her tongue, rolls her bottom lip back, while the officer rolls her upper lip. Does the officer think she's hiding cigarettes in her nose or mouth?

&

The weeks and the afternoons drag on, and while Zarina naps Krystal strips down to her bra and puts on one of Zarina's Depends. Pulling them up as high as they'll go she prances around the room. She poses, beckoning to Lucy with her index finger, come on, baby, want some of this? They laugh until their guts hurt. Krystal manages to get dressed before the officer marches in.

"What's going on in here, Riordan and Weems? Why isn't she out of bed? Don't pamper her." The officer shows off her best feature. Her white teeth. Cold teeth. Like a wolverine curling its lip.

"Get her up from that bed and into that wheelchair," she demands. The brownie bowls aren't washed yet. "What's this shit, Riordan? Clean it up!"

&

Krystal isn't sure she can trust her new friend even as Lucy begins to share her darker stories. Lunatic dealers hitting dead women, overdoses. Heroin, you're gliding, your feet not touching earth, and then one summer you're homeless, sleeping in cars, fucking and blowing men, tens and tens of them. In the beginning heroin isn't just need, it's swimming with a lover in a pool nude, and it's driving at midnight in chlorine blue. It's your make-up and the streetlight giving you beauty.

Never into heroin, Krystal liked weed. Her addiction was Draymond Coleman. She shares with Lucy how the detectives charged her with kidnapping and luring the soon-to-be-murdered girl back into the hotel room. She really doesn't want to explain how it felt leaving Weehawken after Jennifer's body had been left in a dumpster, how she and Dray were in the cab heading to Harlem and the heat followed them inside. The air conditioner leaked soupy air, and she buzzed the window down but the hot breeze blowing in irritated him. His forehead broke into a sweat. "I had to quiet her. That wasn't me in that room." That wasn't him choking the life out of an 18-year-old girl.

Krystal had to light his cigarette; his hands so gouged with scratches he could hardly use them. His head hurt. He wanted his mother. His mother!

She hopes Lucy will understand the good things with the Draymond she called Dray. For her birthday he treated her to the Mexican restaurant she loved and in the candlelight his beautiful skin was the color of her fajita. They stuffed themselves, rolling the morsels of beef and pork into red-hot salsa. "You're the only girl in the world I'd ever die for," he said. The Draymond who hated the night to end knowing that he hadn't scored a job or money. He swore on his eyes he was trying.

Krystal still finds it hard to imagine the fear Jennifer experienced, but she'll also picture her own paralysis, her disbelief, her lover killing a girl in front of her.

&

Zarina is getting drowsy as Krystal brushes her hair, scratching her scalp with the stiff bristles. "Krystal, do you have any pictures of the beast?" Lucy asks. "I want to see Draymond, the lady killer."

Krystal shivers. Perhaps Lucy too wants to tunnel into the July 2006 Weehawken Hotel room, a little shabby with the shared bathrooms in the hall, where Krystal and Draymond stayed for the sex work. Will she question Krystal about what happened? Could Jennifer have left the room? If she hadn't screamed or fought would the outcome have been different?

She didn't scream, Krystal might say, or else she might describe screams so horrible that she had to turn up the television to drown them. Hopefully, Lucy will not judge her.

"So what happened?" Lucy says, snapping Zarina's emery board against her leg.

Krystal looks away from Lucy, unable to meet her eyes. "I was sure I would be next. Dray snapped, and then he snapped back. He was afraid I would leave him."

These are the phrases Krystal uses to explain the unexplainable. Inside the room Draymond had punched Jennifer so violently, swelling her eyes shut, and yet blinded she fought on, scratching at the brute odor of his flesh, marking his body with her fingernails.

68

Lucy realizes what occurred in the room will stay in the room. In the silence that follows, Candida Moore again speaks, "Ms. Riordan might not have known that a murder would take place that morning, but she did aid Mr. Coleman in kidnapping Jen for the purpose of sexual assault."

&

Krystal lies on her bunk trying to sleep with her headphones when Officer L enters her area. He's a pretty fair guy and gives out more pink sheet warnings than blue sheet write-ups, which go on your record or get you sent to Lock.

"Get dressed," he says, "Macaya's had an accident. You and Weems are needed in the Medical Unit." All the way down the crusty hall she tries to get him to tell her what kind of accident. As soon as they enter the unit, she smells the accident. Zarina has pooped herself and made a stinking mess. Isn't she the night crew's responsibility?

&

When her points improve for good behavior an officer gives her the news: she needs to pack up. She's going to Hillcrest. In an hour. For a moment it's as if she's swallowed bubbles and might rise to the ceiling. An inmate on the transport comes with a hand truck to help her move. Funny, she's been here for years and all she has looks ratty, like it's all been through the wringer. Even her new stuff looks old. Her photographs, her letters, the glittery birthday and Halloween and Valentine's Day cards, the clothes and underwear, her television and headphones. She says good-bye easily to this cell where she smoked her last Newport a few months ago before the No Smoking Policy went into effect and even the guards went crazy with withdrawal. Her transfer from North Hall to Hillcrest where Lucy lives seems like a dream vacation.

&

The first night Krystal stops by Lucy's room the Mess Hall had served a crappy chicken and rice casserole sans the chicken bits since the inmates on kitchen crew had eaten them all.

Krystal asks Lucy if she wants to eat some mac-n-cheese. It's a game of crisscross in the beginning when new friends resemble lovers learning how much their pasts overlap and discovering their sympathies and alikeness. Lucy tells Krystal about her crazy Italian–American family and how after her druggie mother abandoned her 23-year-old father and kidnapped Lucy and her brother, Freddy, how after her father got them back, her grandmother and her aunts and uncles rolled up their loving sleeves to help raise two motherless kids.

&

Krystal's eyes widen and she looks away, almost as if she's forgotten the spoon in her hand. "Neither of us really had mothers but your big family sounds nice."

It almost hurts her to hear about Uncle Rocco, the biker uncle, and Uncle Marco, the bookie uncle, and Lucy's grandmother also named Lucy, and the godmother-aunt and the rich husband. The holiday feasts of homemade Italian specialties. One day she'll tell Lucy how her adoptive mother fed Krystal hot dogs three or four times a week, so many hot dogs that by junior high Krystal had soaring cholesterol. She loved hot dogs then, and still does.

"I had an uncle, too, my mother's brother. He wasn't a good uncle to me," Krystal murmurs. The spoon stays lost in her hand. Her long hair falls into her face, each strand a flame highlighting the symmetry of her features.

Lucy's amazed that her new friend has twelve more years to serve, if she's lucky and the 85% of sentence rule holds, otherwise she'll have twenty-three years. She wonders what could have happened to land Krystal in this dirty place with her height and looks, Krystal, who could have played basketball or modelled or partnered with a man or woman who treated her with respect and love.

&

Krystal will learn of the night terrors that plague Lucy when hunger for her daughters empties her of sleep. They are still months

70

away from deep friendship and becoming bunkies, Krystal lying in the top bunk after lights out, and Lucy's twisting and turning below.

"Hey, I can't sleep," Lucy will say.

Still months from Krystal sliding off her bunk and bending over Lucy, pleating and doubling the sheets until Lucy is swaddled like a baby, and then Krystal tucks her in. Lucy begins to drift into a sleep of lukewarm green. Sweet pickles floating in a brine of seeds and she is floating too. Months from Krystal's black ink drawing that Lucy finds beautifully odd, and barters her batteries for red construction paper to frame. A year from the day officers move Krystal to another unit and Krystal hits herself in the face with a lock and gives herself a black eye claiming she isn't safe away from Lucy.

Don't forget the night Lucy feels depressed, which means end-of-the-world down-in-the-dumps stuff, on Mother's Day when she hasn't heard from her daughters, and Krystal will unfurl a blanket on the floor and chuckle, daring Lucy to get on the blanket, and she will drag her friend down the hall to make her laugh. They will share more secrets of the chaotic ride that led them here, how they'd grabbed for the safety strap at the last second but when they needed it, it flew away like a frightened sparrow. They'll call each other soulmates and they'll laugh and challenge each other to dance competitions. Then like Zarina they'll kiss the six red mouths that bullets have made in each of their bodies and the world's body.

&

Krystal still has no inkling that when Lucy has served her time and leaves for a half-way house, she will, unlike so many others, keep her promise and not forget her best friend.

Krystal won't be alone, not in her imagination; she'll be leading her chestnut mare by the bridle, remembering how men had mounted her and she had ridden them, and neither led to the far away, neither led to besotted flies and happiness, or delirious weather. At first the men rode her gently, then rocking. Hard.

71

In the mirror of the mare's neck she sees her face. In the blackness of its nostrils her own breath. Her feet go into the stirrups although she's not ridden a horse in years, a click of her tongue and off they trot, not like in Poldark or True Grit, fast enough to break your neck, but perhaps enough to break the breeze.

UNION COUNTY JAIL:
SOLITARY CONFINEMENT
Elizabeth, New Jersey

The attorney told me I was looking at 30 years.
—Lucy Weems, Inmate #781192

The officer leans in the window with his dark glasses and shaved head. Sun pools on the hood of the car in undulating halos. Her mind stays quiet and cool, as if the flames shooting up from her childhood have been doused by God. Yes, there are drugs in her, although not enough for even a police officer to detect.

"Lucy Weems?" he asks, surveying the car. He notes the car seat securely fastened and the stuffed bear and frog in back. She was driving from work to the daycare center to pick up her daughters when she heard the police siren behind her and felt that red shiver in her throat, the fear rush. How is it he knows her name?

"Yes?" She puts a question mark at the end of yes. Tiny blue suns pulse like heartbeats in each lens of his glasses. After working as a prostitute, you never quite get accustomed to the uniform. Not much scares Lucy, the woman who used puddle water to cook her heroin when she was low on cash, the woman who climbed in and out of strangers' cars. No dark stairwell in a public housing project spooks her psyche.

&

"Step out of the vehicle and keep your hands where I can see them."

The cop's a youngish guy, maybe Italian-American like her. She gets out of her car, trying to step gingerly, as if a dangerously wide space were opening under her feet. Cars are slowing; drivers crane their necks, rubbernecking. His walkie-talkie crackles from his belt-line, complete with revolver, citation pad,

73

pepper spray, the bulges and bumps of police paraphernalia. "You're wanted for armed robbery and kidnapping. We've been looking for you for six months."

Armed robbery? Kidnapping?

"There has to be some mistake, Officer. I'm due to pick up my babies at daycare. I'm an accountant, not an armed robber," she says, smiling. Stay calm.

He reads her the Miranda warning, and then he handcuffs her. Still, there's disbelief in his voice that such a well-dressed, good-looking woman has committed the crime she's accused of. In the horrible thrill of the moment, you don't yet know this is the tidal wave that rips your feet from under you and sweeps your future away. One day you're an auditor in a pantsuit crunching numbers, and the next, a hooker in a car letting a stranger lift your dress off the hanger of your body. The red spandex that you've slipped on and off—gone.

&

Elizabeth Street Precinct Station. She's lying on a metal bed and nothing else. No blanket. Who will pick up my babies? My two girls. Please help me.

An officer tells her that her ex-husband has come for them. Her bail's set at a million dollars, then lowered to $500,000, and later to $250,000. When she talks to her attorney she'll be truthful, but today she can't stand up. Today she doesn't think about the hotel room where she and two girlfriends lured her dealer, Ramón, with promises of sex. He'd sold her a tainted batch of heroin that made her so sick she thought he'd poisoned her. Knowing he had to be taught a lesson, Lucy went shopping for kidnapping at Home Depot, purchasing ties, rope, and duct tape. For armed robbery, she borrowed a handgun. Easy to get him to take his clothes off once he saw the gun. They tied naked Ramón to a chair, robbed him of money and drugs. He'd recently restocked—weed, heroin, cocaine. "Tell Housekeeping you're a sex act gone badly."

Freed hours later, he calls the police.

74

Heroin and love of it breeds hydra in polluted water, underwater forests of it breathing the oxygen, birthing more stalks with long rag-like leaves. Hydra blanketed by the dark, cloying water suffocates fish. The hyacinth. Like heroin, killing what is most precious—the water itself. Floating on their sides, fish staring into the icy ball of the sun. Rehab and relapse, her cycle of life. Finding a dream job as an auditor, loving it, supporting herself, then falling back into car repossession, eviction, stealing, and prostitution. The hunt for drug money empties her, leaves her in the streets, disappearing from her family for months.

Hydra hung with druggy, incoherent black apples underwater.

Even though I was detoxing from heroin they did not give me
anything to help subside the terrible withdrawal side effects.
—Lucy Weems, Inmate #781192

She's in full-blown withdrawal—vomiting, diarrhea, chills, heartburn, convulsions. She's fed a dry burger on a stale Kaiser roll, and decaf water-coffee three times a day. Her head spins. The cell is overcast like the Florida Everglades, the tour guide pointing out alligators, the ancient reptiles waiting in the scummy green water under the metal bunk. She tries once to tame the nausea and takes a bite of the choke sandwich. Flashing lights explode in her head. Raves, all-night dancing, drugs. A beautiful anarchic desolation. Acid house music, DJs calling her name, Lucy. She can almost taste the blotter acid on her tongue; she's dancing, mesmerized by the contrails her fingers scribble in the air. Then everything goes bad and she's throwing up, the bass drum crashing on every beat in her head. Ecstatic girls, long hair smelling of tropical fruits and flowers. Again, Lucy bends over the reeking toilet.

A cramp hits her like an iron horseshoe. The dizziness comes and goes. When the cramp lets go, she takes a deep breath. The shaking makes her teeth chatter. The walls reflect her putrid choices, streaked with feces and vomit. She doesn't think of her babies, her four-year-old and two-year-old daughters. There were always people who adored her, and yet heroin, which did not care at all for her, earned her love. Heroin carries a thousand silver-handled whips. In the silkiness of the nod, shots cry out. Detox elbowing you through the green glade of puke that keeps erupting from your guts. The night's insomnia eyes hiss and every inch of skin is ridden by ants. Freedom's last gasp.

It was bad enough to feel like the world didn't need you in it ...
but then to feel like an outcast on top of it just ripped my soul
apart.The worst of it was, and, this was all I thought about 23
hours a day in #1313, alone, seeing ghosts, should I, and could I,
off myself?
—Lucy Weems, Inmate #781192

Union County Jail. She's taken to Cell 1313. The jail has 13 floors and she doesn't want to go inside. Number 1313 feels cursed. This is solitary confinement. You spend 23 out of 24 hours alone. All the eyes that stared into these walls; all the buttocks that sat on the toilet, as if to pee away the mistakes that led here. The room is 10 ft. x 10 ft., with a bunk, a sink, a toilet, a desk and chair. A letter slot of a window, 12" wide x 3' high, faces a gray-grit parking lot and a grayer apartment building. Thirteen flights up and the people below are mosquitoes. Wave at me, she thinks, concentrating every ounce of her being. Wave. Mosquitoes, wave at me.

The thing called the past reigns here. Her crime is more serious than the prostitution and possession charges that bring most to County. Number 1313 gives her time for life review. What speaks the truth and what lies?

&

Her high school self roves across the ceiling. That Lucy falls in love with accounting after working summers with her uncle, her

76

natural gift for art, writing, and comedy supplemented by a mind able to find the sexiness in numbers, the art required to make them balance; tidying them up, pigeonholing, and classifying them. At twenty, she marries Michael Weems, who labors as a well-paid Union welder. They live and love well, and then her husband introduces her to heroin. He makes such good money they never have to go without, and heroin isn't the center of their lives. They're chipping. Here in her king-size bed, propped up against the pillow of the cool white wall, her beautiful man shows her how.

The couple thinks little of doing heroin before work and after. He forgets to tell Lucy about heroin withdrawal, about the wild shakes you go through and the drizzle of cold rain in your bones, about the day the sun subtracts you to zero. When she leaves him, she stops using heroin and her body shivers and vomits and defecates. Thinking she has the flu, she visits Urgent Care. The doctor, after he examines her, noting her track marks and listening to Lucy describe her symptoms, informs her that she's going through withdrawal.

&

It hasn't stopped—pooping, vomiting, insomnia, and heartburn; fierce rushes of acid in her esophagus, sweating, and shivering. She begs for a TUMS and the guards laugh.

"Deal with it. You did this to yourself."

Twenty-three hours of alone time. One hour to shower, make phone calls, the single hour called "recreation time." A radio is allowed in and a friend sends three books a week, most of them by James Patterson. Solitary confinement seems to be the kingdom of psychotropic medication. A kingdom where the Constitution's prohibition of cruel and unusual punishment falls on deaf ears. To keep prisoners from going stark raving mad, they are medicated. Her public defender warns her that she may be looking at 30 years.

&

Lucy senses the curse of #1313, the narrow window, and the

bars. Shadows begin to take on corporeal form; they flicker in the corners. Instead of swallowing she begins to cheek her medication, and then hides the capsules under her pillow. She licks the rain pebbling her cheek and sings to quiet herself. Not rain but sweats. In a heat wave of detoxing, the skin sweating sounds like a downpour rolling through the canopy. She ruminates over her life, the heartache she's caused her loved ones, the wreckage of her choices. The ceiling fills with images: a wedding, her pregnant mother, 16, and her father, 18. Freddy is born and in two years, she arrives.

The young Lucy Basso's first four years are spent in the bosom of an extended Italian-American family, and then there's the day when her mother's drug-dealer boyfriend loads their beds into a van and moves them and their mother into a dingy loft. The six-year-old boy and the four-year-old girl hardly leave the apartment. She can see her brother growing skinny like the room. Their hair is matted, they don't bathe or brush their teeth, and after the boyfriend leaves, strange men come and go. Lucy sees her mother poke the silver gleam of a needle into her ankle. "What are you doing, Mommy?" she asks.

"Giving myself medicine," her mother answers, injecting the silky sleepiness into her pretty leg. On other nights her mother dresses up and becomes a stranger in a leather skirt and goes out, while Lucy watches from the window. Like she is watching now in the shadowy cell, watching a woman in high heels getting into cars. Lucy stays watching for hours. The window, the ceiling. "Mommy, come home."

The beautiful woman with big eyes and hair the color of melting chocolate calls up, "Honey, just a few more cars."

&

She eats the stock of pills she's cheeked, and for all her desire to escape and end this hell, she wakes in vomit in the jail's Medical/Psych Unit. The next day she undergoes ten minutes of counseling, in which the psychiatrist explains his version of karma and how Lucy is experiencing hers. Just deserts. In essence, the biblical reap-what-you-sow admonishment. He prescribes Haldol, the drug-of-choice if the zombie state is desired, which turns naturally vibrant Lucy into a slow-motion slug. She tries four more times to die.

&

Her four-year-old daughter, Hope, hates the cold and holds on to her undershirt when Lucy tries to take it off her. I be cold. I be cold, little Hope pleads. Then when both babies contract poison ivy, she pours purified water into the basin and lifts first Hope, then Faith, easing their bottoms into the water. Their cheeks shine, raw red, and they squirm while Lucy soaps them. It hurts. I know it hurts, my darlings. The scabs open no matter how gently she works her fingers.

"It's almost over," she murmurs, and then she sings. Lullaby and goodnight. When she kisses their softness, the love she feels for them is almost unbearable.

&

Things still flit in the corner of her eyes. A floating arm or leg, not a fish, and a glimpse of something weedy. She turns to stare them down. Sweat is crying at her temples and leaking down between her breasts; her body feels like a greasy ice cube.

&

Days turn into weeks. The medication piles 40 pounds onto her petite frame.

&

She can see everything in the ceiling and walls where the past lives. The past holds the loft. When her mother nods out after shooting up, the men stride into the children's room and the six-year-old brother tries to stop them from touching his sister. In the cell she is undersea and the man's eyeglasses are floating on the water's surface. Underwater is warm and cloudy and safe, like her name. Lucy, her grandma's name; Lucille, her aunt's.

The man pulls her out of the water, he's touching her, and his finger enters her. She is a meal for the shapes swirling around her. Not that night but another and another it's her brother's turn.

"He's gone," her brother gulps. She wants to sink into the bubbles and never return to the surface.

"You're the softest thing ever. I bet you like this. I bet you do."

The man's finger hurts her. A Popsicle stick lifting her toward the ceiling. "Does it hurt? I'm not hurting you, am I hurting you?" She pictures lasagna, the pool of red sauce giving a bath to the yellow cheese. Mister Cheese. He talks into her ear, his lips tickling, and bits of words blowing into her ear. His breath in her ear makes her stomach sick. The rest she no longer cares about.

&

Mostly, Lucy cares about food. Her stomach is hungry and there's nothing in the cupboards or refrigerator. Her brother discovers a neighborhood grocery a block away and they go there and smell the air. The wood floors give off the aroma of sawdust and cold cuts. They inhale the bologna and salami, and let their noses eat. They smell the cold blueberries and the strawberries in their frozen bags. When customers keep the old man busy sacking and the woman checking them out, her brother steals a loaf of bread and they run and gobble it. "My brother shared it 50/50 always. Sometimes he would roll the bread into balls and we would pretend they were meatballs," Lucy says.

All this she pictures on the ceiling of the cell, her eyes open or closed. She's flooded with love for her brother, her protector. For a year, they possess only the shoes they left their father's house in. They're young and they're growing and the heels of their feet are covered with bloody sores. They don't have socks, and when Lucy steps on the back of her shoes to loosen them, her toes shiver. For a year they don't brush their teeth and their mouths fill with cavities.

&

She closes another detective book, lies down, and looks up. College student Lucy's in the ceiling bent over her calculator and peering into a computer screen at the trial balances and statement of activities, at the crimes and malfeasance in each number until they balance. The ceiling swallows one Lucy and spews out another and another.

Seven-year-old Lucy takes ballet and ruins the recital by dancing her own routine while the rest of the ballerinas look on. Ten-year-old Lucy discovers the flute and practices "London Bridge" for hours. How she loves the slender silver stalk, her breath giving birth to trills. She loves the aperture her lips form, a secret tunnel. Her infatuation with the flute lasts until her first recital, where she plays perfectly, and then it's on to another challenge. Thirteen-year-old Lucy adores her karate class and the instructor, earning a Second-Degree Green Belt, winning tournaments until she can't break the brick with her one blow.

&

The tray arrives and she eats 1 hot dog, ½ cup mixed vegetables, 3 slices of bread, 1 cup decaf-water. Yesterday, chicken and noodles, ½ cup carrots, 1 muffin. She tries to push thoughts of her daughters away; she doesn't want to dirty her girls by even picturing them in #1313; she doesn't want to feel the crash of guilt. But her girls come; she sees herself cradling her babies, first Hope and then Faith. All the while each of her daughters had been inside her womb, she'd stayed clean—she'd felt Hope's soft head, her hands preparing to touch, and Faith's lungs working to breathe, her ears listening. She's pressing her palms to her nine-month stomach, her fingers listening to her baby's heartbeat. The miraculous life inside her.

&

It would be better if there were cell bars instead of a locked fortified door with a tiny window in the center; better with bars, as the officers would have to see you and hear you. With bars you wouldn't hear your own breathing. One of the officers sometimes rolls a cigarette under the door—if she flashes her breasts at him and he's looking in the window. Barter.

Alone 23 hours a day, it felt I was in a cursed room.
I had gotten delirious and started to see shadows
and movements that were unexplainable.

She's still gaining weight from her medication. No exercise, a diet of sugary carbohydrates and few fruits or vegetables, only the preservative-laced tasty foods of the Commissary offer sweetness to the mouth and mind. Before it is over she'll gain 100 pounds. Her teeth throb. Cavities that hot or cold liquids stab with their tiny pitchforks. A lightning bolt of pain in one of her incisors and she almost passes out. One tooth, another tooth, needles of pain. No dentistry here but extractions. Lucy loses four teeth.

&

The officer has walked by on his rounds and won't be back for an hour. She ties a sheet to the vent. The cell, which wants to claim her, throws its haze over her eyes—especially the left one—and the cave-darkness of the future. The hair rises on her body as she ties the sheet around her neck and climbs the desk. It feels like escape; she only has to move her feet and walk into the air; she takes a deep breath and sends love to her babies, her big-kid dad, her brother, her stepmother, her godmother. She kicks herself off the desk, wades deeper into the air, suspended now, and knowing suddenly this isn't the way.

She tries to get back, but her feet can't reach the desk. The sheet tightens around her neck. The more she struggles, the tighter the sheet, and then mercifully, she blacks out. Night falls and Lucy hears it stumble and her brother, too, listens to the light losing its footing.

Night is there, breathing, on the other side of the room. Go to sleep, their mother says, opening the door, then shutting it. Her mother can be no older than 24. Lucy and her brother are hungry, and when the dark truly comes there are others who seek food—bugs skittering, hunter-gatherer roaches exploring the walls. Mosquitoes, with their ballerina legs, descend onto the children, drawn to their blood. Outside, the diamond stickpins of asteroid belts blink, but here, bugs are the dark stars shining from the wall of the room's night.

&

Out there in the hall one footfall, then another. Miraculously, the guard making his rounds has turned back. Turning back, he glances in the window. Seeing her hanging, he pops the door and cuts her down. He's annoyed. No county jail wants to deal with a suicide and the spotlight of an investigation.

&

In the air, kicking off from the desk, the sheet tightening and knowing in that moment that your daughters need you, trying to get back to the desk and you can't and then blacking out. Coming to, Lucy wakes to a real hospital, her neck with its deep lacerations bandaged, she wakes to actual nurses and doctors. Blessed two weeks in a psych ward with caring counseling.

After she is released from the hospital, they bring her back to #1313. No, she begs, she fights. I can't go back into that soulless room. The door clunks behind her. Her medication increases, medication to blur the real.

&

Her tongue in her own mouth becomes a stranger. Long, pink, and rough like a cat's licking at the corner of her dry lips. Perhaps she's becoming more catlike. The pills tumbling through her are listening. Three times a day the prisoner who has been appointed tier-worker distributes the medication. The door pops. Three times a day she lines up in front of the tier-worker for the Dixie cup of pills and the cup of water.

Her night cocktail's haul of eleven pills holds up the line. Eleven pills she has to choke down. Like the mouse in her cell has to swallow the balls of bread she leaves for it. The women behind her grumble. Listen, she wants to say, you're facing 60 days in county jail and I've got a real crime. I'm looking at 30 years in prison.

The District Attorney wants the names of her two co-defendants, the women who helped her tie up Ramón, but the crime was her idea and she refuses to give them up.

&

The day comes when her mother's habit takes the sun from her and her beauty is a smoldering coal that heroin pisses on. She can't feed the children and so she calls Lucy's father. "Bring me a thousand dollars and come pick up your kids."

Her father and godmother-aunt drive to the bum apartment and walk through the ganged-up-looking guys hanging around outside. Lucy knows the moment her father lifts her into his arms that the horror has ended. Lucy's godmother shakes her head. "What did they do to the children? Their ribs are showing."

&

Home. Lucy and her brother are bathed and barbered and fed pasta and meatballs and chicken primavera and three-cheese pizza with five toppings. The siblings eat and eat, and Lucy's grandmother makes them dreamboat biscotti and Zabaglione. They gain weight and will always have to fight the desire to stuff themselves. When Lucy opens her closet a wave of heat surges through her and she can't go any farther. She fears being shut up inside and the door locked behind her and the skittering things raining on her feet and hair.

Therapy, counseling, doctor visits, dentists; no expense spared to heal them. Freddy refuses to talk about what happened; Lucy can't stop talking.

Lucy's father is no more than 26 and a single dad. Grandmother and aunts and uncles pitch in, giving care and love. Angel hair linguini, clam sauce, Italian wedding cake soup, tricolor cookies. Lucy, an extremely intelligent girl, is kept back in the first grade. Her year of dogs barking close by as if they were starving or being taught to fight, of sirens, black shapes, and nauseating gulps have deprived her of language—singing, speech, counting. Those subjects didn't interest her mother, only heroin.

Her brother never allows his guy friends to flirt with his sister. When he enters junior high, he walks a mile every day to meet Lucy at her intermediate school.

Her father's a big kid, and tells them to hop into his vehicle because they're going to the diner. Not their favorite eatery, but okay. They ride off in the sea-green Monster Truck or the red

Beretta or maybe the souped-up Jeep, but it's not the diner with its cabbage and old-grease reek, it's Chuck E. Cheese.

Somehow, the angels' wings kept me alive long enough to find out I wasn't doing 30 years, but sentenced to nine years.
—Lucy Weems, Inmate #781192

Her father, alarmed by the Public Defender's 30 years, manages to hire a real attorney, and then everything changes. The facts of the case become distortions. He examines the evidence and gets much of it thrown out—blurry video footage, tainted DNA exhibits. The plea deal's 30 years gets dropped to 15 and then to 9. Lucy accepts the 9 years and will be transported to Edna Mahan Correctional Facility for Women to begin serving her time. Ramón, the hard-core dealer who bullied his customers and sold tainted dope, shows up at the sentencing and claims he'll be traumatized for life.

&

In the doggie wagon van the sun has gone out, and Lucy sits with her head bowed. There's no room to straighten up without hitting the van's roof. Better to contemplate the shackles around her ankles and the handcuffs encircling her wrists. Soon she'll add inmate to her list—a college graduate, a flutist, an artist, a mother, a wife, an accountant, a heroin addict, a prostitute, and an armed robber and kidnapper.

Maybe it rains only inside her or the doggie wagon. The same kind of van that Animal Control transports stray dogs in. All afternoon it's been the gray overcast that makes you feel like you're floating inside the steam that rises off a kettle. Yet she's high on being out of Cell 1313. She's interested in her neighbors, her fellow prisoners, and the noises of the interstate. Instead of how the jailed world sounded—the outside muffled and half drowned. After being in solitary confinement for a year, the breathing and shuffling of her neighbors being transported to prison is music.

&

You can feel the highway but not see it. One of the other prisoners says she's from Newark and the other from Camden. The Newark girl violated her parole and she's on her way back to EMCF. This is her return trip past the cliffs of Weehawken, past the sea-oats sloughs that once flourished and now are a toxic nothingness that ducks putter through.

So long, Newark, all dying cathedrals and abandoned factories. So long, tall clusters of trees, poplar and hickory. The Ironbound section—foreclosure storefronts, mosques, flu shots advertised $24.99. All the doggie wagon ladies have tasted the dark matter bubbling at the universe's core, the trapdoor that leads to the street, the homeless shelter, or prison. Like Lucy, the other shackled women bow their heads and to God, glancing down from the clouds, it looks like they're praying.

ROGUE WAVE
EMCF   Clinton, New Jersey/ Cary, North Carolina

To some extent, we all construct and reconstruct our lives in the stories we tell and the images we share, but Facebook exists in a special twilight realm; a world village gathers here to drink from its trough of images. Although I have never met Lucy in the flesh, I consider her a close friend, and Facebook lets me skim through her life, her life before. Life Before always holds a great fascination for me.

Lucy might be years away from her last download or posting, but her 2010 is captured. There's Disneyworld, there's Christmas, and the celebrating mother and daughter won't leave these frames ever. There's the husband, Jimmy, now her ex, embracing Lucy in her red holiday sweater, there's her smiling blond stepmom and her father, there's daughter Hope in a pink parka, surrounded by a snowbank of presents, shimmering gold and silver bows.

There's 2009, a babyish Hope on Easter in pink gingham sashed with white feathers, and, Lucy, the mother, wearing white as well, her dark hair and eyes shining as she holds her swan daughter. Both mother and daughter look ethereal, as if they've been floating in clouds; the love-glow beams out of both. Fast forward to Faith, in pink heart-shaped sunglasses at Disneyworld, being hugged by a tiger, Faith in a peacock dress and matching hat of blue, yellow, and green. I view her Facebook friends and read her chat. After 2010, everything stops.

&

There's a trajectory here. I sense a downward spiral from the Facebook photo galleries holding Lucy's stepmother and brothers, husband and daughters, as though heavy cream in silver pitchers. Nothing has yet been spilled, and then it does.

Lucy mails me a striking 8 ½" by 11" glossy portrait in which she sits on a bar stool in a finished basement. It is clear that Life has happened. Wearing a salon-gal dress of spaghetti strap, flounces, and vintage boots, she smiles. Wryly. She's no longer the beatific mother in pink and white of 2010. Behind her the bar with its bottles glint in a mirror the size of a picture window. The bottles float in reflection like crescent moons on the surface of a lake. Her daughter Hope is older, no longer a toddler; she sits on a stool next to her mother with a book in her hands. The baby, Faith, is not pictured.

Lucy holds a revolver lovingly in her lap, admiring its barrel, the weight, the smoothness of its nostril. It will make her shine like an asteroid belt.

I study the photo for some time, fascinated. Lucy asks for copies of the photo, which I make and send, but Lucy learns that they've been destroyed by the EMCF mail screeners. Photos with firearms in them are forbidden.

&

Many people sail through their lives on fairly calm seas, passing through the occasional storm without lasting damage. Others grapple endlessly with leaky boats and turbulent waters; they struggle, they swim—or they sink.

An unlucky few of us are hit by rogue waves. If there was any warning, we missed it—or dismissed it.

I count Krystal among these. She had spent enough time with Draymond to know he was as flawed as he was charming. But the sudden snap, the violence that squeezed the life out of Jennifer Moore, seemed to come out of nowhere, she says, unexpected, suddenly appearing, and a threat to anyone within range.

&

Looking at Lucy's photo, I chose the pinpoint pupils of the bad girl and saw Lucy's grip on the revolver as my friend letting the gangster in her out. I took what I knew of her life and imagined her heading into the storm that ultimately washed her into EMCF.

88

Years later, I asked Lucy about the photo and the gun. She said she'd simply been vacationing with Hope and Hope's father at a Wild West-themed motel, and posed with the props they'd provided.

I didn't tell her what I had assumed. She knows my story, so I probably wouldn't need to explain why the appearance of a gun in the hand brings up the spectre of my forever mistake, my rogue wave.

We stopped at the end of the driveway before going up to the door. This is where and when I mentioned to you that I saw a red glow about the house, and maybe we shouldn't go in there, turn back, or go do something else.But you didn't see it.You said, "But they are all your friends, right?"
—Michael

"Where are you from, honey?" he asked, his southern accent blended with a bite of sarcasm. I told him Iowa. The little piggy in the center of the nation. When he laughed, he meant it.

I'd spent the summer after high school hitchhiking across Canada. In Montreal, my ride dropped me on St. Catherine's Street and I found my way to St. James the Apostle Church where the transients hung out.

Determined to slough off the skin of my innocence as fast as I could, I was only looking for a place to crash; instead, I found Michael, a 19-year-old Black Irish, pale white as if his skin never saw the sun, handsome, tall, and unkempt. I had no idea that "Black Irish" referred to dark-eyed, dark-haired Irishmen. He wore high-top sneakers and a turtleneck with ragged sleeves. He was from Cary, North Carolina, a town outside of Raleigh. He was a writer, he said. He was everything my mother hated.

When she did meet him in the hospital sitting cross-legged on the floor of my room, they fought. When she accused him of stealing my virginity, he snapped back that I was no virgin when we met. That was the truth of it.

The hospital room was still four months away.

&

Michael and I hitchhiked to North Carolina for his sister's wedding. His parents liked me because I pitched in. After the wedding reception, dishes were stacked everywhere and I washed and dried them all. It took hours.

In the days that followed Michael and I laughed madly, I teased him mercilessly about the sautéed cabbage goulash he ate instead of meat. We held hands and I scribbled on his palms and forearms. Pretend you can't hear, Michael, and I'm talking to you through your skin.

No matter how close we grew, he always let me know I would not be the only one. He would sleep with other girls. In the hard parlance of the time, he would "ball other chicks."

&

Michael didn't ask me to leave but I needed to head back to Iowa; I had plans to go to college. I took a Trailways from Raleigh to Cedar Rapids, where I spent three weeks attending classes.

But when a letter from Michael arrived, I left school and hitchhiked alone through five states to see him. Standing next to a highway when the sun had set, seeing the taillights of a car braking, not knowing, opening the passenger's side door and sliding inside. Like Krystal on the street, clutching at the fear in her stomach, the car stopping, never knowing what she was getting into.

How silly my red Maybelline eyebrow pencil and the pink Estee lipstick. The comb and my coin purse, the $5 inside. The can opener with the spiral corkscrew—my weapon of defense.

&

The old tobacco farmer who gave me a ride from Asheville tried to hand me a ten-dollar bill and I asked him to put it away. He wanted to make sure I ate a full meal once I got to Raleigh and suggested the Char-Grill. I told him he'd shared something better—an education in horticulture. He'd pointed to the passing fields with their peculiar yellowish-green plants. Some of

90

the leaves looked like the dried skins of giant lizards. Tobacco country, where the long-boned drying barns shied away from the highway. He did everything by hand, from weeding and harvesting to barning tobacco. He did topping and suckering, too. Breaking the yellow flowers off the plants so the soil fed the leaves. We travelled a long way together and I lit a cigarette and learned how it all worked.

&

When we got to Raleigh, the tobacco man dropped me off at the bus depot near downtown. Shouldering my Army surplus back-pack, I passed a ghostly Woolworths where the lunch counter sit-ins still lingered. Between the storefronts and parking meters an auto parts garage emitted the sound of wrenches hitting met-al. Dusk was falling. Even the fronds shading the asphalt looked weary, their petals brittle. The pearled petals cracked off into hard black chips.

Michael sounded giddy when he heard my voice on the phone. "Honey," he said. "I want you to meet my best friend, Charlie. There's a party tonight."

No questions about my trip, it was as if I'd walked across the street.

&

There were four of us, Charlie, his girlfriend Janet, Michael, and myself. She was a shapely blue-eyed girl with flowing hair and a southern accent that burbled out of her mouth. She flirted with Michael, and he with her. We strolled on the University of North Carolina-Chapel Hill campus where Charlie went to school. His light brown hair parted on the side fell over his face onto his shoulder. His eyes, I'm not sure. Blue, more likely hazel.

I saw him only on two nights of my life; this night would be the first. He was meatier than Michael, who was rail thin. The fir trees and oaks, massive and towering, surrounded the beer kegs that had been delivered to the quad next to Charlie's dorm. The early October air smelled of cedar and damp earth and roots uncoiling, snaking above the ground.

The three of them filled their plastic tumblers with free beer, once, twice, thrice. Janet took off her indigo cape and draped it from Michael's shoulders. They laughed, and played matador, taking turns being the bull. The clean-cut fraternity boys who hosted the kegger smirked and pointed.

I stood alone under the trees apart from the others. I hadn't yet learned the art of liking beer.

&

In Charlie's dorm room, he popped in an 8-track tape of the Rolling Stones Let It Bleed. Through the long night, it would play over and over, an endless loop of "Love in Vain," "Midnight Rambler," and "Country Honk."

His roommate had left for the weekend and the room looked as if no one lived in it. Two beds, two desks, two textbooks, one candle, and little else. I sat on one of the beds, and Janet took the opposite one. She got up and lit the candle. We didn't speak. Charlie had taken Michael aside, they stood near the door, and then Michael returned and dropped down beside me.

"Charlie wants us to switch," he said, lowering his voice. "I'll be with Janet and he wants to ball you."

He waited for me to respond. You've been ignoring me all night, I wanted to say but even that would be admitting too much.

I was complimented in some weird way. Like Krystal telling me that during those first months of sex work she never felt so beautiful. I was round-faced, slender, 18. An Iowa farm girl. Pretty, but not beautiful, except for large (nearsighted) brown eyes.

"You have cow eyes," Michael had said.

&

Chuckling, Charlie pulled off my boots, yanked the legs of my jeans and slid them down. Already naked, his hair falling in his face, he told me how he could go for hours, that chicks had to beg him to stop.

Part of me had already gone to sleep, but the rest of me was there to please. Charlie was thick, solid. He rolled me onto my stomach, lifted me onto my knees, picked me up.

How many times did I hear "Gimme Shelter" before the bed where Michael and Janet lay, both of them fully clothed, disappeared completely? On my stomach, on my back, my side. "Love in Vain."

Again, he plunged into me. Now I understood he wanted to hurt me with it, he wanted me to bow to the strange fuck heat seeping into my blood. I should push him away, make him stop. This was work, this was tying the tobacco leaves and being thrown into the curing furnace.

Had Michael agreed to this, even before he asked me?

Had I agreed?

&

Hours later, both of us drenched in sweat, Charlie told me to wrap my legs around his waist and he carried me into the bathroom while his dorm brothers opened their doors to watch the procession. We showered in the nozzle's rain hot, then cold. Not cleansing.

He told me I was pretty cool. The Ioway chick. He should have said that reptiles were jumping from the moon.

If I had never seen Charlie again, if the second night had never happened, the dorm room with the candle and the 19-year-old who wouldn't stop, who wanted to hurt, who seemed not to care he was doing this in front of Janet, the girl he would marry, in front of his best friend, Michael, I might still feel this lingering shame.

It looked like you had a good time with old Charlie. Michael has reminded me over the years of that night and that room.

&

I do not want to think of how afterwards in Michael's house on Normandy Street we argued and wept and talked endlessly. We agreed this would never happen again. We had transgressed against each other, only my sin was far worse.

I had gutted our love, only you could not ever say that word. The dirtiest word there was.

&

Love. I could not and would not say the word either, ever, or not for a very long time. Never to Michael and he never to me.

That is the dirty word that carried me home on the Trailways from Raleigh back to Vinton, Iowa and to work in my uncle's dental office.

I knew the route but this time I watched the towns and the names that might be oracles. Snow Camp. Thomasville. Rougemont. Passengers, white and black, getting on and off the bus like hymns. The bus driver, lanky and red-haired, wanted me to take the seat behind him. He asked my age. Kimesville. Liberty. The driver's looks reminded me of shacks and goats eating lonesome crabapples. The driver kept raising his eyes and mouth into the mirror to smile at me. Youth itself must be what this older man craved. Who knows why I remember the Winston-Salem supper break? There was nothing to eat in the depot except the vending machine's triangle-shaped tuna salad and egg salad garnished with Tom's pork rinds. Sandwiches that glowed green and tasted like janitor-in-a-drum. More towns. Climax. Hiddenite. The ghosts of grey wolves.

We crossed into Virginia. I saw a sign for Roanoke.

1587, the mystery of Roanoke Colony. Virginia Dare.

The Blue Ridge Mountains were out there. Old Jim Crow laws. Unicorn root. The bus was winding its way up the velvety blue shadows of ancient mountains. None of it felt real, only the shame and the goodbye to Michael. In the hollows poplar and hemlock, the oak's yawning bones. Then West Virginia and more towns. Oceana. Looneyville. Wick. Lynching happened more in the low-lying counties but here in the hills as well.

I pictured a boy and his two sisters hanging in the branches, fingers cut off. If you dream of us, the sisters seemed to say, even without our fingers, we will touch you.

94

&

Vinton, Iowa. I stayed with my aunt and uncle on Riverside Drive where college brochures awaited me. Days, I worked in my uncle's dentist office, half-heartedly filling out applications— Minnesota, Nebraska, Iowa, whichever school had the easier enrollment requirements. Although I'd been on the honor roll throughout high school, I only did what came easy to me.

I couldn't think about the future. I lived in the moment. I wanted to experience the grittier world, but I'd learned the hard way that in that world there were rules, too. Sex was expected of girls, no attachment, no strings. Guys claimed their freedom, and chicks were little birds, second-class citizens.

&

The letters from Michael started coming in, one every third day, fat envelopes filled with his poetry and ink sketches, but nothing personal, as if one of his alter-egos, an alias, had messaged me from his medieval dungeon.

A note from Charlie had been slipped in: Remember me? I'm the dude with the white Toyota and we partied that night in Chapel Hill.

He mentioned another party, the one he would be hosting at his place on Thanksgiving. I was invited. His parents would be in Paris for the holiday.

&

Over the years, I've given a lot of thought to both Charlie and Draymond, and to the forces that shaped them.

Although Charlie was raised as an only child in affluence and Draymond spent his boyhood shifting between foster homes, unwanted, the two men shared certain tendencies. Both required constant stimulus. What lights up the brain of the ordinary person stays dark in the brain of a psychopath. To Draymond and Charlie, a word like "rape" likely resonated as little as a word like "pear."

I have read that without an inner emotional life, the psychopath struggles mightily with boredom, that emptiness of thought marks his inner space. All is external excitement. Impulse.

I'm completely unqualified to diagnose, of course. But I see parallels in these men. The threesomes Draymond insisted upon. The girlfriend swapping that Charlie engaged in.

The burst of destructive rage when thwarted.

&

A girlfriend dropped me on the I-80 entrance ramp and I lifted my face into the cold and felt a few snowflakes. I watched them sparkle in the headlights of oncoming vehicles, blue minnows, whirling. I stood with my thumb out. No gloves. I hadn't packed any.

&

A sports car, metallic-gray, and low to the ground stopped. The driver, in his late 20's or early 30's with fleece-like silver hair, announced himself "too tired to talk." He said, "All I ask is that you talk and keep me awake. The coffee thermos is next to your foot. Cups too."

I poured, drank, prattled on about Chicago being the great Midwestern city. My father's hometown. My aunt's house in Morgan Park was now on a street too dangerous to walk down. Did he know Longmont Drive? He didn't have to answer. I was 12 the last time we visited. My mother wore a polka-dotted turquoise sheath with pearl beads. My deeply religious mother had legs like Rita Hayworth. Time to eat. At the table, a tossed salad in a wooden bowl with homemade vinaigrette, and then came the rare steaks. Each plate held a T-bone; at home one steak fed four. I told the driver with his fleece-like silver hair that we didn't eat meat rare in my mother's family, anything animal had to be toasted into a burnt offering.

The snow still fell softly like a Saturday afternoon rain, but it was snow. It was approaching 10:00 p.m. according to the clock in the dashboard. In the world of the Volvo no longer reachable from where I sit 11:00 p.m. will never arrive. I have no idea what I said only that I rambled and when I stopped he ordered me to

96

keep on talking.

The driver called me T-bone when he dropped me at an Indianapolis east bound entrance ramp. "Thanks, T-bone, you did good keeping me awake."

&

An overheated blue Volkswagen beetle picked me up. The Puerto Rican husband hunched over the wheel while his European wife and their baby navigated. His brother and his brother's buddy shared the back seat, and I squeezed into the buddy's lap. We traveled across Indiana and into Ohio. The car by-passed Hammond and Gary, Indiana, the steel mills' orange smolder, sparks flying from the smelter stacks like huge fireflies. Slag heaps.

We drove on, into the legendary Thanksgiving blizzard of November 24th. Soon it seemed our headlights were the only ones on the highway and they too reached into the swirling white and vanished. Five adults and an infant—captives in the snow world and the wind. Hours later, my new friends dropped me at a Trailways on the Pennsylvania border to catch a bus to Allentown where Michael would be waiting for me.

&

The massive snowstorm could not stop me. Even in this retelling of an event that happened a lifetime ago, I am not in a hurry to arrive at Charlie's party. How much easier for me to dwell in the land of before. How much easier to place Krystal in the time of before she meets Draymond Coleman. The stakes are so high and yet none of the three 18-year-old girls can see—not me, and not Krystal when she first meets Draymond. Not even Jennifer when she turns and spots her murderer.

&

4 a.m. in the Allentown Bus depot. A highway patrolman approached me, "Are you Stephanie?"

I froze; this could only portend something awful. I answered slowly, "Yes."

The Highway Patrol had picked up Michael, trying to thumb a ride in a prohibited zone and took pity on him. He was waiting for me in a cell over at the jail, where the sheriff had been kind enough to give him a bunk for the night. I followed the patrolman outside to his cruiser and got in. He would drive us to the interstate in the morning.

The jail walls were thick stone and the bunks clean. We didn't sleep at all. We were too busy being happy to see each other and planning our route to Raleigh.

&

In the morning, police coffee gave me strength. The black bottom of the pot like static drained off a citizen band radio—a local broadcast, bitter rhythm, thick. We both wanted to drink coffee until it hurt our mouths, until it rushed through us.

On the highway Michael was a little more dressed for winter than I was; he wore a jacket from Army surplus, high-top sneakers, gloves, and his hair a homegrown muffler. It was Thanksgiving, and we should have no trouble getting rides.

Waiting for a ride, we shivered against each other, a good shiver. We held hands, agreeing that at Charlie's party, no switching partners.

&

I do not have to guess how far Normandy Street was (or still is) from Cindy Street or look for the unnamed tiny cemetery where African-Americans were buried, most graves marked by piled stones only. The walk took only 5 minutes now like then and the property values on Michael's Normandy Street are hundreds of thousands less than the 5-bedroom 3-bath, Roman-column houses on Charlie's Street.

Michael tells me we both saw a red nimbus of light around the house, a red aura, and we asked each other whether we should go in. That doesn't sound like a story either one of us would make up but I don't believe I saw it, or else I forgot it in the actual red of the aftermath. It was a large expensive ranch house with columns on either side of the front door that looked misbegotten as if they had run away from a plantation in another century. We walked around to a side door and Michael knocked.

&

The door swung open and Charlie stood in the bright entryway grinning, his hair brushed over the side of his face, covering his left eye.

"Hey, come in, come in," he said, his drawl deeper and slower. He was drunk.

I said hello and smiled but kept holding Michael's hand as we walked inside. The kitchen seemed to radiate light, the bulbs in the ceiling lamps must have all been 100-watt and every lamp had been turned on. The polished-wood dining room table was a forest of Jack Daniels, Wild Turkey, Johnny Walker, wines, and long-necked beers, like a skyline of liquor. Charlie hoisted a bottle of whiskey and drank. "Michael, you've got some catching up to do. Let's get you drunk."

A glass of Boone's Farm Strawberry Hill appeared in my hand. I glanced beyond the bottle forest into the living room, at the three-piece slate-gray sectional sofa, coffee table, and long pooling drapes. Other friends of Charlie and Michael were in the living room all along. All teenagers. Michael dropped my hand and went to talk to them. I stood alone again.

How clean everything was and like my aunt's house, everything in good taste, everything in the kind of good taste only money could buy. A safe house. I chose to ignore the turbulence already churning the waters.

"It's good to see you," Charlie said. He was so close I could feel his breath on the back of my neck. The liquor's swelter.

&

I would not be in this house long and yet every second of every day in the decades since flows from this house. My eyes again take in the kitchen. Avocado laminate countertops and an avocado refrigerator. I'm not guessing at the shade of the appliances, as they matched those in my aunt's house. Not a bit of food anywhere, as if Thanksgiving had no place here except for a centerpiece of squash gourds, Indian corn, and pumpkins.

I took another drink of the sweet wine, wine so cheap the

bottle unscrews rather than corks. The White Castle of wine. I suddenly needed to wash the taste away.

"Can I get a glass of water?"

"Help yourself," Charlie said, snickering. His wolf eyes were glazed, stalking from behind the brown hair in his face, when he again tilted the whiskey. The kitchen floor was tiled in earthen tones. They matched my suede boots, lace-up, and deer-brown, the boots that I would wear blood-caked home months later, and not on a bus, but a plane. I marched to the cupboard next to the five-faucet sink. More money here than even at my aunt and uncle's.

I'd always liked to look at things people kept in cupboards and drawers. Cutlery, dishes, cookware, what they stored in junk drawers. I opened the cabinet to rows of tumblers and goblets, champagne flutes, La Rochère-stamped. A Google search takes me to the French stemware I saw then.

I filled the rose tumbler. The tap water tasted like warm strawberry soda-wine. I stared out the window into the growing dark waiting for my head to clear.

"You forgot to turn the water off," Charlie said. His arm slipped around my waist. I didn't move at all, didn't respond. There were crab apple trees out back that had lost most of their leaves. "Remember me?" he whispered. "I'm the dude with the white Toyota. I sure remember you."

The room in Chapel Hill again, the flickering candle, my legs over his shoulders. The grin. His arms had been strong, and he'd wrapped them around my waist, pulling me up from the middle, and then poured me back onto the bed. His body hard as a car door. "Moonlight Mile" and "Sister Morphine" luring farm girls into the deepest and most dangerous furrows where a boy or girl would be waiting.

"Give me a kiss," he teased, "you didn't come all this way not to give me some soft. You can at least look at me."

When I turned to face him, he kissed me, trying to open my mouth with his tongue. My stomach knotted.

100

When Michael walked into the kitchen, Charlie said, "Tell her, Michael."

Michael looked at me, then at Charlie. After a brief silence he said, "Great party, man. But…she's with me, Charlie."

I asked where the bathroom was. Charlie pointed. "Down the hall."

"Charlie," one after the other of us said, "Put the gun down, we don't need it." And on and on to take his finger away from the trigger. He said he was protecting his friends. And the more he said that the tighter his grip on the gun, and the less I believed him.
—Michael

I left the wine glass on the counter and walked toward the plushy carpeted hallway. Charlie followed me. "It's the first door on the right. I'll show you." His eyes locked with mine as he reached for my hand.

"Charlie, I'm sorry but I'm with Michael now."

The grin dropped from his mouth. The laughter and shouting faded into a knot of noise. The last hall I'd walk down, the last few yards swinging two good arms.

I found the first door on the right. Once inside I fumbled for the light switch but never found it.

I didn't need to pee. Instead I wanted to look at myself in the mirror, to comb my hair, to put on lipstick. I didn't need the light for that, so I just left the door open a crack. The hallway light was bright enough to see by its shine.

&

Was I touching the towels and smelling the soaps? Was I admiring the shape of the sink and the pattern imprinted on the shower curtain? Was I in here because it felt like Michael was about to ignore me again?

Why no light in the bathroom? Now Michael tells me that the bathrooms were always the go-to place to talk in low voices for this crowd, to get away from the madness.

I leaned closer to the mirror until I found my face. I blinked. Did I hear the sound of distant thunder? One boom, then another.

Light from the hall spilled in as Michael entered. "Hey, honey," he said. "Mind if I come in and talk to you about Charlie?"

I sat down on the fur-covered toilet lid. Michael stood next to the tub directly across from me. Paul, another friend of Michael and Charlie, came in and parked himself in the tub. A young guy with blondish shoulder-length hair is all I can retrieve of him. A shadow's shadow.

"Charlie says he's getting threats from rednecks and went for his daddy's shotgun to protect his friends," Paul said. "No one knows what he's talking about. He went outside and shot off a few rounds."

"Everyone's telling him to put the gun up," Michael said. "Honey, I think we'd better get out of here."

Michael, the man I liked, a better word, *like*, than the clichéd and crusted-over *love*, and always would, looked down at me, his black eyes holding all the towns we traveled through south from Allentown, miles swept by in flyspecks. Michael in a brown leather jacket, his hands jammed into the front patch pockets. Under the jacket he had on a tee shirt that showed his stomach. Almost as skinny as mine.

"There he goes laughing in the kitchen so maybe he's over it," Paul said. "But he's armed."

I believe Charlie was intent on shooting you as he couldn't have you and he always had gotten what he wanted. No one wanted to hear that. And the friends soon distanced themselves from the tragedy and were lost in time. As were you.
--Michael

The door thumped open all the way and there stood Charlie holding the 12-gauge shotgun. I had time to glance to my left to see him with the gun, the long gun, almost as if it was slung from his hip.

Michael said time itself slowed. I experienced it as totally speeded up.

The barrel was aimed at my face. I must have leaned forward, must have been looking at Michael, or I would not be here at 6:29 a.m. after an all-nighter revisiting the ghost of a Thanksgiving.

I heard Charlie laugh.

&

Today, perhaps a cell phone video would have found its way onto Facebook for the world to dissect, but for this, Michael gives my eye witness account.

Charlie burst into the bathroom with his shotgun, while the two partygoers who had been standing directly behind him scurried back to the kitchen. From there, it spiraled down quickly. His friends tried coaxing him to put the gun aside. "Charlie, put the gun down, we don't need it. Take your finger away from the trigger! Charlie, take the shells out!"

He kept on about the threats, about protecting his friends, even while Michael pointed out that we were his friends and he didn't need the gun in here.

Then time literally stretched out, slowing as Charlie put his finger back on the trigger.

Michael tried to move, to pull me forward out of the barrel's aim, but couldn't. Paul said later he had frozen in the tub. The gun went off.

&

In my peripheral vision, I saw Charlie burst in with the shotgun. I heard him laugh but I never stopped looking at Michael. I heard the blast, saw the blue snort of fire from the barrels, felt intense heat.

A crack of thunder, a loud boom as a lightning bolt exploded from the gun. The blue flames were in the air a long time that must have been less than a second. I didn't have time to raise my hands. Flames hit my face like boiling grease.

This is what happens in the newspapers. It's happening to me.

The buckshot hit with such strength it boosted me above the tub. Pieces flying out of me, blood and bone, like corn spattering from a sheller. Hard bits. Teeth. I was being harvested. I was straddling the blue flame.

The house vanished into an enormous black. I must have toppled onto the floor because I could hear their voices above me.

"Don't die! Don't die!" Michael screamed. They all talked in screams now.

I was inside the black and I could not breathe or see. My lungs had filled with blood, although I could not know it then. All I knew was I couldn't breathe. A farm girl at my core, I knew I had to get out of the bathroom to breathe and die outside. Following some kind of instinct, I started to crawl, kept crawling and bleeding. No one stopped me or touched me or got near the blood.

They tell me Charlie wanted to call his family doctor, but someone phoned the police. The fire department arrived first. It took three firemen to hold me down. In the ambulance I came to for a moment when the EMS gave me oxygen.

I heard the siren and wanted to laugh that the sound of forked red lightning was speeding me to Raleigh. There the hospital ER packed my lungs and sent me on to Duke University Medical Center, a teaching hospital in Durham. My injuries were too profound for a regional hospital to handle.

My life belongs to those whose names I do not know. The Thanksgiving firefighters and EMS, the doctors and nurses in Raleigh and Durham.

JAILBIRDS
Lyon County, Minnesota

A judge sentenced a former Orange, CT., woman to as many as 30 years in prison Thursday for her role in the death of a New Jersey teen whose body was found in a trash bin in a case that led to a crackdown on New York City nightclubs.
—New Haven Register

The Lyon County Jail is housed in a stone building impenetrable as a granite cliff. I was lucky; my cell in the small Minnesota county jail had a view. A huge oak shaded a window whose bars shone in the sun. Staring into the emerald leaves of the massive tree the bars only made the outside lusher, more desirable.

Another antiwar resister would be my cellmate. Judy Fox, her body like the sleek animal she was named for. I idealized her—her looks, her passion, the work she was doing to end the war. I was secretly pleased at the prospect of spending nine days locked in a cell with her.

&

Once in custody, my bag was opened and its contents spilled into plastic tubs. The bruised eyebrow pencil and lipstick, the clumpy mascara, the musk oil, lemon drops, Starburst fruit chews, Bic lighter, Virginia Slims, a prescription bottle of Darvon, Tylenol, a fat wallet stuffed with miscellaneous and two dollars.

The Darvon the sheriff would keep and bring to me as prescribed. No tweezers, no fingernail clippers, nothing sharp, no jewelry, no cash or coin.

A female deputy took us one at a time into a separate room, the walls the same damp stone. She patted me down and then asked me to remove my clothes, to bend over and spread my cheeks. I reeked of patchouli. A druggy smell. Unashamed of my nakedness, not at age 18. I hoped she wouldn't notice my arm. I

105

even tried to hide it from her.

"Your arm is limp. What happened to you?"

I almost laughed. I never heard it phrased like that and never would again. "Limp," meaning flaccid, wilted, a noodle. My arm was rigid, a soldier fated to salute for half a century, angular. She told me to get dressed.

I knotted a red halter and slipped into my jeans which hung on my pelvic bones. My jail uniform for nine days.

&

Judy Fox went first to be fingerprinted. We rolled our thumbs in black ink, the sheriff asking her for the right and left thumb and nodding at me to give him two right thumbs. This was July of the summer the harbors and mangrove swamps were mined, and when we pressed our thumbs into the sheriff's blotter, I admired how they spread in ink like swirls on underground rivers.

A white sheet had been unfurled behind us for our mug-shots to be taken. Both of us smiling. The war was the backdrop of our childhood and adolescence, always there but not there, the rice paddies and wild orchid forests, the napalm and B-52s, blooming and exploding in our cornfields and school lunches.

We climbed narrow stairs between cornmeal-colored walls. Like prisoners everywhere we each carried a blanket, a sheet, and a pillow. The stone locked a lavish coolness into the jail.

&

The sheriff escorted us into one of the bedrooms of his stone house. A tall man with wide shoulders, handsome in a strong-jawed way. Not like the surly officers Krystal must deal with, the ones who delight in saying no, who don't give a fuck and say so. The cell door opened, two bunks, one on each side and chained to the wall, a sink, and a silver toilet on a raised platform. Home for the next nine days.

"Three meals a day," he said, locking us inside. "Every two days you'll get a shower. Dinner my wife makes, and she's a pretty good cook. You can ask the rapist and stick-up guy across

106

the way and the assault and battery fella down the hall, if that isn't so."

He grinned and a dimple showed in one of his cheeks. "Okay, girls, enjoy your stay. Judy, if you need anything let me know."

I could see his dark eyes travel over Judy, not leering, but in an admiring way. I too appreciated her unruly beauty, her thick kinky red-brown hair, her husky voice the ear drank in.

"He's nice," Judy said, unfolding her sheet and blanket.

I stretched out on my bunk. "He is nice."

Krystal was admired by an officer too. They would meet in a closet and kiss. He wrote her love letters, brought her glitter and gel pens, he made her feel special. When her bunky Shaun found one of his letters, she tried to blackmail him for gel pens and an 18" gold chain. He was caught up in the EMCF sex scandal, fired, and later arrested. Krystal never spoke out against him. Her loyalty as ever her angel and her demon.

&

My eighteenth year was proof I had not learned the lesson the shooting should have taught me. My impulsivity, my flinging caution to the wind, and my throwing my future away drew me to Krystal, who had also thrown hers away. Whatever was yet to come had been ruined.

She spent years in Hudson County jail awaiting trial, perhaps thinking this would count, that she would have served enough time and be let go after the plea or the trial. She kept waiting for Draymond to proclaim her innocence and clear her name, to tell the truth of how she had nothing to do with Jennifer's kidnapping and murder, nothing to do with any of it. Instead, he dragged her deeper into the cauldron, the ravine overgrown with sticky webs and roots.

She apparently does not know that he accused her of having had sex with Jennifer, as well as him, before the bludgeoning began. I cannot bear to be the one to tell her.

&

Nine days in the Lyon County Jail. Breakfast: coffee, milk, Kellogg's corn flakes, white bread toast. Lunch: a bologna-and-mustard sandwich and coffee. Dinner: home-cooked by the sheriff's wife, yesterday's chicken and biscuits, corn-on-the cob, and fruit. Lights out at 9:00 p.m.

&

Proud of our arrests, Judy mounted the raised platform and sat on the toilet as if a ruby-jeweled throne, her red hair like rope unraveling over the shoulders of her ribbed purple top. While she peed she talked about wanting to adopt bi-racial children, the ones left behind in Saigon, she wanted to elope with a silka deer. In front of her lay a future.

She made friends with the prisoners across the hall. The men loved her, especially her sultry voice. The rapist and stick-up guy rolled lemon drops across the hall into our cell.

The sheriff brought us books other prisoners had left behind. In the slow afternoons when light slanted in, we read aloud passages from Harold Robbins' purple sex prose and laughed. Longhorn cattle drives and a Latin gaucho lover, jungle birds, panties going moist every four pages. The sheriff too wanted to be near Judy, to listen to her voice. Nights he would carry a footstool upstairs and set it outside our cell, or squatting down like the Vietnamese did, he and Judy discussed the politics of protest. I snuggled up with a penlight reading Fire in the Lake, Francis Fitzgerald's Pulitzer prize winning history of Vietnam and the American intervention.

We each had our own war.

&

As the lemon drops rolled across the floor, we drank from plastic cups our mangrove swamps of coffee, and cleaned our trays like we did in grade school. We would resist. We would make the world change.

Judy and I talked through the nights, the ember of our cigarettes glowing. We were both running from our mothers. She had written essays on the Midwestern mother, on a generation of women before feminism, who saw other women as rivals, including their daughters. Especially their daughters.

Kali Maa, the Mother Goddess, the Teeth Mother who devoured her children, the Buckboard Wagon of Criticism Mother, angry and strong pioneer women marooned in the 20th century. The Cult of the Great Mother, the oldest religion of all, Cybele, raised by panthers and lions, her love too intense for her mortal prince who went mad and castrated himself.

Our mothers' love was too much for us, their daughters. We spoke of grandmothers and wondered if they had been Teeth Mothers once, worn down by the water of work, softened.

Judy remembered being a shy girl, wishing the grandmotherly neighbor who babysat her had been her mother. She told Judy that tiny maidens lived in the castles of sugar and flour and rode through the baking powder clouds on the backs of grasshoppers. The kindly woman taught her the secrets of dough and pie lattices. I loved my grandmother, her kindness, her kolaches, apricots and cherries and poppy seed.

&

When Judy showered downstairs that's when I mounted the throne to poop. Girls don't do that dirty business openly, not easily.

I was lying in my bunk when the sheriff suddenly appeared, telling me I had a visitor. He opened the bars and led me down the stone stairs through the hallway into the jail's visitor's area. It was just a few tables and chairs.

Lips painted white, patchouli-drenched, with copper bangles on each arm, I had metamorphosed into someone and I was thrilled that I had a visitor to witness me in my anti-war glory. Did I have enough eyeliner and mascara on?

I saw my mother rise, leaving her purse on the table, her arms that smelled of brown sack and celery at her sides, eyes staring wide. Who was that with the bare stomach in hip-huggers? She grabbed for the cigarette I was smoking, knocking it to the floor and stepping on it. "This is what I sacrificed for, scrimped and saved. In jail. A daughter of mine in jail."

Her mouth a sharp thing, mine even sharper. Jeans dragging, I pranced to her, batting my ghoulish lashes. She had been 75 miles away at the Bible Conference in Storm Lake, and decided to drive up to Marshall to see me. Her blue eyes looked watery when she flipped her clip-on sunglasses up.

"You look like a haggard whore," she whispered, smoothing her injured dress.

She was fifty-eight. This was my last chance.

&

I should have said sorry, I should have wept, but my lips felt numb. I hit my thigh with the flat of my hand. My eyes burned, but no tears came. I was eighteen with a scarred face and one useless arm. I had rebelled against her strictness, and a fellow long-hair had shot me.

&

On the day Krystal walks into the courtroom for her sentencing, she is shaking. The parents of Jennifer Moore are present, as are the Riordans, her adoptive parents. On the advice of her Public Defender, Krystal has pleaded guilty to the charges leveled against her. After Jennifer's mother reads a devastating victim impact statement, the judge asks the defendant if she has anything to say before he pronounces his sentence.

She faces the Moore family.

"I wish this never happened," she says, in her throaty voice. "I'm not going to say I'm innocent because I know what I did was wrong, but at the time I was scared, and I did fear for my life."

Jennifer's parents show no change in their expression, but the Riordans weep. Only after the judge sentences my friend to 25 years for kidnapping and 5 years for hindering apprehension, do Jennifer's family cry tears of joy.

&

I never mention to Krystal the nine days I spent in jail for demonstrating against the war.

110

Not the Gulf War or Afghanistan or Iraq, but the Vietnam War, which was for my generation "the war." Nine days in a county jail such a spit compared to the fourteen years she's already served. When my nine days were up, I walked out under the leaves of the oak, free, without probation or parole.

Somewhere, a road was left open, not left or right, but a crooked road.

NATURAL BORN KILLER
New York City

Dray was funny and liked to laugh. He was really attentive when it came to me. It was like I was brainwashed. I thought I couldn't live without him.
—Krystal Riordan, Inmate #661387

At first he showers her with attention. They talk outside the apartment, where they go to smoke cigarettes. When her friend's boyfriend decides to sell her to another pimp, "That's when Dray stepped in," Krystal says. "He fought for me."

They leave together and she begins working to support them. He is charming, funny, and sweet. He makes her feel beautiful. When his fingers explore her hair, she notices the clove scent of his hands. Her lips please him most, the plump lower and heart-shaped upper. Draymond pimps her; he goes out with her at night to watch over her. She calls him Dray and she admires his strength. "He didn't like how a guy was leering at me and he fought him."

Under the peculiar rubric of the pimp/prostitute relationship, Draymond can live on the money she makes having sex with strangers, yet still beat up a man who looks at her too long. She believes she loved Draymond more than he'd ever been loved. "Dray was a pimp and I was his moneymaker," Krystal says. "He would bring girls over on a regular basis for threesomes. I always did what I was told by him."

For Draymond, she gave up not only her body to strangers, but every dime she earned. Bloggers report that Krystal cheated the Cookie n Cream Escort Service out of their fees, handing all her trick money over to Draymond, who called every hour. She obeyed him, she says, because she loved him.

"She was tall, blond, blue-eyed, and white. The guys loved her. Not much of a chest on her, but she had a pair of hips," says Jasmine, the booker at the escort service. "She never smiled, and she was terrified of him. I felt sorry for her."

&

Krystal uses condoms with strangers but not with Draymond, so when she misses her period for the second month, she takes the pregnancy test. A positive. She tells him the news and he's happy, but he's going to see to it she keeps working. Her belly incubating life means little to her except a change in her size and having to buy larger clothes.

She's not a druggie, although she likes to smoke weed. Draymond keeps her on a short leash, which she interprets to mean he loves her. He must. But he never loses his thirst for more women in the circles of midnight, in the hangover of morning turning to afternoon.

&

Pregnant, her clothes feel like cardboard and chafe against her. Her dreams turn green and things keep budding. Ants build humongous castles. Inside, separated by a thicket of blood vessels, the old miracle takes place; sperm and egg meeting, carrying the double helix, the chromosomes for sex, eye color, and skin, height, bone structure, potential and possibility. The fetus absorbing its mother into the womb-trance.

The baby wasn't real to me until she was born.
—Krystal Riordan, Inmate #661387

She gives birth to a healthy girl. The past doesn't say hello, or goodbye either; it expects you to do all the work of bringing it back. It requires curiosity. The baby becomes real when she leaves the hospital. How long before Krystal's working again? She's still bleeding, still stitched up.

She hardly has her long, this girl-child. One night she returns from work to find her daughter gone. Draymond has called

Child Services, telling them to come for the 'unwanted' infant. She stops caring. The 19-year-old is under Draymond's control. Friends have questioned this story, telling me the mother's signature would be required in a closed or open adoption case. I suspect that Krystal, unable to face the truth of how she and Draymond lost custody of their child, has revised the story. She herself had never felt mothered. Her birth mother neglected her, her adoptive mother's strictness never made her feel loved. What a sensation to hold a baby, and when the newborn is your own child, there's nothing like it. I'm not sure Krystal could feel it.

Years later, she will ask me to look for her daughter on Facebook. She would be a teen now, with a birthdate of May 6, 2005. Although I searched and searched, I found no trace of a girl named Tiana Sade. The last picture Krystal has of Tiana is a photocopy of a photo taken when her daughter was four. The child of Krystal and Draymond is a mix of white, black, and Hispanic. She inherited her mother's long legs and expressive lips—lips like eyes. A beauty. The baby Krystal gave birth to is so distant, her daughter might well be a waking dream.

&

She slips her tongue between this one's lips and into this one's small ears. She howls and whimpers, she's on her knees in men's room stalls, she's spreading her legs between forests of overflowing garbage. The men tell her that her hips are made for sex.

When work's over, she tears wrappers off chocolate bars with her teeth, wolfs down peanut butter cups, starts in on M&M's. The sugar hitting her bloodstream feels like a heat wave inside, the sultriness that drugs and makes you numb. You're like a boat gliding through the men, filling your mouth and hands. Sweet oysters, eating one, putting two in your mouth; buckets of oysters, the taste of the sea and come. She smokes some weed and relaxes. Who cares about the stopped-up sink? About the marijuana, social workers claim, was found in her baby daughter's bloodstream?

How long did you have her?

114

Not long.

&

The Krystal who lives behind bars seems freer than the ba-by-faced prostitute trapped between her pimp/boyfriend Dray, the funny charmer, and Draymond Coleman, the killer ex-con. Letters still come from him. "You showed me true love and I didn't know how to handle it. I thought it was all a game, but it was true. You put my name on your body. You had my baby. You gave me everything. Now it's all gone, thanks to my stupid ass."

There are paragraphs of complete sentences with no mis-spellings, letters written in a delicate cursive. "We'll be Natural Born Killers," he told her after Jennifer's last breaths. It surprises me to see the handwriting and think of the same hands stran-gling a young girl. Yet Krystal has never forsaken him.

The night of his arrest, Draymond claims that he'd picked up a working girl at the Port Authority. "I am not a wholesome man," he tells police, "but I am no murderer."

Wholesome. Such an odd word to choose. My mother's generation used it to describe a good girl, a wholesome girl, what they hoped for in their daughters. Krystal pictures Draymond, his forehead glistening with moisture and his smile showing his dimples. He wasn't all bad, she insists; something had snapped in him the night of the murder.

"After he killed Jennifer he broke down crying and kept saying he was sorry," Krystal explains. "Then he said he did it to prove he loved me." Nostalgia for the minute before Draymond half-carried Jennifer up the stairs like a wounded bird.

Stephanie, when you love someone too much, you can't see past that person. That's how I felt about Dray. I thought I couldn't live without him. I can't compare the way I loved Dray to the way you love Rob. But if I did, I hope that wouldn't offend you.
—Krystal Riordan, Inmate #661387

Rob and I had been together for over a decade when my relationship with Krystal began. In my second letter to her I introduced him and mentioned that he was a brilliant writer as well as the publisher/editor of our small literary journal.

We'd met in a writer's workshop. I was 43 and he 27. We liked each other's writing first. I was impressed by his images and metaphor-making ability. Workshops were held on Friday nights, and on Saturday mornings I would sit in my reading chair and drink my morning coffee, reading over the poetry from the night before. His was so good it gave me goosebumps.

As I learn more about Krystal, she learns more about me. She's heard about my work at an accounting firm as a one-armed word processor, that I'd written and published books, and lived with Rob and two black felines, Sally Joy and Vallejo. She's heard the whole story of how Vallejo had been adopted from an animal shelter. We'd hesitated to adopt this long weird Slinky toy of a cat, burned with battery acid and terribly scarred, but I kept thinking of his scars, and my own. We finally went back a third time, forked over $125, and loaded him into the pet carrier. In the cab ride home, he let out a plaintive meow and we fell instantly in love with him.

In our phone calls and correspondence, I share my life and my story with her, and she slowly opens up and shares her own.

Money, work, scars, relationships. Love, and the tangles it can get us into.

Krystal and I would seem to have taken very different paths, but if you trace them backwards, there is always a point of convergence.

&

Sometimes Krystal remembers how the guys asked for her—the tall blonde, the blue-eyed goddess who doesn't smile. Sometimes that's the time she longs for. The hooker-goddess who works her mouth to pleasure men, no matter the push and gag, the strong odors.

The trees shed their leaves on the long-ago streets. The

116

work smells of the window left open, no, the window broken; it smells of all-nighters, a hot room where it snows in the closets, the money neon-green as the slop water at the bottom of a boat.

&

Krystal sees herself as the victim, the abandoned, the unloved, the beaten, the raped, the robbed, the cheated on and lied to. There's the knife to her throat, the rope around her neck, the fist in her face. Her part in her own fate erased. The ultimate is invoked.

She is arrested in a Harlem hotel, alone when police break down the door and put a gun to her head. She's naked.

The detail of being naked is the embellishment. Who doesn't understand her impulse to claim for herself victim status? She's been judged for her sins. When she speaks of Élan, her disappointment at being sent there, and the end of her basketball mastery, and how she waited for Dray, her Dray, to speak up for her, I hear truth. Naked truth.

&

In prison she has time to consider Dray's love for her. No more designer clothes. No more rental cars. The money goes to him. She keeps spare change for snacks and Cokes and cigarettes. She works the street, Craigslist, Inc., escort services, and their own low-rent hotel room. She gives him loyalty. She holds his head in her lap and massages his temples. Together, their arms and legs entwined, his eyes are a dark milk running over her face. He lifts her buttocks and she fits in his hands.

Even after the murder, I love you, I love you. She sees marked-up girls. Faces welted with dark red streaks; cheeks, fist-smashed into maple leaves. Pimps disciplining their inventory.

I love you.

&

Sometimes she dreams of returning to the weathered buildings of Weehawken—its sooty cliffs. The Park Avenue Hotel in Wee-hawken, a single-room-occupancy five-story brick dungeon in the middle of the block, is gone, torn down after the "notorious murder of an 18-year-old girl" in one of its rooms. A senior center has taken its place.

Thelonious Monk spent the last years of his life in Weehawken. And Monk's syncopations might have been playing on WBGO in the taxi ferrying the soon-to-be-murdered Jennifer and her Good Samaritan through the Lincoln Tunnel and into the cliff city. The jazz musician's genius—tinkling the piano like the bebop stirring of ice in a mixed drink, like one of the many— the blue licorice, the amaretto—the doomed teen had consumed that night. Across the street from the now senior citizen center, there's still the Dunkin' Donuts where Candida Moore wishes her daughter had sought shelter.

"Please, come back," Candida calls to the girl in white mini and black halter. Who doubts that Jennifer is still out there, alone, wading into the darkness?

CRIME AND PUNISHMENT
EMCF   Clinton, New Jersey

I was the one who brought them straight to Jersey and showed them where Jennifer's body was. I showed them where Dray threw everything out. I told them everything. Without my help they would have never had any of that. I told them I was scared for my life and would do anything to help.
—Krystal Riordan, Inmate #661387

I read the Superior Court of New Jersey's decision on Krystal's appeal online, print it out, and mail it to her. The edge of the paper where the judge's signature appears could cut a throat.

The case summary raises the dead. Once again Coleman muscles Jennifer Moore, his teenage catch who barely tops the scale at 100 pounds, to the seedy room he shares with Krystal. Again the beating starts. Blood is squirting from Jennifer's nose, but the soccer captain fights hard; she scratches him and he hits her. Her fingernails are her only defense and she uses them fiercely. He hits her again and again. He starts to strangle her; he wants to quiet her. Krystal freezes. She remembers Draymond's fingers around her own neck, squeezing, how she couldn't breathe and it felt as if she were drowning. Jennifer rises up from the bed and down she is pushed. Her eyes have swollen shut. Her fingernails rake his hands. A fingernail breaks.

He murders and then rapes the 18-year-old girl; the twelve hours Jennifer was in the room constitute kidnapping. The last morning Krystal and Draymond spend together is a panicked one: washing her body, clipping her fingernails, then folding Jennifer's body into a suitcase and closing the lid on her life.

I have put in my petition for a sentence reduction. I did my best with the papers but no one helped me. I think I had bad advice at trial. Everyone says I shouldn't have pled guilty.
—Krystal Riordan, Inmate #661387

At her 2010 penalty trial, Krystal was sentenced to 25 years for kidnapping and five years for accessory after the fact. In May of 2015, The Hudson County Appellate court judge announces the defendant failed to show she had been denied her constitutionally guaranteed right to effective assistance of trial. Sentence Affirmed.

&

Krystal falls into a profound depression after the court's ruling. She dreams of Draymond. He approaches her as if he's being led from the 10th Precinct. In a blue T-shirt, his shaved head is bowed, his massive shoulders ripple with muscle. The last time she saw him, two stocky detectives stood on either side of him, each grasping an arm, and the strain of trying to hold him back creased their jowly faces. Now he comes to her with his hands cuffed behind his back, a key clenched between his teeth.

I loved your face, your eyes, and your hair. Unlock me, Krystal. You've never turned your back on me. You put my name on your body. You had my baby. Clutch the table, hang on, the rain starts to fall. In the dream, Draymond says, Baby, that wasn't me that evening. This is me. He'll say it in the same soft voice he used at his sentencing. Like green Jell-O starting to melt. Her whole life winnows down to a man's fingers at someone's neck. Yet she remembers Draymond in the beginning. His sweetness.
I will not tell her what she doesn't know—the call Draymond placed from the murdered Jennifer's cell phone, the one to his mother, was to find out his former girlfriend's number. The calls Draymond made to his ex-girlfriend the day he hoisted the suitcase with Jennifer inside it into a dumpster were the calls that led to their arrest.

You are where you are because of my stupid ass.
—letter to Krystal from Draymond Coleman

"Lisa?"

"I'm right here," she answers in her low voice, as she opens the door and invites the man inside. The heat is suffocating, and he too opens his mouth to breathe as if Draymond had his hands around his throat. Each time she moves she has to pull her feet or arms through the glue—the room sticks to her body, a syrupy honey bear. The air conditioner blows hot air only.

She closes her eyes, and what flashes by is Draymond and Jennifer and the sun staring at them. The mosquitoes keep lighting on her shoulders and she feels them drinking her like they want her and would take parts of her to share with strangers.

&

The day's sounds gather force, a purple river of trucks backfiring and fire engines honking. She offers him the $150 special, his choice of two, but he only wants oral. When he unzips, she cuddles his sex and licks and blows him especially nicely. His crinkly hairs have an oregano scent mixed with nutmeg, as if he had washed himself not long before. That kindness makes her eyes tear. She brings him to his climax easily.

"Baby, how can you stand the heat in here?"

There are two more men. The younger white guy wants the special: anal, oral, vagina. His crotch tastes moldy, maybe of Gouda cheese. In the future stretches her 30-year prison sentence.

&

Time to leave the befouled Weehawken. Krystal's lips look caught in mid-tremble as she gets into the taxi. Her frightened eyes speak their own truth, or hide it.

The driver is a Pakistani, and Dray tells him to take them to 112th Street in Manhattan. They now have money for the New Ebony Hotel. The cab's air conditioner leaks tepid air and she buzzes the window down, watching the New York skyline rise,

121

the tall buildings already glowing with light. She doesn't feel anything at all. She's walked through a wall of jagged glass into another world—where you go when you've committed a mortal sin. Do you reach over and squeeze his knee or fumble a Newport to your mouth? *I didn't think I could live without him.*

It's Draymond who lights a cigarette. His hands tremble. They're gouged with scratches and he notices her staring at them. "I had to quiet her. That wasn't me in that room."

&

Detectives testify. Not telling the judge how Krystal cooperated and told them everything; where Jennifer's body had been left and where Dray had disposed of the murdered girl's things.

Her attorney talks about the abuse Krystal had suffered at the hands of her birth parents. Molestation. Her night terrors. The judge asks if she has anything to say before he pronounces the sentence. Her tear-stained face is delicate as a lilac bush in the rain as she at last speaks for herself.

"I'm not a bad person," she tells the court in a trembling voice.

The judge listens, then says, "There's only one victim here." He sentences her to the maximum.

When I get out I'd like to help prostitutes. I've seen many young girls get picked up by pimps, fed drugs, get beat up, and afraid to leave.
— Krystal Riordan, Inmate #661387

Krystal at her sister's wedding

Krystal (far left) and her sisters on the first Easter following adoption.

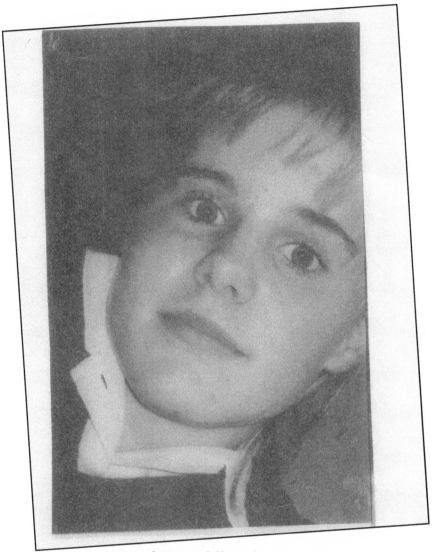

Krystal in Middle School

Krystal entering EMCF

Krystal (#13) with her St. Mary's basketball team.
Fundraising (bottom). With chaperones at the National
Championships in Florida (top)

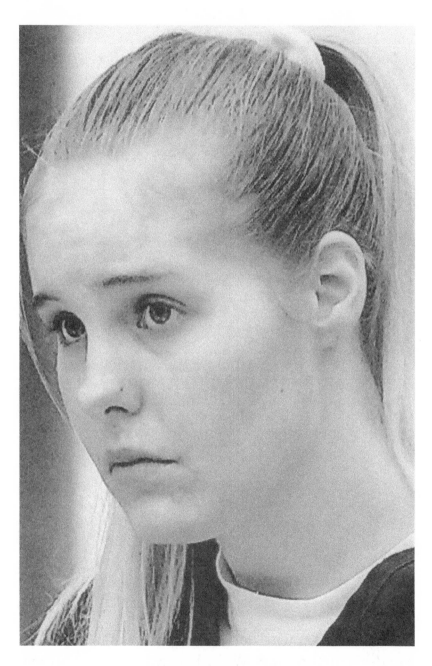

Krystal in court

Draymond Coleman
Mugshot

Krystal at EMCF - Age 33

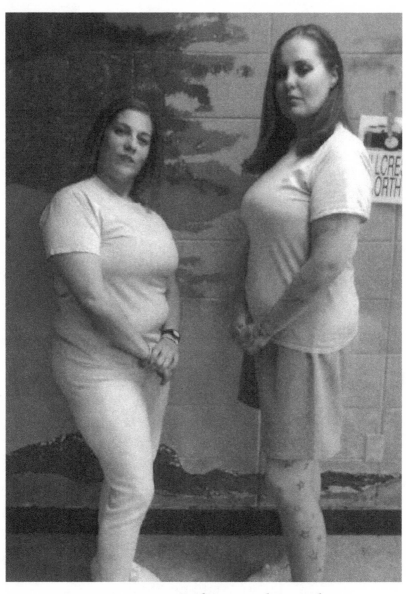

Lucy Weems and Krystal Riordan
Showing off Krystal's Tattoos
EMCF

Lucy's Wedding Photo
after her release.

Krystal and Lucy showing off Lucy's tattoos,
inked by Krystal.

Lucy's post-release job search.

LOVE IN THE RAZOR-WIRE WILDERNESS
EMCF Clinton, New Jersey

Dear Nickel Cone, I still love you and look for you through the fence. Remember when we were in Detention/Segregation together? I wish I could do all my time like that with you.
—Krystal Riordan, Inmate # 661387

Krystal likes women and had slept with some before going to prison. To be Draymond's girlfriend meant threesomes. Krystal kept hoping he'd settle down. His predilection was for two girls, one man; master of his own universe when two women gave themselves to him, flat thick noodles he could wrap around his fork, and then direct what they would do to each other. Use your finger to scoop the plum sauce from that clam. The triangle titillated him, not just the flesh but the violence, the rule of three releases.

Maximum Compound women have hundreds of years to live through. Krystal doesn't have a choice but to serve her years, and hope for parole. After decades away from the world, will she recognize it when she's free? New inmates coming in bring the streets with them; they bring tales of Facebook and Twitter, the latest dope talk. The world is moving fast: Facebook using artificial intelligence to categorize what you write, smartphones listening to what you say. Krystal tries not to let the place change her. "I'm a nice person," she says, "so that's how I'm going to stay." The outside does change. How long before the inside feels cozy as home? For many, the home that never was. The rules comforting as an overprotective parent. Whom should you really watch out for? The outside world? A girlfriend is the best meal. You can talk about food and sex, lie about your crimes. You can beat each other.

&

The women help Krystal forget how much time she's done, how much time she still has to do. The years she's served are evidenced by the tattoos blossoming on her arms and legs. Growth rings in a tree. Noticed no matter which wing she's moved to, the girlfriends come and go.

Maximum Compound women sleep with someone they've known for a day, and then sleep with their new girlfriend's friends. Officers call it the animal kingdom. Inmates fight constantly to claim their mates as property, they fight to claim who is next for the washer and dryer. Women with dark marigolds for eyes, inked women, muscular women, soft women fattened by Commissary loot, women with sideburns and goatees, women who have killed with golf clubs, women who have tied their husbands up and stabbed them sixty-two times. There's always something to want. Inmates steal and stockpile. They sell their private Commissary Chips Ahoy for double the price.

Some of the women turn to anger, especially the lovers who claim each other, and when one of the claimed women cheats, there are fist fights. Sometimes it's the cheating lover who punches the faithful lover out of guilt. In this ringed world, this planet Maximum Compound, relationships don't kindle, they burst into flame. Ex-girlfriends, referred to as "exes," abound. So many rules, so much deprivation that there's a hunger for touch. The dalliances can take place in plain sight, those deep eye-kisses that can be had in a glance. Make no mistake—there are friends here and love abounds.

Hey Krystal, I love you! I'm here as your friend and as your champion. I hate to write so that's why I've been quiet. I love you deeply.
—Rikii Davis, Inmate #75466FD

Krystal has a weakness for the tough new inmates. The studs. Draymonds in female form. Although she's white, she sometimes identifies as black.

136

In Maximum Compound you might glimpse your girl-friend through a fence or in a window. To be in love in Maximum Compound there must be opportunity, and to mate with someone in North Hall when you live in South Hall, you find where both inmates have reason to be, say, attending church services, or researching in the law library. As the outside recedes, you love the one you're with, and you have so little to call your own that the one you're with belongs to you. If word reaches you that your girlfriend has hooked up with someone else, you've thrown fight blood on the floor.

Krystal wants Rikii to belong to her, and she wants it with desperation.

&

Rikii Davis's mugshot shows a pretty, brown-eyed, full-lipped 18-year-old Paterson girl. She's just pleaded guilty to aggravated manslaughter, a plea deal in the killing of Ashlee Ernesto, age 19, and her boyfriend, Rhett Cash, age 24. Her sentence, twenty-five years. While any tough-looking chick that comes into the unit attracts Krystal's eye, it's Rikii who has her heart, and when Rikki gets sixty days in segregation, Krystal breaks rules too so she could join her in Lock. Two women segregated from their units, two women to a cell.

&

Alone together in Segregation, or Lock, as inmates call the detention cell, they talk about the past that keeps happening and the crime that is never behind you. Rikki tells Krystal that at 16 she'd been chosen by Jules, the local Paterson Bloods gang leader, to be his girlfriend. When Jules calls her Kii, everyone does. Lots of respect comes from being Jules's lady. There is swagger in his gait. The light gamma rays from his mouth when he says Kii. "What's on your mind, Kii? Hey, you're silky-fine."

On the murder day, the gangbangers gather in a shabby row house to party. Jules doesn't feel well; he's got a cold in his ear and feeds it a dropper of sweet oil. He can't hear anything out of his left ear except the ocean, waves ebbing and flowing, Atlantic

City, high tide, the boardwalk.

Jules's talking about Rhett Cash and he's riled up. He's sure his rival is setting him up for a drive-by. "It's my life or his. That pussy says he's a Blood and then gets seen hanging out with Crips."

The weed's good and Kii is laughing at her friend Larnelle down on all fours pretending to be a horse. "Larnelle, you never seen a horse in real life. TV don't count."

Murder is already in the air; they're talking it, thinking of it. Before long, Cash is knocking at the door. "Let that sucker in, he's not walking out." Jules loads up his weapon. Shit, he's brought his girlfriend with him.

Cash takes a toke of weed, then he and his Ashlee get in on the dancing. His pretty girlfriend, with her almond eyes and head of Shirley Temple curls, looks like a swimsuit model who's been airbrushed. She's a high school graduate who's going to community college.

"Ever eat oysters, Jules?" Cash asks, like he's bragging. "A plate of four raw oysters costs $27. They're some nasty, salty gray snot. But Ashlee liked them, didn't you, baby?"

More smoking, and then Jules gives the order; Cash has to die. Now the murderous snakes are unhinging their soft wide mouths.

Cash denies he'd ever turn against Jules, but they gag him. Jules shoots him twice then orders, "Kii, you help Larnelle rough up Ashlee. Take her down to the basement."

Down the dark flight of stairs, Kii half-heartedly punches the girl, who raises her arms to ward off the blows. Larnelle hits her with a baseball bat.

"Finish it!" Jules calls down the stairs. The beating goes on until the girl slumps to the floor.

"She don't want to die," Larnelle says.

&

The word love is used constantly in this world. In segregation, Rikii and Krystal trade stories and wish their crimes had never

138

happened. That Jennifer and Ashlee were only names. They tease each other. Pretend to carry each other's luggage into five-star hotels. They talk. Krystal tells her about the first time Dray saw her when she wore a sweater-dress with a V cut-away back.

"You're a goddess," he whistled.

They give each other guided tours of their bodies. Here's where Krystal fell, body-slammed the floor on the basketball court and skidded, taking the skin off her knee and bruising her calf layers deep, and on her ankle the blister that left a crater. And there's where she cut herself. The old cut is a cold room, the window left open; it smells of roaches, it snows in the closets.

Rikii points to those places where her skin darkens from chestnut to reddish-brown and dimples bloom heart-shaped. There's a crosshatched scar on her chin, and one on her eyelid, from when the Paterson juvies pushed her head-on into a tree. There's that day in the row house, such a forgotten town, half the police force laid off, no funds to pay them, the gangs taking over the days as well as the nights.

"I love the scar on your eyelid best," Krystal says. "It left a mesh of pinkish nicks. That's what I'm kissing right now; I'm showing you how much I care."

Krystal also kisses the long scar on Rikii's arm, a black jagged line where the girl going to community college used her fingernail to scratch Rikii practically to the bone.

"Go rough her up, Kii," Jules, her boyfriend had said. An order. A fingernail that ripped her life apart.

Krystal and Rikii pretend they're inside an Xbox video game called Planet America, the nightclub where panther women carry trays of drinks. Sometimes they both dream of peacocks. In their sleep they meet; they listen to the male's heavy feathers drag, they watch the peacock fanning its tail, hundreds of aqua and black eyes, gold- and kohl-encircled.

&

Krystal dreams of Rikii dressed in the moist red of apples. They sit holding hands in the cab of a pickup on a dark street—the truck Krystal bought at 18, when she first started hooking. Krystal wears white, even her shoes. High heels. The first time in ten years she's slipped her foot into anything but a sneaker or boot. Her feet start to giggle, and then she does. Rikii slips Krystal's promise ring on her finger. They are both laughing. It rains—rain falls in through the open window like violets. Rain carries light from a thousand skyscrapers into the truck, making them shimmer like tiny galaxies.

Krystal turns the engine over, asking her lover where she wants to go. Alaska? Montana? We're going to believe in each other wherever we go.

&

What Krystal and Rikii never talk about is getting-out-day. Added together the two women will serve over half a century. Fifty-five years. There is all the time to make up, the stopped time. It's too painful to think of time starting again. When they get out, they will be middle-aged. To them that day is too far off to believe in and too painful to think of. Too painful to envision freedom day, the blessed day of no rules, the day of sleeping as long as you want, eating good oven food, relaxing at a table, taking a long hot shower, dressing in reds and blues, tight clothes. Getting-out-day is the day you will fill yourself with walking, letting your legs take in the sidewalk, going to a basketball game, snacking on popcorn and red licorice. The day you'll feed yourself a lavish supper of spinach tortellini and red sauce, Häagen-Dazs Rum Raisin ice cream melted in the microwave. You and your girlfriend will marry there in the happily ever after of when-I-get-out. She is in her gang colors and you in pearls and tattoos.

LUCY IN THE SKY
Newark, New Jersey

There's a sisterhood among street prostitutes.
A very jealous sisterhood.
—Lucy Weems, Inmate #922870C

Krystal and Lucy talk about how easy the money feels at first, how there's an allure, a flamingo feather boa that sex work tosses over your shoulders. In the beginning you're younger, prettier, and healthier than the competition; you're the tiara-shiny 200-dollar girl, not the mucked-up 20-dollar whore. Those escort service days when you're doing crazy things with your tongue on celebrity basketball players and rappers. Sex Apps order you in along with Jamaican jerk chicken and sticky rice.

Then it all comes down to cars moving sluggishly through the troubled streets and shabby hooker hotels. Krystal rarely thinks of the smell and taste of those men. She handed her earnings over to Draymond Coleman, who hounded her for money even as she made it, the pimp-squeeze at her neck. Those soft body/hard cash transactions. The stories she makes up to erase her guilt.

I was in Hudson County jail for 4 years. When I first got there I was still in shock. I was put in a private cell because of the severity of my crime. I was in jail with some high-profile prostitutes from Long Island.
— Krystal Riordan, Inmate #661387

Krystal sometimes studies the old news articles and photos that friends have printed off the internet for her. She shows Lucy the 20-year-old Krystal being led before the judge to be arraigned on kidnapping and accessory-after-the-fact charges. Her eyes downcast. Her long blond hair, showing its darker roots, is pulled tightly back into a ponytail.

"Isn't it weird we were both charged with the same crime of kidnapping? Do you think I look evil?"

Lucy smiles. "You can see the comb marks in your hair. It looks like you haven't shampooed in a week."

Who could shower in that filthy shared bathroom in Weehawken, and then after the 16-hour interrogation following her arrest? She heard Dray fell asleep in the holding cell after his interrogation. He fell asleep, while she wondered if she'd ever sleep again. Her baby face appears haunted in the old photo that is forever new online.

"You look like a cheerleader," her friend says. "Preppie!"

&

Krystal hates to even look at her 24-year-old self at the penalty hearing after she'd pleaded guilty.

Guilty. What a heavy word, one that she has to carry to the end of her days. In a Hudson County green prisoner's uniform and wearing glasses, she stands beside her public defender, a bearded African American who also wears glasses. Taller than her attorney, whom she trusts, her shoulders broader, she appears to loom over him.

The pounds she's gained make her ashamed; more shame floods her face as Jennifer's mother reads her victim impact statement, especially the damning sentences about the hotel's video footage showing Krystal buying soda and snacks while Jennifer is being beaten, those words nauseating her. All that weight she has gained going against her. Her hunger. Her rice-ball cheeks.

Candida Moore points out the closeness in the two girls' ages but the distance in experience. She points to Krystal's selling her body to support a man she knows could be violent. In the court's eyes, a prostitute's soul must fester with fist holes and bones, weeping glass, and ripped-up car seats.

Lucy wants to read Jennifer's mother's statement, but Krystal says no.

"Your hair looks beautiful and thick in this picture. You

142

curled it, didn't you?" Lucy says. "You look like you're on your way to church."

Krystal nods. Her life in the offertory plate. "The Long Island girls curled it, thinking it would help soften me."

I vowed never to speak of it, for my aunt's sake.
—Lucy Weems, Inmate #922870C

Lucy's uncle penetrates her. It hurts. For her virginity, he pays the 14-year-old 800 dollars—a sexual route to earning an expensive pair of sneakers.

The money and the sex go on for years.

What do we see spawned in the shallows of violated girl-hood? The too-early warming of mid-Atlantic waters?

When she was 15 and 16, her uncle would pay her to work with his accountant and she grew to love the flow of numbers, the sexiness of debits and credits, how they must equal. In the end, everything must balance.

Lucy attends the University of Connecticut and Kean University, graduating with a BS in Accounting.

&

Lucy's in her early 20s and on summer break between her junior and senior college years, when her uncle—the same uncle who molested Lucy at age 14, the same uncle who said he would be gentle and that the money would always be there within reason—approaches her with another commercial opportunity.

He knows a Madam in Bridgeport, Connecticut, who owns a condominium and employs girls for two weeks minimum and four weeks maximum. Maggie, the Madam, a slender ash blonde, all coiffed and chic, reads Lucy the house rules. No drugs. She'll have sex with at least three men a day, earn $1,500 for one week's work and keep all tips. Condoms required and their usage strictly enforced. Maggie orders take-out every night and the girls can cook at their leisure during the day.

Like everything in her life, Lucy's journey into the world

of prostitution is an unusual one.

It's hard to get off the hooker hamster wheel. I've given blowjobs for $400 and anal sex for $20. If you're dope-sick, you'll do anything.
—Lucy Weems, Inmate #922870C

Here Lucy's in her late 20s and wearing heels and a halter dress walking down New Haven's Ferry Street, broke after buying heroin. A man pulls over and asks Lucy if she wants to make some money. One hundred bucks and the taste of easy money translates into 8 bags of dope, food, cigarettes.

But now she knows better and her price is 200 dollars for a guy to sleep with her. Twenty minutes tops and her clock is running.

&

One day, over a decade and more in the future, everything she sees—the sinks, the toilets, the hallways, the bunks, will be moldy, filthy. The denizens of this place don't seem to notice the dirt or the stench. Her first meal is breakfast. "Fifteen minutes to eat. Now let's move it, Ladies."

Into the clatter of trays she walks for a cup of grim coffee, a splash of juice, a cup of cottage fries, 2 boiled eggs, and a spoon of margarine. In the Yard the sky's overcast, the color of iron ore, has smothered the sun for days. The mouth and throat tingle. Time to reflect. Seven years of time.

&

But for now, we are in the world of cushy chairs, pastel bedrooms and king-size beds, large-screen TVs; here, all money transactions, except for tips, Maggie attends to. From full frontal, oral, and anal, to the more rarified station stops on the sex-for-hire line, each has a different price.

The men are divorced, married, and single; they are businessmen, doctors, lawyers, politicians, men of means. Money is their common denominator. One man so admires Lucy's skills

144

that in her two weeks, he requests her four times. Her fingers flow transparently over the beauty of the body. Maggie requires that Lucy shower between men if they have intercourse, and if she performs oral sex, then she must brush her teeth and gargle with a fluoride mouthwash.

Greed never pays off. Share the wealth with other prostitutes because when you start being greedy and overworking yourself, the quality of your service declines.
—Lucy Weems, Inmate #922870C

Newark on Frelinghuysen and Evergreen, and Lucy's looking for dates when a Rolls Royce pulls up with a driver and a man in the back seat. The night gathers around her as he steps out of the Rolls like Old Hollywood and sweeps toward her in red velour sweats and gold rope necklaces. His hair is braided in neat rows, and when he introduces himself as Prince, not the famous musician, she notices his blue eyes.

Hellos are floating along as he motions her to the car, offering her a place to stay, drugs at shift's end, protection, bail. The quota $600 on a weeknight, $800-$1,000 on weekends. If he keeps his word, she'll work for him.

He forbids the girls working for him to snort or shoot cocaine. To make top dollar you must be clean and beautifully dressed. No fishnet tops or purple jeans, no tangled tresses, etc.

The drug I was in love with was heroin—the worst of them all.
—Lucy Weems, Inmate #922870C

One night, a Mercedes pulls over and she hops in.

The thirty-something man asks if she'll go with him to New York City to The Vault, a sex club, and she calculates she can charge him $800. He agrees.

First stop, her dealer's, where she buys heroin. When she goes into the Projects to buy her dope, she drops her sexiness and pretends to be crazy; mumbling, biting her arm, pulling grass, flailing her hands, and shouting. People cross the street to avoid her. If she's made $100 tricking, $90 goes for dope and $10 for cigarettes, a bag of chips, and a soda. She walks, moving with reptilian slithers. She stares at her shoulder.

More shivering. Sidewalk too close, the curb follows her with its eyes, and the shrill insects drink from the same night as her.

On the main floor they offered a buffet, free and unlimited. It's crazy because theoretically they had food out & exposed around a bunch of nudie people & and it seemed like no one wanted to touch the buffet because of the idea of nudity & food. But do you think this stopped me? Absolutely not. I'm a fat girl at heart.
—Lucy Weems, Inmate #922870C

They cruise into the city and the club's exterior of grilled storefront and side-entrance buzzer hardly looks promising. Her entry fee is $150. Her date's a member. You must come as a couple. Lucy has to sign waivers. No alcohol is served, since the law forbids even consensual sex if you're drinking. Alcohol renders you unable to give informed consent.

Blond hair hangs to the back of the hostess's kneecaps. Her beautiful cheeks don't have a dimple, pimple, or bruise on them. She gives out unlimited condoms. While her date signs in, Lucy sinks into the cushions and sips the cold carbonated seltzer, the color of camellias and naked bodies. Everyone who passes wears only their skin, and like the thong-clad sunbathers on the beach, some bodies verge on perfection, while the rest fall into the normal range between pudgy and thin.

She undresses in a sparkling clean locker room and goes to meet her date, who laughs at her when she stops to eat a cheese cube speared on a toothpick and a water cracker. There's a buffet that people seem to be avoiding, as if there's something taboo about eating while nude. No one is touching the food. Lucy has

146

it all to herself and chooses little pigs in a blanket and meatballs.

&

Then he takes her hand and they climb the stairs into the demimonde; "sex and debauchery city," Lucy terms it. Room upon room with high ceilings, low ceilings, deep carpets, black lights, divans, rooms of minimalistic art and beanbag chairs, a room of mirrors.

She picks the arty black-light room. Her date likes watching the others as they sink into the soft carpet and he penetrates her doggy style. A brunette woman asks to lick Lucy while her date has sex with her. The bodies begin to blur. Almost dawn and the moisture is steaming off her, the unsteadiness. She showers in the locker room, all toiletries provided.

&

A BMW pulls up and a tall, handsome black-haired man offers her $500 if she will defecate on him. They drive to a hotel, where she runs her hand down his chest and he pushes her away. He wants only to be defiled. She crouches beside him, then over him, squatting. Heroin is the great god of constipation, and transforms the bowels into a lock-and-key box.

Lucy's a sport if she's anything and promises him she'll try, and so she strains, drinks warm water, and finally, after an hour, a pellet, a raisin of shit, is born from her. A tiny dark moon shining over the stricken heart.

If you're good at what you do, you should never charge less than the woman who is toothless, smelly, or dirty. When you are well taken care of and good at your craft.
—Lucy Weems, Inmate #922870C

Jersey City, Atlantic City. Hot spots in the dating game. One weekend night business is slow and police sirens keep scaring her dates away. She's made $650 but needs $150 more. Prince insists she keep working.

She tells him to bugger off and rents a hotel room, buys a supply of heroin and kicks back. Her lighter heats the spoon that cradles her heart's desire—heroin and drops of faucet water. Her mouth goes wet. The powder liquefies. Tap, eject the air, and tie off, needle destination. Mocha cream in the mind. The sink, the towel racks soften. In the mirror she appears luminous.

&

Lucy learns survival skills on the streets of heroin and prostitution. Heroin, which revolves on its turret, its long tail wrapping around you, its strands of seaweed swaying like a bridal veil. A seahorse tango. The shame of heroin. The crazy expense. Her father, godmother, brother—carved chess pieces, their heads of beautiful horses watching her. All those burnt offerings. Heroin clothes you in a gunny sack. Sex work lathers you in the sweat of anus and ambergris. Egyptian incense smoldering across a tub filled with toilet water. Men in rotting jeans—sex work sets her on her knees for her mouth to receive.

Heroin eyes swimming upside down, seconds before another mosquito eats her, a lanternfish with tiny pearls of light sewn up and down the lips of her vagina. Heroin dances for the homeless encampment. Lucy, exceptional at her trade, knows her value and learns how to outperform competitors and how to protect her turf.

&

She leaves Prince to freelance. Heroin-hair matted to the pillow's blue stripes having nothing to do with sleep. A mirror breaking, jagged glass on the tile floor. Melon rinds used as ashtrays. Her daughters packed off to their godmother's. Sirens. The worst taste in her mouth, her own sweat. A foreboding of need—black shapes in white trees. Day of the crazies. A tooth aching. Head, a bursting beaded purse. Mouth, the boil of rotten shrimp. Mind, a cesspool. Mottled black.

Her shoe-fetish date she sees regularly. Lucy wonders no longer what she looks like in six-inch spike heels, as her weekly trick carries in his car trunk women's shoes in a variety of sizes. He likes his women to wear garter belts and black nylons, he likes watching Lucy jiggle the nylon over her toes. The fetish world

148

seems less strange and adventurous than it does cliché, a fixed-ness, a rigidity. The ordinariness of the extraordinary.

Lucy knows she's a thrill seeker; she tempts the fates and she chooses to be homeless. There's nowhere to go to the bathroom, except to try the El Cantina's "customers only." She orders some tortilla chips in green jalapeño sauce and reads the horoscopes because she likes to know what's in store. Here among the mismatched tables and chairs, the quest isn't for the Holy Grail but a bathroom the homeless and sex worker can use without fear of arrest.

Newark Broad Street train station, and stench of soiled winter clothing, slept in, shat in, of ripening papaya and green beef. The stalls are filled with homeless women and sex workers, and she feels a great compassion for them, but she's about to vomit.

In the food court, also brightly lit, the familiar names you can count on, welcome her. It's hard to clear her nostrils, so she wolfs down a salty cloud of mashed potatoes.

&

When the Newark sex workers would see the vicious prostitute who called herself Sherry strutting down the street, her scowling whiskey face thickened by black eyebrows, they'd clear out of her way. According to Lucy, the other ladies couldn't haul ass the other way fast enough, the crazy whore ready to jump them and steal their money.

Lucy stows her drugs and money in her sock and keeps walking. Sherry wears a lace half-shirt and hot-pink skinny jeans, with not a crease, except for the canyon between her legs, where the men unloaded their fantasies. Dirt Baby, Lucy tags her.

Sherry grabs for Lucy's bra, trying to shake out her drug stash. Sherry lands the first punch, and then Lucy gets in the second, third, and fourth. Sherry takes off running and loses one of her shoes, which Lucy picks up and tosses in a dumpster.

Later, after they both ended up in Maximum Compound, Sherry apologizes. "I was crazy," she admits.

&

One lady of the night says, "You can get AIDS if your date ejaculates inside you, especially your mouth, and then you swallow." For Lucy, the dark side of prostitution isn't an arrest for loitering or being attacked but her date's condom breaking. She's grown up after the disease's first wave of death; the mysterious plague that goes by initials had already spread across the land. Although much more is known about transmission and treatments, the prostitute sisterhood fears AIDS above all other STDs. Few engage in the highest-risk behavior—unprotected anal sex. Lucy never has. Ever.

> *Whores are hungry all the time.*
> —Lucy Weems, Inmate #922870C

Few talk about the hunger a prostitute often feels, a gnawing hunger because the stomach hasn't been fed in days. The hundreds of dollars Lucy earns feeds the drug-beast almost exclusively; cigarettes, a few bags of potato chips, and a couple of Cokes escape its maw.

Her routine is to stay awake for three days, then sleep an entire day. Often her dates take her to motels and after the sex they offer her the room for the rest of the night. If she's at the end of her three-day run, she might accept and sleep around the clock or she might tell him she's not done partying and ask for a ride back to where he picked her up. She's thin and her ribs show. Sometimes a date will pull over at a convenience store for a sandwich and buy her one too.

Once she goes with her hunger into an Italian supermarket and the brightness of the fluorescent lights burns her eyes. The light gapes at her cleavage and the needle marks on her arms. How can she slip something into her mini when all the white-aproned men and women behind the counters are staring?

The monkfish and oysters stare too. In a tank behind the counter, three lobsters lift their pincers, their other spectral

150

limbs knock against the glass, as if asking Lucy to let them out, or inviting her in.

&

She finds some weeds behind an abandoned daycare and bends to the task of finding a vein, when a man taps her shoulder and wants sex.

"Give me a minute," she says. She told him to give her a freaking second because she needs to find the mist that moves through the cooled trees, and only heroin in a vein does that.

Thanks to him, she misses the vein. He pushes her down, orders her to blow him. Her hair feels like an escaped convict, crazy and full of twigs. When he's moaning, her hands find his pockets and she takes his ciggies, 85 bucks, and a lighter.

No one sent me the memo that the season had changed.
—Lucy Weems, Inmate #922870C

Halloween passes and Lucy has no idea why the little ninjas carry plastic pumpkins and keep hollering Trick or Treat. "I thought the varmints had been let loose to mess up my high."

Weeks later, maybe a month, she shudders in her tank top and short shorts. The white sun too far from the earth means no more warming of the sky. The dirty-gray crusted to the curbs and manhole covers is ice. Her bare legs and heels go skating over the sidewalk cellars and subway grates. A frozen world.

Lucy visits the nearest Costco and shops for a jacket and heavier clothes. She tears the plastic ring off the hem before she walks out, wearing a new ensemble.

&

Then she's in Newark, it's Evergreen Street, and she's been up for days shooting cocaine and heroin, the taste of the blood from a sunset on her lips. She's wearing a halter dress and her head swims. Birds and fish take turns circling her head; you're the tourist ship of flesh, the funhouse. She can't pass out on the street to be raped and robbed.

She stumbles into an Emergency Care clinic. The knife flashes keep swimming around her head. Everyone sitting in the waiting area stares, heads turn, and she feels the track marks glowing like kryptonite on her arms. Before she reaches the receptionist's desk she blacks out and wakes in a wheelchair being rolled into the ER of a hospital. Again, everyone is staring at her. She sees her breast has fallen out of her halter. "Haven't you ever seen one of these before?" she blurts.

&

What Lucy doesn't see is still off in the future. The doggy wagon parks inside the prison compound. Off go the shackles and handcuffs. "Okay, Ladies, everything comes off. Bra, panties, socks."
She's given 2 uniforms, 5 panties, 2 bras, 2 socks, a blanket, a pillow, and a sheet. "Put on your uniform and leave your clothes here." In the dormitory holding tank, she notices that women are sleeping with their sneakers under their mattresses. "Newbie, you better stick your sneakers under your mattress or you're going to lose them." The heat is sticking to her and she can hardly breathe.

Women crowd around the fan. The heat is swaddling her. She can't escape or swim away so she'll have to go down in the stifling black water.

Lucy thinks about the skills she acquired when working as a prostitute. "You learn to value yourself and in business people will pay whatever you ask if that service is worthy of that high cost." She fights her way to the fan.

&

The prostitute sisterhood peers up at the murky Newark sky, or is it New Haven or Jersey City, and the moon is shining over them. "Once you know your service outclasses comparable services, never reduce your price," says the blue rabbit that lives in a moon crater.

Valentine's Day Belongs to the She-Wolf

EMCF Clinton, New Jersey

She's really beautiful. Can you find some I Love You Cards and send them to her and just sign my name? I have a teddy bear being made and a matching ring earring and necklace set.
—Krystal Riordan, Inmate #661387

In Maximum Compound the holiday that captures the barbed wire universe's essence isn't Thanksgiving or Christmas; those nostalgia holidays subtract you to zero. Turkey and yams you bastardize in the microwave. When you bow your head and give thanks, it might be the microwave you're most thankful for. Thanksgiving belongs to the free world; a leftover, like the sweet potatoes saved from Mess Hall to be doctored with brown sugar and syrup. Voila, glazed yams. No Cubano sandwiches on Christmas morning, the meats piled so high between slabs of French bread that you need double mouths to take a bite. As for the wild party of New Year's, noisemakers and drunken cheers are against the rules, so the inmates toast their off-brand vintage soda to that yardstick of time served.

&

Valentine's Day is Maximum Compound's signature holiday. The love-day celebration that topples the walls made of rules: DO NOT TOUCH ANOTHER INMATE, DO NOT REACH FOR AN OFFICER, DO NOT LEAVE YOUR AREA, DO NOT SPEAK DURING COUNT.

This day the flicker between eyes is celebrated; this day, girlfriends are made to feel special. This day the inside expels the cold and rain an animal coming in from the wild shakes over a room. Girl-love is celebrated and even the officers can't spoil it.

Outside, in the world I know, the space between people grows; we live in digital capsules, three-screen universes, and our lovers receive the least of us. The opposite is true in Maximum Compound among the murderers, the father killers, the kidnappers, and armed robbers. For Valentine's Day, the inmates go all out, ordering hand-painted cards, stuffed animals, origami bracelets, and watercolor portraits for wives, girlfriends, and side chicks. Everything made by inmate artists gets sold on the black market. Women cheek their medications and save them for their girlfriends for the holiday of love.

&

Since Krystal was locked up in 2006, worlds have risen and fallen. The women she has loved mark her time, not the calendar. While wars rage in Iraq, Afghanistan, Yemen, and Syria, Krystal meets Tiny, not even 4'9" tall to her 5'9". Tiny treats her right, the two of them midget and giant.

While Krystal hurries to be in full uniform with ID badge by 7:30 a.m., refugees are fleeing droughts, sea-level rise, and phosphorus bombs. She winks at Isla in Mess Hall while wildfires ravage California. A tsunami hits Japan, and Fukushima Nuclear Power Plant melts down.

By 8:30 a.m., Krystal reports for her work detail and the last white rhino on Earth dies. For eyeliner she uses the black watercolor from her art supplies. Rikii kisses her in church. Her sweet-tasting papaya lips. The Boston Marathon bombing. Epidemics. Ebola. Heat waves and Australian highways liquefying. Rikii and Krystal scarf down macaroni glop and touch each other later, unhurriedly. The sub-prime housing bubble has grown, mortgages happily displayed like expensive crown jewels. Isla, with her long neck and fig-like body.

At 12:30 p.m., Krystal mops the common area. While she performs extra housekeeping duties for a rule infraction, Lehman's brokerage house declares insolvency. Financial collapse. Recession.

Done at 3:00 p.m., then exercise in the Yard. Election of the first black president, Barack Obama. The best part of her 24 hours, meeting Valarie by the fence.

154

Supper, fish square, 4"x4", ½ cup carrots. A new disturbed inmate hits her in the face. Shake it off, Krystal. Don't hit back. Mass shootings: Newtown, Miami, Las Vegas. Schools, bars, concerts, churches. Krystal falls in love again with Isla. Isla, why are you dating that cracker? More shootings: Virginia Tech, Dark Knight showing in an Aurora, Colorado, movie theater. Rat-a-tat-tat.

Early-evening snacking from her Commissary trunk, real food like peanut butter cups and Cheez-Its. Kiosk time to type emails, ask favors, send lovegrams. Election of the first real estate mogul/reality-show president, Donald Trump. Count. Hurricanes Harvey, Irma, and Maria.

Nights, listening to headphones to block out the noise. Lights out. Smartphones, Uber, the gig economy. Through it all, Krystal has worn the beige inmate uniform and the gray sweats, and has added more tattoos to her flesh: names, sunrises, and shooting stars. She's had sex with a throng of women. She's worn no earrings or rings or bracelets. Only the cross necklace with its regulation chain.

None of the Outside's cataclysms seem real. Except for trips to St. Francis Medical Center in Trenton, she has not traveled a mile outside of EMCF in years.

&

Love's an obstacle course that sometimes ends in blood. Girlfriends come and go, and relationships flare, only to turn to cinder.

In Maximum Compound, when fights erupt, they are usually about cheating. Couples bond and then break apart, but here love is celebrated on Valentine's Day. No matter that the prison is haunted by women who have killed their lover's ex-girlfriends, those who have stabbed and smothered and thrown lye, the same women later murdered here. The February sky shrinks and the afternoons are gray in their winnowing away. Temperatures drop and inmates put on sweatpants, sweatshirts, and tie-up ankle boots.

In the exercise yard, Isla and Lucy, their breath white in

the icy air, pass the word that Krystal's been taken to Lock on an assault charge. An officer is involved, making it serious.

&

The disturbed inmate hits Krystal again, and this time she defends herself. An officer steps between them. When there's a fight, no matter who threw the first punch, both women are taken to Lock.

Even before the assault charge, trouble had brewed for Krystal. Her arms are nicked by cut marks, and she can't seem to stop the urge to cut when she's been rejected. The pressure builds and the urge grows, until she can think of nothing else.

Her friends tell Krystal to stop her cutting shit or she'll end up in Isolation and they'll throw away the key. A few days, okay—and if you're with your girlfriend, better. But no one wants to be walked down the long hall with doors on each side with only a square window the size of an officer's face.

You want that, Krystal? Keep slicing and dicing on those arms. It'll be no Thanksgiving. The holiday they all save their carrots for. Carrots, the color of autumn. The real outside. The day they cook with cinnamon and sugar and syrup and call it yams.

&

In Lock, you're allowed your tablet and headphones, but you'll need batteries, and they're $4 a pack. Isolated inmates are permitted to spend only $12 on Commissary per month.

She gets a cell to herself. The first days pass like a spoon through mashed potatoes. She can afford not to eat the trays of watery noodles and wax beans they slide in. The tray sits on the floor looking disappointed. *I wasn't good enough*, the pale green bean says, finally free of its can. The puddle of instant potatoes has nothing to add.

&

She's losing track of how long she's been here. A month? More? Her birth mother enters the cell. Eva. What are you doing here? Has she brought Krystal a red devil cake with cream cheese frosting? *Who are you?* even the corners of my friend's mouth ask.

Krystal has only questions of this woman whose bow-lips are replicated on her face. French, she guesses, and a sex worker too. Her helmet of glossy black hair matches the ice-cold sparkle in her burning black eyes.

Why did you bother having kids? A welfare check? Eva's smile gives off the light of a full moon. Everyone knows the moon eats babies too.

Why did you let your brother, my uncle, molest me? Why did you steal from me when I finally found you? Joining Eva is Krystal's real father, Charlie. He blames the Riordans for keeping them apart. The furrows on his forehead look ridged but he smiles. She blinks: neither parent, the cell empty and quiet.

&

By the fourth week she shouts for the lights to be turned off, shouting at the lights themselves, sure they can hear her. The lights hate her and stay on throughout the night. At dawn her mind turns the lights off and all goes dark. Her hands slip into black velvet gloves. *I must look at and touch nothing.*

She returns to the nights after the Riordans first adopted her. The night is huge for the six-year-old in the spacious Connecticut house. Her mouth hardly knows how to speak. Her fingers talk, each digit speaking with its own music; her index makes a pointing, pinging noise, her pinkie coos, and sometimes barks. She's so thin she's almost transparent. Her new mom talks too much and too loud. Her mom's voice seeps from under her fingernails.

&

She stands in the shower. The officer's voice sounds sluggish. Her words are tied together by cord—an endless step-by-step of a sentence so slow that Krystal can watch for a hundred miles and the words come no closer.

The officer says, "Two minutes. Finish up."

By the fifth week she's deep into her head. She's pushing into the forest that looks on fire, huge bark trees soaked in white smoke. Someone crouches behind the trees. A girl's arm brushes aside the smoke. Jennifer. Her broken jaw and half-closed eyes. That's when she starts to shout.

I'm not a bad person. More words—golden flecks on large black-winged birds.

I'm doing a redo Valentine's Day because we were in Lock on February 14th.
—Krystal Riordan, Inmate #661387

When you are isolated in Lock, the officers stop by each cell in the morning, asking who wants to go outside. Time outside lasts two hours. Many cells are occupied by women locked in solitary for 100 days, and most stay in. Isolation's haunting of the mind works its evil.

Handcuffed, inmates are marched to the enclosures. Four women fit inside each roofless cage, where they're uncuffed. If it rains, they must still sit for the scheduled two hours, no exceptions. No matter if rain clouds darken the sky to a stormy green. If not rain, the hours spent in the unshaded sun make your head beat.

&

In the dog cage, Krystal meets the beautiful Camila.

Or, the two meet in Lock, not in the same cell but neighboring ones. Thirty cells side by side, two women in each, and the noise never subsides. The yelling from cell to cell, and the shouting to get the guards' attention, goes on around the clock. If your girlfriend's also here, then you're afraid she's having sex with her cellmate. You're on half-rations and irritable. Every third day you rise again from the stink of Isolation and are brought out in handcuffs and escorted by two officers to the shower. You're carrying shampoo and soap and clean underwear. The rain you lift your face into cleanses body and soul. Reminds you today is not forever.

She's really beautiful. I want you to see her. Lucy said this is the

158

only girl she has ever approved of and liked me with. It is 50/50.
She's a sweetheart and makes me feel special.
—Krystal Riordan, Inmate #661387

And so, for my inmate friend, Valentine's Day is the awaited-for day. Even if she must create it from her almost bare Commissary trunk and State pay, she'll give her new girlfriend a Valentine's Day to treasure.

Krystal tells me Camila soothes her. Is her voice like smoking a cigarette when you're lying in bed and it's a cool morning? Bare, peaceful, explaining-things lips.

&

Chaucer spoke of the mating season of birds, and men and women. Or Valentine's Day could be pagan. Lupercalia, a Roman festival of fertility and coupling. A priest would cut the throats of a goat and dog near the sacred cave of the she-wolf. The mythological she-wolf who nursed the abandoned twins, Romulus and Remus. The good lupus mother. The hide of the goat was then sliced into strips that were soaked in blood. Half-naked young men would dance through the streets of drunkenness, flicking pregnant women with blood. The blood was thought to safeguard the mother and ensure the live birth of the child.

&

Krystal wants to care and be cared for by this woman, this Camila, arrested for attempted homicide. Like Krystal's crime, Camila's homicide attempt occurs on a hot July day. It involves a male friend who has been staying in Camila's apartment. The town is Tinton Falls; once called the Iron Plantation, where slaves were brought to labor in the ironworks. The ruins of the grist mill seem to be the town's only tourist attraction.

Camila is angry at the man, shouts for him to leave. He packs and carries his gear out. On either side of the street, milkweed and red cedar grow from the silty-clay soil. She rummages in the drawers, finds two large butcher knives, and chases him down the sidewalk. After throwing one knife, she stabs him in the chest with the other. Not far away, wild turkey and wood-peckers wander the marshlands. The police are called, and an ambulance rushes the bleeding man into the red dusk. And now, Camila experiences the hunger of Krystal's love.

&

What drives Camila to assault someone she invited into her apartment? There is her daughter and her dog Charlie, whose head likely breaks through the skin of canine sleep when he hears the shouting and the clattering of the knife.

Did he beat the hell out of her? Did the idiot think she'd squirreled that money away in her stomach, and that's why he kept hitting it?

No boyfriend was going to go through her body drawer by drawer, swinging his fists.

&

When Krystal asks me to go to Facebook and print some pho-tos of her new girlfriend, I already know the process of elimi-nation. It won't be Camila from Rio de Janeiro or Buenos Aries, not the news editor for the New York Yankees, not the IT consul-tant Camila with a multinational corporation. It will be another Camila, whose online life stopped in 2015.

This Camila is beautiful, and her apartment looks airy, as if a flutter of ship's sail has passed through it. In a short black strapless club dress, she blows wasp-stung kisses. One of her ad-mirers lingers in the social media bushes, wowed by her legs. Camila's daughter and dog are shown sleeping in her bed.

"Two babies," she comments in her post.

She exudes late-night drives when the stars are bright as magnolia blossoms, and you want to reach up and pull them out of the sky and eat them. There are more photos of night-clubs, darkening places, padded leather doors, deep booths, smoke-polished maroon wood. Billie Holiday crooning through the murderous hip hop. Hoop earrings, gold-flake eyeshadow.

&

The she-wolf who exemplifies instinct and loyalty, the unselfish she-wolf mother who suckles abandoned children can become the she-wolf, devourer. Women who have been wounded horribly sometimes wound others. Sometimes fatally.

Me and Camila broke up. Yesterday she told me the real reason is because she got a crush on someone else. The lady she's got a crush on looks like Shrek. I don't get it. She said everything she told me she meant and she really loves me. This is the reason I always feel like I'm not good enough and ugly.
—Krystal Riordan, Inmate #661387

The imprisoned body is the chapel or the toilet to be adored or shat on.

Krystal told me of Camila in the joy of new love, followed too soon by the crashing disappointment of seeing her girlfriend with hickeys on her neck. Krystal is sure those love bites are aimed at her heart. Idiot. She must be ugly; she must be unlovable. She pictures herself as a lizard.

The thirst of this place is going to drink Krystal into it.

&

Krystal needs to talk to her Camila. She needs to be comforted.

It is 1 a.m. at the correctional facility when the fire alarm goes off and all the units march outside into the Yard, where the inmates are supposed to stand in silent lines. The inmates are talking, guessing who pulled the alarm or started a fire. Maybe the moon shines, and after midnight it's a fat scoop of ice cream you want to lick.

Everyone talks, then someone yells Camila!

Krystal is waving her arms crazily. The moon is filling their bodies with love. The mermaids of after-midnight are swimming.

Camila turns away.

Most real couples in prison will buy each other tons of gifts and may even have a sexy outfit sewn for them on V-Day night in the

privacy of the nasty bathroom.
—Lucy Weems, Inmate #922870C

There are three Counts a day, at 8 a.m. – 8:30 a.m., 11 a.m. – 11:30 a.m., and 4 p.m. – 4:30 p.m. Mid-afternoon, Krystal goes into the bathroom with her BIC razor filed away.

What does she see in the mirror? The mucky walls, her time? A summer girl shrinking into winter, a 20-year-old when she was arrested, she'll be in her 40s upon her release. Where is the way out, the way away?

She wants motion; she wants to flow. Madly heading somewhere. First the nick and then the trickling begins. If she's brave, the shimmering red taillights of her veins will open. Have to do this. Have to struggle the blade in, no stopping. No creeping. Claustrophobic nearness of the walls. Her heart pulses where her bunkmate Lucy's name is tattooed. They had inked each other's name on their left wrists, the arteries that run directly to the heart.

&

She cuts her left wrist, deep; the deeper the cut, the better she feels. Nearness of music. Blood is streaking her hands and thighs. The cuts are forgiving her for the *I Love You* cards and the necklace set; the teddy bear. Krystal remembers touching the mole on Camila's back. Pressing her thumb into the mole's blue softness.

The last endorphin rush feels like a gentle, loving mother. An inmate finds her and runs to tell an officer to check on Krystal in the bathroom. She's on the floor and lying in a pool of red running from her left wrist. An inmate stretcher crew arrives and they carry Krystal to the Medical Unit. She receives both internal stitches to tendons, as well as numerous external stitches.

Her history of cutting and depression goes untreated.

&

In the outside world, there is Valentine's Day as well. Tepid, well-dressed couples get in and out of taxis and Uber cars, and they walk on the sidewalks lined with bursts of bergamot and jasmine.

Restaurants fill with musk-fragrant suited men, and young women dressed in sheaths, the smooth silver of an ice shaker. Hair, heels, electricity. Credit cards. Couples with cheeks like glowing shots of amaretto. The inhabitants living on the continent of freedom celebrate romantic love.

&

Inside Maximum Compound, Valentine's Day celebrates love of the she-wolf. What the officers learn of the inmates is nothing compared to what the inmates have learned of each other. Strange things lie on the bottom of us all, things we are ashamed of, and yet most inmates believe that what love embodies reigns supreme, even in the barbed-wire world.

GIRL-WORLD / LUCY
EMCF   Clinton, New Jersey

On my very first day at EMCF in reception, I looked down at the bunk bed diagonal to mine and saw the first of hundreds of public sex acts. A woman was making ridiculously loud noises with her head between another woman's legs. No one else paid a bit of attention. One day in the future I would look past it and even be a public sex act myself.
—Lucy Weems, Inmate #922870C

Born in 1977, Lucy's older than the average inmate, who's in her early 20s. Her online rap sheet tells the viewer she's 5'3" and weighs 110 pounds. Her arrest mugshot captures her long, tangled hair, some ringlets pinned to the crown of her head, other ringlets dangling haphazardly to her shoulders. Her brow furrows as she looks with bored expression at the photographer. She's high. Lucy's narrowed hazel eyes peer out of a face that seems to be judging the photographer, absorbing him just as he is fixing her for all time. She looks like a February morning-after on the Jersey Shore, with gulls circling the empty bottles and cans. Every hangover you've ever had.

Her two daughters, Hope and Faith, whom she left behind in the world, live with relatives. Different sets.

Her sentence, nine years for assaulting and kidnapping a drug dealer, seems a walk on a white-sand beach compared to her new best friend's thirty years. Yet, when you're a mother of young daughters, you'll miss their growing up. The oldest has been taught to call her Mrs. Weems, not Mommy.

&

Lucy still shudders, remembering her first day at EMCF.

There's a line you follow. "Single file and no talking." "Move it or lose it!" the Officer had snapped.

164

She marches toward the metal detector behind the women on her unit, one at a time through the detector, and then between the officers, male and female, three on each side. The tiny hairs on her body rise like iron filings magnetized. Her eyes follow the streak of sweat across more than one officer's cheek.

Lucy's arrival at Maximum Compound coincides with the day cigarette smoking is outlawed at EMCF. Most of the officers and many of the inmates smoke heavily and are undergoing nicotine withdrawal. Everyone seems on edge, a hair's breadth from rage. She's passing between the force fields of appraising faces and feels dirty with experience, weighed down by the heaviness of her own life.

Left right, left right, toward the metal detector, one at a time through the gauntlet past the armed officers, male and female, two and three on each side. Like walking through enemy soldiers.

Once she was among her fellow inmates, the way some of the women had gazed at her with eyes like hard black seeds made the breath catch in her throat. A few of the older ones seemed kind, but the young ones asked her straight out whether she had family sending her money to order stuff.

"I already knew better than to offer any financial or personal information," Lucy says. "I was among the piranhas."

&

Krystal can't remember her first day at EMCF. Jail muted her arrival here, and hasn't she spent her entire life in one form or another of incarceration? For most others, like Lucy, it's a shock when you are transformed from a citizen of the free world into an inmate in custody of the State. Free world, free will.

You carry nothing in with you; no driver's license, no credit cards, no clothing, no medications; nothing except your troubled past and your eyeglasses, if you wear them. "Shut up, Ladies, while we process you," an officer snaps.

"Okay, Ladies, everything comes off. Bra, panties, socks. Bend over, squat, and cough."

Naked in the thin light, it's the same sallow light you wake to after being up for days, you can't escape your own face wearing caked mascara and greenish fish-gut eye shadow. Strip. The Officer wears a rubber glove to explore Lucy's privates, making sure her vagina and rectum aren't smuggling in contraband. She's given 2 uniforms, 5 panties, 2 bras, socks, a blanket, a pillow, a sheet. "Put on your uniform and leave your clothes here."

&

Some of the older, experienced inmates would tell Lucy what she had done wrong; these unselfish women help all the new girls adjust and learn the ropes. Doing wrong is a dangerous thing.

There's Thea Pena, almost finished serving her 25-year sentence. She speaks in a soft, motherly voice and quietly warns the new women to hush. You don't ask what her crime was; you'd rather get to know her first, but she offers up her past. The husband she tied to the bed, he expecting kinky sex, sees too late the knife's silver gleam. She brings it down 41 times, this fine-featured Dominican, this exotic-looking woman who has served a quarter of a century in prison.

He threatened to take her children and beat her again. Did she want that? How often does she wake in a cold sweat, believing she's in her Fort Lee apartment, her children missing? Lying in wait is the year 1994. The crickets sing madly—you'll never see your daughters again.

In her sleep she keeps asking where her babies are; she's trudging from town to town. Knocking on doors answered by all different shades of faces, from high yellow to dark.

Nobody's seen them. 41 times. Blood.

&

Lucy shares her story with few inmates other than Krystal. The contours of being married twice, the first time in the Bahamas and the second in New Jersey; Michael, the first, and Jimmy, the second and Hope's father, both cheaters.

She pictures herself pregnant and ecstatic with Hope, and not getting along with Jimmy, so she moves into a YMCA-run home for expectant mothers. Given her own room, counseling, mothering classes, and surrounded by so much love and support, she could have been strolling through a field of sunflowers. It must be the way the guards are standing like guests at a wedding when the bridal march plays that causes Lucy to imagine her teen parents on their wedding day. Two Connecticut kids in the late 1970s about to become parents. Her dark-eyed Ava Gardner look-alike mother soon gives birth to her brother, and two years later, Lucy comes along.

She's always been told she resembles her mother, but she has no photographs of her. Her mother is said to be alive somewhere. Somewhere she inhales and exhales.

&

Lucy claims that officers sometimes look the other way if you and your girlfriend are caught in flagrante delicto; others just look, and a good many write you up. There's a thriving subculture in Maximum Compound. Love affairs and sex-fueled blood fights. You take big risks meeting your girlfriend in an area not your own. Isolation. Investigations.

The Prison Rape Elimination Act (PREA) makes informed sexual consent by a prisoner impossible. Unwanted touching is a zero-tolerance offense, as is any act of sexual violence. Prisoners legally belong to the State during their incarceration and therefore have no agency. It's against rules to be seen giving and receiving affection or using sex toys.

With so little control over their own lives, it's no surprise that as soon as two women talk to each other, they claim the other. It's like this. *Don't leave me. Please, please, please. Love me, Isla/ Gabbie. Chyna. Naty. Love me, Bitch.*

The Yard, the Fence, Church, Mess Hall, the Bunk, the Bathrooms. These are the geographical locations for a rendezvous. The blueprint for couples and love-talk.

Meet me in the Yard. Are you going to Church?

My niece said, "Grandpa! Did you get to meet Aunt Lucy's girl-

friend? Do they kiss a lot?"
—Lucy Weems, Inmate #922870C

Four years into her sentence, Lucy feels the attraction of the glance when Topaz, a gangbanger from Newark, strides into her work area.

"Hey, beautiful. They tell me you're smart."

Upper lip shadowed by facial hair, she projects masculinity of an off-brand sort. Topaz brags she could be a chef, and then proves it. She seduces Lucy with yummy spring rolls made in a microwave with low-quality Mess Hall and Commissary ingredients. Keep calling me your spring roll, Lucy, and I'll keep rolling over for you. Gifts exchange hands: chocolate chip cookies, Frosted Flakes, taco bowls, Hershey's Kisses. *Bite my lip, Bitch.*

&

Lucy laughs about an ex-internal auditor/ex-accountant/ex-prostitute making love to an inmate affiliated with the Bloods, a large girl of 22 with a lovely white-toothed smile. Topaz poses in her beige sweats, a black-beaded cross around her neck. Although it's forbidden, she surprises Lucy in her room. She unfastens Lucy's pants and slides her hands down her girlfriend's thighs. They drape sheets over the bed and create their own cave, their own aloneness. Before Topaz leaves, she kisses Lucy on the cheek.

Topaz chats up the Unit Supervisor, giving advice about the sautéing of shrimp. Topaz loves them, even the fat blue grass shrimp, the kind used for bait. Why didn't Mess Hall serve shrimp fried rice? Ramen shrimp doesn't count.

"Topaz would talk to the officers on the way out with the smell of my pussy on her breath. Later, we'd laugh and laugh."

Pussy is the word of choice in Maximum Compound for the vagina and clitoris, the pleasure wilderness between a woman's legs.

&

Should we experiment with a strap-on?

Why not, they decide, and Topaz attempts to make one.

A monstrosity like a great coil of a tree root is the result, a sex toy that would puncture Lucy's lungs. They hang Topaz's elephantine device in the bathroom as a trophy, and consult Krystal, the village toy-maker, who produces the perfect toy. Topaz falls in love with the dildo, wearing it like it's hers. You offer what you can as tokens of your affection. You've become part of it, like in the old days on Ferry Street when you opened doors to strangers' cars, your hands slowly squeezing the handle, joining your date in the privacy of the driver's seat.

Officers who find toys hang them in public areas or tie them to a fence to embarrass us. We lost our shame at the door. The day we were arrested and told to strip in front of an officer was the last of our shame.
—Lucy Weems, Inmate #922870C

In Maximum Compound the rumors circulate endlessly. Gossip is many-headed and its tentacles entangle every inmate; the crime, what brought you here, what else you've done to have been banished from the human pack. Lucy is told that Topaz's online rap sheet charges her with having had sexual relations with a 16-year-old.

Murder's understood, even forgiven, but crimes against children follow and hound you, giving off a foul scent. Still the affair goes on until Topaz asks for a threesome and flirts openly. Maximum Compound couples rarely seem to last. Lucy forgives her girlfriend, only for Topaz to cheat again. This time after they break up, Topaz marches into Lucy's area and throws a punch at her. She charges Lucy and they swim around each other. Another jab, what would have been dead center of her nose. Lucy's head buzzes with anger's red flush and she starts to land her overhand punches. Her Uncle Pauli taught her how to throw boxer's punches; legs apart, knees bent, and fists loose. Topaz is reeling. Punches are flying, now everything's allowed: kicking and biting. Neither will give up and there's blood everywhere. Both women are in the blackout zone, unaware that officers have entered the cube and are pulling them apart.

When couples break up in Maximum Compound, there's a good chance fight blood will be shed. Inmates experience so much prison tension that fighting becomes another forbidden fruit, its own sexual release.

Krystal was suspicious of Morocco.
—Lucy Weems, Inmate #922870C

An inmate named Morocco transfers into her unit. Every time they pass, Morocco's dark eyes harden and she gives Lucy looks like throwing a fist into a wall. Her eyes could be stones breaking from the earth's socket and tumbling down.

It seems Topaz had been seeing Morocco at the same time she'd been romancing Lucy.

"I'm not your enemy," Lucy finally tells her. Morocco's face softens. Her eyes turn to smoky kerosene.

There's a real charge between the two. The flicker. Soon Lucy wants to feel her body cooled by Morocco's breath. Her hair's cropped close and her voice deep and musky—a Jersey City god. They make a handsome couple, a study in contrasts. Lucy's face lifted, once again almost beatific, her waist-length hair decorated with thin ropes of braids, her dark eyes that sometimes look gray-green. Morocco, a head taller than Lucy, her thumbs-looped-in-pockets stance, broad shoulders, a prettiness in her face and closed-lip smile. Morocco: her name is music.

Her stomach somersaults at the sight of her. Morocco's skin is smooth, except for the darker puckered places: the mouths of scars, one just below her left shoulder blade and another at the small of her back.

"What happened?" When Lucy kisses the scars, a tenderness inside her.

Lucy has a great heart and I'm not going to break it. I have been

170

thinking about marrying her.
—Morocco Lawrence, Inmate #911442D

They celebrate their seven-month anniversary. Lucy's in love. She worries about their age difference because she's once again the older woman in her mid-thirties and Morocco's much younger, in her early twenties.

Lucy's underground art business of creating hand-paint-ed greeting cards—Valentine's Day, birthdays, Mother's Day—explodes. So many inmates order cards and want specific messages that Lucy becomes overwhelmed. Morocco runs interference and protects Lucy from too many requests. That feels good, almost as good as the sex. Morocco wants to brand Lucy, ink her with—MINE OR DIE. Those thumbs hooked to her belt make Lucy thirsty for her. Being around Morocco makes the air taste buttery. Someday Lucy will take Morocco to the flower gardens.

If you're wondering if I have any goals when I get home, well, I do. I want to get into real estate. Lucy has me looking at the bigger picture. I really love your friend and I do want to marry and build a family with her.
—Morocco Lawrence, Inmate #911442D

No lookout, but the officer has made her walk-through. Morocco is going down on Lucy and Lucy touches Morocco's cropped hair, fingering her head. "How come you have a nicer shaped head than me?" Lucy asks playfully.

Morocco's tongue is a fluttering fish, and then she lifts her head. "Because you're an acorn-headed dago. You knobby, pointy-headed thing." Now Morocco's flitting tongue is teasing her and she's arching up on her haunches.

"Whoa," a man interrupts.

&

Lucy blinks, sees an officer's boot inches from her head. He might write them up. He might want them to run their fingers over his chest.

Instead, he tells them to keep going. "Don't let me bother you." Lucy decides what the heck; we're getting in trouble anyway…

She loves Morocco's shoulders, her confident cool emanating from Jersey City's dark streets. Morocco forges on and Lucy orgasms, her outer layers melting away, while looking into the officer's eyes, pools of glittery bacon grease. Getting caught by an officer who then watches is a turn-on. No write-up.

Draping a sheet from your bunk is a great way to get privacy for sex, but it also lets other inmates know that you are having sex at that time, of which you risk the chance of snitch inmates running and telling the officers— which you wouldn't know because you're busy in the act. That is why it's important to have a friend looking out for you while you're busy.
—Lucy Weems, Inmate #922870C

Lingering rumors about her lover passing notes to an inmate in North Hall causes Lucy to go to the source. She pays in batteries and snacks for one of the notes, in which Morocco talks about missing the inmate's face.

"Hey, lady, it's great to see your beautiful face!"

When Lucy shows Morocco the letters, her lover grips Lucy by the neck and starts to choke her. Lucy kicks Morocco in her sore knee and she lets go. Then the punches start, the hooks and jabs.

One of my friends named Apples knew I was an art aficionado and gave me a contraband wooden ruler. I seldom used this ruler for artwork and slept with it under my mattress to whip out when my girlfriend Morocco got out of line. It did the job.
—Lucy Weems, Inmate #922870C

Morocco asks for another chance and Lucy readily agrees to give her one. They go on. Perhaps they have twin souls. When they

172

get out they won't be together, not at first; Morocco will be re-leased a year before Lucy.

Will Morocco wait for Lucy? Morocco had said she want-ed Lucy for her lawful wedded wife.

Morocco, soon to be paroled to a halfway house, is trans-ferred to Minimum Compound.

Not a note left behind. Gone.

&

After the 2019 scandal in which multiple male guards are charged with sexual abuse of the inmates of the Edna Mahan Correc-tional Facility, only women officers are allowed to supervise any Maximum Compound unit. Love weaves through the darkness at the far end of the heart's street, then disappears.

Lucy goes through a phase of sexual heat when she be-comes involved with Toya, an older woman with Jimi Hendrix's exotic looks who loves oral sex. *Anywhere, anytime!*

Toya's crimes of possession with intent to sell stolen goods seem minor in comparison to the kidnappers and armed robbers around her. It's a chump change rap sheet but felonies add up, so she cycles in and out of EMCF.

&

Medication keeps Toya's mental instability muffled but some-times it flames out. She loves to feed the birds and saves her food from Mess Hall and Commissary for the feathered beings.

In the Yard, Toya announces, "It's Little Bird Day." She scatters bits of bread and seeds, and the sparrows and the pi-geons descend. They know her, and the air quivers with wings.

"No." She shakes her head violently, as she grimaces and bites her thumb. "Go away, Big Birds. This is Little Bird Day."

Her words drown in the river of birds. The birds come from the free world. In her disordered mind, the Big Birds are purposely disobeying her. A song sparrow floats by like mist. Lit-tle brown birds with long tails. She screams and throws cups and dirt at the big birds. The little birds smell sweet, like scabs all the neighborhood boys picked from their knees.

Krystal refuses to hang out with nutty Toya, who is clearing the yard with her launching projectiles; sweet Toya, who is drooling.

&

Lights weave through the darkness at the far end of the heart's street, then nose down an alley and disappear. Who gets a life sentence on the dirt planet and who gets life on a pleasure planet? The sun goes down and it's the hour the night shift begins. You're the sex nurse. You're the hearer of bodily fluid confession. You're the facility that has installed 93 cameras throughout the grounds to avoid blind spots. You're the blind spot where girlfriends find privacy. You're the sheet hanging down from a bunk to shelter lovers. You're the delight that darts through cubes and crawl spaces. You're the T-shirt perfumed with grape jelly and sardines, you're the dark rings of sweat.

You're the hands that pull down my pants and the ceiling that giggles. You're the golden currants—M&M's sex fruit. Your fingers swallow your own beating heart. You're the moss. The hair. The entanglement. You're crushing me. You're hurrying my clothes on. You're the exquisite. The overlarge voice ringing in my ears. You're the waking and the wondering. You're the love.

GIRL-WORLD /KRYSTAL
EMCF   Clinton, New Jersey

I love you and I'll be in Yard soon. I love you, CRAZY BABY!!! I MISS
YOU! Listen, Blacky. Hey, White Krystal. Crazy Fool!
—Inmates EMCF

It's 46 degrees in Stowe today, the new unit where they've moved
her. Even inside two pairs of socks her toes feel like hailstones
about to roll away. Blue ice. She shoves her hands inside her
sweatshirt and warms them. She wishes she was astride a horse;
not the real ones she never rode, but the ones she imagines. Freedom horses. Her feet in the stirrups, her legs against his flanks.
She lifts her rump from the saddle and the trot begins. The reins
ripple like water through her fingers.

&

Krystal feels like a stuffed sausage in her two pairs of sweats as
she walks to the common area and waits for a phone to free up.
No phones today.

The last time she called home her dad mentioned he'd
seen an old friend of hers. Her father likes to reminisce about
Krystal's natural athleticism. "Remember the friend who took
you horseback riding when you were younger? We ran into her
at Trader Joe's," her father said.

Krystal had taken to horses from the beginning. Mountain Valley. Flat riding fields and trails.

"How's she doing?" Krystal asked, her stomach knotting.

The friend's name was Gia. Her first girl crush. She remembered the two of them riding. Fast. Faster. Something had
spooked her mount; the horse, spinning, galloped toward a
mucky place of tarry leaves and tires. Gia, riding behind her, was
calling out, "Flex from your shoulders, Krystal; bring her un-

175

der control." The fence appeared suddenly in front of them, sun shining through, each slat a rainbow-like silver arm. The horse rocketed up, jumping, and Krystal, no longer afraid, rose in the saddle. It felt like flying. Like sex someday would.

"She's teaching riding and had her little girl with her," her mother said. "She asked after you."

Krystal's pulse had quickened, she wanted to know: what did you tell her? What could they have said? Lower their heads like horses do when they're sad, and tell her that Krystal, the natural athlete, became the Jen-Slay Hooker and has served 14 years in prison? That she's hoping for parole in 6 years? The one who wanted French-manicured fingernails and a Porsche.

But her parents never talk about her crime.

Her father adds, "And she mentioned your natural horsemanship."

It all had come so naturally to her. From flat riding fields to climbing trails. Why wasn't she born four-legged? Horses liked to stand muzzle to muzzle, their nostrils breathing together. Sharing the air. Sitting nose to nose, Gia and Krystal pretended they were horses sharing the air. Both girls were tall with straight long legs and blond manes tied into ponytails. First their noses touched, then giggles and hiccups, then kissing. Pale brides. Tongues pebbled with roses.

Yes, she liked women even before going to prison.

Her father brings up her oldest sister, their real child, the married attorney. She pictures the Riordans' property. Far back from the road, trees obscuring the stately house, a stream meandering across the lawn. Her ears hug her parents' voices, even if they loved their adopted daughter less than their natural daughter. One, a jailbird; one, an attorney.

Daddy, your beautiful hands. The forest of your fingers. Wasn't I your favorite? What would happen if she said that?

Laysha, hey beautiful, what happened? I heard you're in Lock for a fight. I was so happy to be going to be able to see you. Now I can't. I hope it's something you can beat. I really miss you and love you.
Write me. Love, Krystal.
—Krystal Riordan, Inmate #661387

Back in her new room Krystal begins settling in and filling her trunk with the few Commissary items she has brought with her. Some red-hot Slim Jims and Market Pantry oatmeal cookies, the vanilla wafers, and chocolate kisses. She picks up the stuffed animal one of the inmates made for her from a ripped T-shirt, a sewing needle, and embroidery thread. She presses the little cloth bear to her cheek and imagines it warm and alive. I love you, little bear.

At last they've gotten the heat on. The pipes are throwing out dirty steam and making a banging sound.

&

Hearing laughter and someone punching the wall, she turns. It takes time for the sounds to unstick themselves from her knuckles and roll through the still frigid air. An inmate is standing in the doorway lifting her fist and knocking, and she's a looker. Krystal takes a deep breath.

"That knocking isn't going to hurt you, Riordan. May I come in?"

Her skin is the color of mink. Long straightened hair and teardrop nostrils. Beautiful, and she knows it. Like she knows more than Krystal's name.

"I'm Laysha," she says, plopping herself on Krystal's bunk. She picks up Krystal's mail and waves it. "You've got two letters here. Expecting good news? Your people writing to tell you they put money in your Commissary?"

Is she one of those inmates who figure you're only good for what you can give? Her otter eyes open wider. She places a hand on Krystal's knee. Funny, for all her soft, the palms of her hands are hard. "I heard your parents are rich. Must be nice."

Was she for real? "They help a little," Krystal says.

"How little?" Laysha asks, the corners of her eyes crinkling up. She pinches the envelopes into her fingers.

Krystal snatches the envelopes back, chuckling. Her head starts to ache, as if she drank hot cocoa and an ice-cold Mountain Dew at the same time. The first ride and Krystal, five years old, is standing on a mounting block. The roan, so gentle, breathes white into the snow air like falling diamonds while her new father checks the bridle buckles. The reins are put into her left hand, and now, take a bit of mane. The mane she would not let go of.

&

Laysha. No facial hair, no boxer's body, and that disarming smile. Feminine in a world where many of the sought-after women are broad-shouldered and bearded, where testosterone in a woman is prized. This Laysha tempts Krystal with her smoothness and, in the beginning, she doesn't ask for much from Commissary and JPay transfers and black/white soaps and hot chili with beans and a warm riverbank to picnic on.

This Laysha knows Krystal's low self-esteem and entices her with sugary words. Krystal, I can hear your strut even in this doghouse and bet you made money on those busy streets at 3 a.m. You turn the air even in this shithole (excuse my language) when you walk by.

Once again Krystal became involved with this Draymond in female form. While she weighs half as much as Dray, this woman stood out on a 3 a.m. exit with an off-duty cop and pistol whipped a 17-year-old girl. This WOMAN we are discussing has a hold on Krystal.

—Lucy Weems, Inmate #922870C

Laysha enters the digital record with the headline WOMAN OVERSLEEPS AND MISSES HER SENTENCING.

Her attorney argues that she's just recovering from surgery and has no intent to escape the court's jurisdiction. Already convicted of kidnapping, assaulting a minor, robbery, and weapons possession, it's the judgment she sleeps through.

She'll trade seven years of her life for a stolen cell phone. It's 4:29 a.m. and Laysha rides in her lover's gray SUV. He's an off-duty cop, a 13-year veteran of the force. A 17-year-old girl, who they claim they're bringing to a halfway house, rides in back. It's good to be in with the law; perhaps Laysha feels she can break the law and come to no harm. She is an extremely pretty woman, with plum lips and slanting brown eyes; her skin and her white teeth shine. You might take her for a lawyer or minister; she gives off a hymn-singing glow; it's her teardrop nostrils.

The nostrils that Krystal loves and hates. A minute later, Laysha tells her lover to pull off at the exit; she's done this kind of thing before. She points the gun at the 17-year-old girl, and tells her to empty her pockets and hand over her cell phone. The police revolver in her grip has real weight, superior to chrome, a cheap silver-plated street gun, the kind you use for muggings and stickups. This revolver is heavy as a judge's gavel.

Now Laysha tells the girl to get out of the car and perhaps the teen calls her a bitch. "You'd better hope we don't run into each other again."

They do run into each other again, in the line-up, when the 17-year-old identifies Laysha as her assailant.

Goodbye, Laysha, pretty as musk soap.

Tampons are roughly $7.00 a box so we do make our own. At the end of the month everyone runs out of toilet paper. Women save candy bar wrappers.
—Lucy Weems, Inmate #922870C

Toilet Paper Day occurs every 30 days, when the guards distribute eight rolls per woman, which most inmates wisely lock up. The thirty days pass and then another week and still no toilet paper.

You're a ripe fat fruit and every pound Commissary has put on your hips looks delicious.

Day 44 and still no toilet paper.

"You don't happen to have any toilet paper in your trunk?" As an act of love, Krystal gives her last roll to Laysha and uses candy-bar wrappers for herself.

"All the ladies get lost in watching you, beautiful. Let me wear your cross necklace."

The cross necklace is the only jewelry allowed in Maximum Compound, a simple cross on an 18-inch regulation chain. They are lying together on the bunk. Laysha traces the chain, then drops it between Krystal's breasts.

Krystal knows that once it's off her neck she'll never see it again. She wraps her hand around her only piece of jewelry and shakes her head.

Laysha curses. Soon, she will exact her revenge.

&

In the end, she takes from Krystal everything she can. *You tickbird. Your face is regurgitated turtle vomit. I'm going to bounce you out of here.*

Her friends insist that Krystal could be loved by a hundred people, but she manages to find the one person who can't love her. "Watch out for Laysha," her friends warn.

She hides razors under Krystal's bunk and snitches to the officers. When the officers try to write up Krystal she fights the contraband charge. She tells them she's been threatened and requests a transfer.

"You are a stupid chick, Riordan," Laysha says. "You're so hungry for a wife, you're scary."

Nickel Cone, I was going through my stuff and found letters from you. I wish you were with me right now so I could do some things like we did in Lock. I didn't want to leave. I could have done my whole time with you in there. I miss you. I love you so much. Al-

ways, Snuggle Bunny.
— Krystal Riordan, Inmate #661387

Laysha's words hurt.

Krystal still craves Rikii, the gang girl with the scent of cinnamon on her neck. When Krystal hears that Rikii has been taken to Lock, she decides to stand by her friend. Loyalty outdoes everything, even self-preservation.

To be taken to Lock, she needs to break some rules. She goes to an unauthorized area outside, just off the Yard, and marches back and forth. The sky, so blue and cloudless, runs straight at her; the sky hurts her heart with all its freedom.

"Riordan, come inside. Knock it off, or else we'll be calling a code on you."

She keeps marching because now all the blue has put its freedom in her.

When ten officers burst in from the door, they let her have a run and then they tackle her. Afterwards, her chest hurts like she's broken a rib. When she raises her right arm, the pain almost frightens her, but she's got her heart's desire—30 days with Rikii.

For a month in Lock they're together. After they touch and love their bodies, after the luxuriousness of sex, they lie in the summer grass of each other's arms and whisper. Although no one can hear, they keep whispering. Rikii sometimes dreams about the girl floating facedown in the river. The girl whom Rikii had been ordered to rough up was a year younger than she, a high school graduate headed to community college. The girl's death smelled sweet and thick, like perfume bleeding.

Rikii shakes and tells Krystal she sometimes hears the girl whimpering for help.

"I love you, Rikii. I love you," Krystal whispers. It's what she has. Only that.

&

The ceiling thinks it's the dark side of the moon. To be unlovable is the nothingness that can grab you by the throat and shake you from sleep. It has no bottom and can put its fingers through you. Krystal believes no one loves her because there is something so damaged, so wrong with her, that she can't be loved. It started with her birth mother and then her adoptive mother. Neither loved her; not really. Not even her best friend loves her.

Valarie has been my friend for ten years and wonders if you can go to Facebook and print her pictures out. I trust her more than anyone.
—Krystal Riordan, Inmate #661387

A bedroom selfie shows a well-kept room, old-fashioned wallpaper trellised with pink honeysuckle, a picture of the Virgin Mary, an insert of her red heart in blue flames. Not exactly what you would expect from an illegal gun seller.

Valarie's cold blue-gray eyes are frightening dreams of the tight dark garage where the guns are kept inside the rebuilt carburetors. She's a muscular Sicilian-American, a fine-featured toughie, who wears a do-rag. Head cocked, thin lips pursed, eyebrows pierced with silver studs, she's showing off her gangster moves. Her post states *I'm a good old boy and I hate a clingy bitch.*

&

Krystal tells Valarie about that twilight after she was taken from her birth parents and put into foster care. A Jehovah's Witness couple with two kids of their own took her in. Strict.

The watchword of her childhood. Strict fosters. Strict adoptive parents. Ultra-strict Élan, where there was a bathroom schedule and only certain times she could use the toilet. "I remember having to pee in the middle of the night and when I would try to go to the bathroom, I would get hit, and if I peed the bed, they'd beat me."

She tells Valarie about the mares and their ruler stallion. She saw pictures of them and made up stories in her mind. The foal named Chestnut for his rich color, how she hugged the pretend pony's neck and stayed beside him all night. Even then her loyalty was everything. She invented an early-March barn where the foal lived. Forgetting the chill, she ran barefoot into the night. The stars tumbling out of the sky. The barn smell, the rise and fall of her breathing. Waking to the bed wet beneath her.

Krystal shadowed a girl around last night when the girl just wanted space, and they were yelling at each other, so when the officer stepped in between them, and told Krystal and Valarie to go separate ways to cool down, Krystal put her hands on the officer, I think she shoved her arm or something, to get at Valarie. The officer called a code and now Krystal is in Lock facing an assault charge.
—Lucy Weems, Inmate #922870C

Krystal follows Valarie into the Yard, the 3:30 p.m. exercise hour. "Talk to me, Valarie."

She doesn't want to say the word; she promised herself she wouldn't. The cringe-worthy word.

Valarie keeps walking, hands stuffed in her pockets, head rocking too, that street swagger Krystal's crazy about. She doesn't want to tell anyone how she keeps thinking if she folds Valarie's clothes just so and makes her bed perfectly, Valarie will love her. "Don't walk away." Valarie's hair cropped, showing off the beautiful shape of her head. "Please."

Hearing the forbidden word, Valarie turns, her thin mouth pressed into a line. "I hate *please.*"

Krystal reaches for Valarie, to pull her back, to pretend they are outside in the night.

The sweet dark that inmates rarely see wraps itself around them. *Please stop. Please let me please you.* The moon is shining down out of the dark heaven, where the astronauts say it is black like you never imagined. That is the unknowing. *I love you like the sun splitting through the leaves of a newly planted tree. I love you pretending to sleep, I love you shaking awake. Your thin mouth and hawk-like face. Please, I don't recognize where I am. The pit of my stomach is caught on a bone. I look across the Yard and a sob breaks from my throat. Please, I am choking on that word.*

&

Dangers in murky water. She senses her girlfriends' dark auras, whatever it is that people give off. That feeling of stepping off the edge of the known, the comfortable, into a wild rough place that stinks of flies and mosquitoes, the soil of her thoughts threaded with worms.

She thinks of her friend Gia teaching her to balance herself like the black mare who was always aware of its body and so awake she could hear the shiver of a gnat land on her white markings.

&

Around Christmas, Krystal makes Valarie and the rest of the women on their wing watch Julie Andrews in The Sound of Music. Torture for some, the corniness of the Von Trapp Family, the goodie-goodie two-shoes Julie Andrews, but Krystal sings along, knowing every word for each of the songs.

FIGHT BLOOD ECONOMY
EMCF Clinton, New Jersey

JPay also has a tablet of sorts, which we use to manage music, emails, games that we purchase from a kiosk. Each tablet requires 4 AA batteries that give the tablet 6–8 hours of use before dying. Batteries are $3.64 for a 4-pack. The average inmate has a monthly budget of $30.00 if they get no outside help.
—Lucy Weems, Inmate #922870C

With the privatization of prisons in full swing, more companies are discovering how much money can be siphoned from the incarcerated and squeezed from their families. Chief among these is JPay, a privately-held Miramar, Florida corporation; Securus Technologies, a prison communications firm, is their parent company. Securus has developed a system that can track any phone in the United States.

JPay has a captive audience, and once the company saw how they could price out inmate emails, the prison only needed to set the picket fence of rules around it.

Through the tablets they supply to inmates, the company offers a digital smorgasbord—email services as well as money transfers and music downloads, which cost 30% – 50% more than iTunes. Each single-page incoming or outgoing email costs $2, and additional pages accrue additional charges. For good behavior inmates are granted kiosk time at the computer for five-minute stretches to compose and send missives.

Eventually, JPay proposes to end in-person prison visits and replace them with Skype sessions on the JPay-provided video tablet. This service will cost the inmate and their family an estimated $20–$30 per session, with the prison taking a cut as their commission on each session.

185

At this writing, Maximum Compound no longer allows in-person visitations.

&

Having once been an accountant, Lucy is able to keep a running tab on the dollars the system collects from her incarceration. Monetized bodies might well be minnows circling the prison pond, propelled and fed by money transfers. Minnows gulped by the big-fish shareholders collectively create great corporate wealth.

When families are able to transfer only $10 from their bank to their inmate's account, JPay adds a processing fee of $3.46. The more money you send, the less onerous the JPay fee. If you send $25, the JPay fee increases to $6.95; at $50 or $60, the fee remains $6.95.

&

To make phone calls, inmates and their families must use Global Tel Link, ("GTL") which allows deposits on phone numbers in small or large amounts. GTL's website tells us that the corporation services 2,300 prisons, processed 900 million credit card transactions in 2019, and logged 3.89 billion in inmate call minutes. GTL has been in business for 31 years and claims 74% of America's inmate population uses its services. Whenever I called GTL to buy minutes, which I did often, I was greeted by the same user-unfriendly recording. Except for occasionally raising the processing fee, the recording went unchanged. When you are buying $10 or $20 worth of phone minutes, the processing fee ($3 and up) may feel burdensome.

Inmates, like it or not, are now under the JPay/Global Tel Link canopy. While the company sings a catchy tune, insisting that their services make prison time bearable for inmates, their lips are smeared with the golden nectar of money.

It's all about the money.

&

In Maximum Compound's parallel economy, tablet time and music downloads substitute for money, and you make that money selling what you're able to.

Since inmates aren't allowed to exchange money or Commissary credit, everything happens on the underground market. Commissary items are a large part of EMCF's currency. Toothpaste, Dove soap, caffeinated coffee, T-shirts, sweatpants, salsa, Doritos, Dinty Moore beef stew, hot chocolate, tinned sardines. Three-way phone calls can be set up for a dollar, meaning a Hershey Bar. Taking a T-shirt or other State-issued clothing and making a stuffed animal, contingent on the artistry involved, could garner anywhere from $3 to $20. Designing greeting cards, drawing pictures and portraits, or creating bracelets and jewelry can net you between $3 and $20. Portraits require the most skill and sell for the most Commissary. Washing dishes for other inmates gets you a small gratuity of ramen soups. Cooking for others rates you a seat at the table and perhaps stamps and a hot chocolate pouch. If you decorate envelopes, two envelopes equals a stamp.

The Art supplies need to ARRIVE before the end of July, as this is the new rule ... every couple of months they pick a month for us to receive our art supplies. I think the next month is October ... The person's name is the same (as I am not allowed to get things, as I have been a bad, bad girl and they pulled this privilege from me).
—Lucy Weems, Inmate #922870C

Lucy has established a flourishing underground economy of her own. Her colorful birthday, Valentine, and Mother's Day cards using poster paper and colored pencils and markers are in great demand. She conducts her business in the Yard, taking inmate orders and making deliveries. Inmates are allowed to receive art supplies twice a year—in October and July. If you've been involved in disciplinary actions, the privilege is revoked, and then supplies have to be routed through another inmate, who delivers them. She's seen the niche and moved quickly to fill it.

Krystal's and Lucy's lives revolve on the merry-go-round

minutiae of rules.

It is against the rules for one inmate to email another, just as it is forbidden for one inmate to transfer money to another inmate. EMCF deposits the wages earned by inmates into their JPay accounts. It could be $50 a month, or $68, but nothing higher. Or it could be the minimum State pay of $30 a month. Lucy's customers send EMCF checks addressed to an outside friend, who then deposits the check and makes a money transfer into Lucy's account.

Prison is a pay-as-you-go operation. Either the blowing tinsel of your misbegotten riches or the wretch and stink of poverty follows you inside. If your family can't help, you have to make money.

This is the land of the off-brand, and nothing is free. You pay healthcare deductibles; you pay for aspirin. And when you can't pay—or won't—you fight.

I don't like violence, not one bit, but here it is sometimes mandatory. Grappling is best because it doesn't leave marks, but really hurts. I am kind of good at it.
—Lucy Weems, Inmate #922870C

Lucy's been brawling all her life. She never backs away from a confrontation and rarely loses, since respect and reputation must be maintained in Maximum Compound. Fights are floating dice games about money.

Fight blood gets spilled over cheating, over the green-eyed monster of jealousy, over women who carry themselves as if they are dressed in black chiffon and sipping rum from a rapper's fist; fight blood is spilled over an insult, over lying and gossiping, gang affiliations, over hand signs and tags, debts and Commissary, over hard looks and soft looks.

Women convicted of sex crimes keep their offenses on the lowdown or else they will be marked for fight blood. These are the women who have been sentenced for child molestation or for pimping underage girls to pornographers; some of these women have been convicted of bestiality and performing fellatio on calves. Insinuation follows them like the click clack of stiletto heels. They keep to themselves. Untouchables. The manslaughter girls would bloody these women if they knew the truth. There's a reason it's forbidden to send inmates information about another inmate's crime.

Since they made it against the rules to smoke there's been a lot more fights here.
—Krystal Riordan, Inmate #661387

Krystal, the people-pleaser, swims in the fight-blooded waters more easily than others, yet even she's been assaulted in Mess Hall and in the Yard. Krystal fights when it's necessary and backs up Lucy without question. Strong-willed Lucy speaks her mind, but it's her body that has been jumped, kicked, punched, her jaw almost broken, her eyes blackened.

A girl swings at Lucy, who ducks, and so she misses with the first punch and the second. Missing when you swing makes you look weak; stupid, even. Missing still gets you tackled by an officer and thrown into Lock. How you look when you strike out to defend your honor counts. To fight smarter, Lucy has learned the art of grappling. Lucy doesn't believe in fighting on-camera, since that leads to trouble, to Lock. You have to discipline yourself to wait until you're alone to fight. Away from the cameras and witnesses, where the real fight blood is shed.

Lucy got into a fight and is in Lock. I'm hearing a bunch of different stories, but they all say Lucy was bleeding a lot. The girl beat her up badly on the unit. I really hope she beats this charge. Please write her and tell her I love her and am worried about her.
—Krystal Riordan, Inmate #661387

You can serve a fight cold, as in a quiet storm, or you can serve it hot.

Lindsay owes Lucy $30, and in Maximum Compound, $30 is a bunch of money. Lucy walks down the hall, where buckets slid into corners collect water from drips in the ceiling. Under the inmate noise reverberating from the walls, she listens to the squeak of her sneakers and wonders if her feet will ever fit into heels again.

Lindsay is biracial and has almond eyes and beautifully arched eyebrows you can comb. She's lying on her bunk with her arms above her head and barely nods when Lucy walks in. "Hey, you still owe me $30," Lucy says. "We can work it out."

Instead of being civil, Lindsay plays it nonchalant and cocky. "I don't owe you $30. Maybe $20, no more."

Lindsay could order something from Commissary that Lucy needs, like Cool Wave toothpaste ($2), Fresh scent roll-on ($.80), a hair brush w/o handle ($3), toilet paper ($1.30), tampons ($5.50); how about a Rawlins Urban Low shoe ($24.99)?

Lucy brings her list, along with the prices, and tells Lindsay she can pay it off over time. Payments like on the outside.

"Urban Low shoe," Lindsay says with a snort. "Are you kidding? I'll pay you back when I get around to it. Urban Low, you're not hurting."

This is the hot fight brewing and about to blow.

"Urban, my ass." Lucy shrugs, anger licking hotly over her skin. "I'll be back in a second."

She leaves to warm up her mug in the microwave, and then returns and throws the hot tea on Lindsay. "I think we're even. Who's the Low Shoe now?" Lucy says, taunting her.

But by Maximum Compound's rules of respect and revenge, they're not even. Hours later, Lindsay sneaks into Lucy's room and punches her repeatedly in the face until blood gushes from her nose. Lucy's head feels too large to hold up.

"I hope I broke it," Lindsay says, breathing hard. "Now we're even."

Krystal rushes into the room. She's crying and trying to

190

catch the blood still running from Lucy's nose. This all occurs off-camera.

&

Fights can take shape between clans or prison families. It's common to hear a younger girl call an older woman Mom. The prison clans are intergenerational mothers, daughters, sisters, and cousins. These are the inmates who call out "Mom," "Daughter," "Sis," "Grandma," and "Cousin." Clans absolutely stick together in fights. Those thin columns of kindling that spontaneously erupt. Lucy and Krystal have both fought clan women in quiet storms. Two or more inmates want to fight and they agree on a time and place. The women might decide on the bathroom and post a lookout to warn them if an officer approaches. Human behavior no matter the time and place tends to mimic older customs, like a 19th-century duel when honor is at stake and blood must be shed to defend it.

In Maximum Compound, if either of the fighters suffers bruises, scratches, broken bones, or profuse bleeding, officers will cause trouble. Before you fight, you must arm yourself with an excuse.

"The locker hit me," or perhaps, "I slipped and banged my head, my hand, my elbow, and my foot on the bunk."

&

Sometimes a new inmate has a special gift for mischief, for pouring fire-oil on already troubled waters.

After she and Krystal break up, Laysha finds work in the kitchen, the coveted $68-a-month job, but then she loses it. Once again she's on Krystal's unit. In the same share cube she shows my friend her disarming white-toothed smile, a smile that makes you forget. "Krystal, wait 'til I'm out, and I'm going home a lot sooner than you. You'll see me in videos."

This is Laysha, one of Krystal friends, I'm not sure if you remember me or not but I'm writing you to inform you that I had someone send some money out to you that I need you to send back in to me through JPay in my name. Thank you and enjoy your holidays.

—Laysha Burton, Inmate #797185F
Upon request, EMCF will issue checks for inmates to send family members or friends outside the prison system. I would rather not be their go-between banker, as this kind of funds transfer is forbidden, but they are my friends and I understand how senseless and suffocating the rules can seem—a wild growth of choking vines.

&

My role as go-between leads to trouble. I receive in the mail a check for $80 from an inmate whose name I don't recognize. It is how Lucy often has checks routed to me for monies owed her for her artistic creations that she sells to other inmates.

I am expecting no check from her and believe this to be the check Laysha emailed about. I deposit the check and transfer $80 into Laysha's JPay account. The next day a letter arrives from Lucy telling me to expect a check for $80, and with a sinking feeling, I realize I deposited the monies into the wrong account. I transfer $80 from my own bank account into Lucy's JPay. Then a check for $40 arrives from an inmate whose name I don't recognize. I tell Lucy and Krystal that I'd already given Laysha her $80.

They beg me to deposit the $40 into Laysha's account. She has already turned a whole wing of inmate women against Krystal and threatens to fuck Krystal up. The female Draymond is a slender pike fish; her silver scales glisten. She seizes you by a sudden sideways slash.

That 40 dollars is mine and if I don't get it I will have my best friend track that money order and get Krystal in trouble and whoever else that has something to do with my money being missing.
Thank u.
—Laysha Burton, Inmate #797185F

Krystal and Lucy argue, and Krystal claims Lucy told her to go slit her wrists.

According to Krystal, Lucy kept saying it. "I'm trying to forgive her, but it's hard. I don't look at her the same. She was the one person I trusted."

Every time they get into an argument, Lucy throws Krystal's weak-mindedness into her face, taunting her about the trunk where each inmate stores her Commissary items and hygiene products. "That's why your trunk is empty. That's why I'm going home in April and you're still going to be here."

It's not always possible to get a truthful reading on either Krystal's or Lucy's statements. Only they know the context of their words, the body language, or tone of voice. Like all of us, they sculpt truth to serve their own needs or to portray themselves in a better light.

And, yet, the bond of their friendship doesn't sever. Krystal protects Lucy and vice versa.

&

In the Yard, Krystal is confronted by Chyna, a young inmate whose advances she has rejected.

"You're too young," Krystal says, trying to calm the waters.

The girl's knuckles tighten, making fists.

Is this how it has to be?

Krystal remembers Draymond's fingers on either side of her robe's neckline. He said, "Say goodbye to this turquoise crap," then ripped the polyester until two halves hung down.

She took hold of his shirt, a $300 shirt, her gift to him.

Her hands dropped, but he punched her anyway.

When she got up from the floor, he pommeled her again.

&

Chyna hits her and Krystal raises her arms to defend herself. They're on-camera and Krystal knows she can't hit back.

The girl punches again and again. Krystal tries but can't always block her fists. Her mind drifts past the girl: her mother punishing her, hitting her, a downpour of fists. Then she hears the echo of a soft voice from months ago.

"I want to give you the moon," Laysha says.

Chyna puts her leg out and trips Krystal. Forearms catch the fall.

The moon—when's the last time you saw the moon without someone telling you what to do? Not even in your sleep; a full moon is as forgotten as the diagrammed sentences of high school.

&

This is Maximum Compound. Blood pooling, teeth lost, officers running.

The most violent women of New Jersey, the Camden girls, the Newark and Jersey City manslaughter girls. Still it surprises me how quickly slights and confrontations can turn violent.

The worst fight both Krystal or Lucy saw was a group of four women who ambushed an inmate named Danny. They kicked, punched, bit and scratched, caught their breath and kicked more. They used a broom to beat her and broke her eye socket, her nose, her jaw, and ribs. Danny's girlfriend thought Danny was cheating on her. Blood splattered everywhere, even on the ceiling. The unit closed until the cleanup crews could get in.

&

The women here have beautiful names. Shonda, Cinthia, Markita, Helen, Nicole, Tahleemah. Fight blood is the heat rippling and roiling; it's all in the punch, the devil-white bail setter, the sentencing judge, a slaver, no matter his/her/their gender or color. Fights are the sugar in a Hershey's chocolate that makes you feel higher than the Empire State Building. Who cares who is president? Papa Obama or Papa Trump, both have a mouthful of money promises, and none of them include you.

In the Medical Unit
New York City/ EMCF   Clinton, New Jersey

"How is that possible? You don't even drink!"

Cirrhosis. It is an unusual word, a dirty word. Neither of us know anyone who suffers from it. I am where I always am, at work in front of the computer, but when I see our home number on caller ID, I answer, already afraid.

"They don't think I'm going to make it," Rob says, in a rushed voice. "I need to get to the Bellevue ER. Meet me there." His vulnerability, expressed in the simplicity of those words, staggers me. The love I have for him chokes up in my throat, "Of course, you're going to make it. Of course, you'll make it."

Never did I believe he wouldn't make it.

&

I've known Krystal for more than two years when Rob is diagnosed with a life-threatening autoimmune liver condition. Lucy and I are now correspondents as well. Her letters, arriving in envelopes decorated with watercolors and blooming with hearts and flowers, have planted the seeds of another friendship.

At first, I am hesitant to share any problems in my life with women who have been through the hell that both of them have survived, women whose daily life in prison holds stresses and dangers I can only imagine. But real friendship can't exist as a one-way street, and these two are as real as they come.

They both know my history. And they know about my partner's illness, from the beginning that Thanksgiving when Rob came to the festive table set with Indian corn, gourds, and a paper turkey. He was unable to eat, unable to stop scratching his chest.

"I woke up with this itching. I don't know what it is." Red welts from his nails, his skin showing no rash. The itching around his ankles that he scratched until he bled.

In letters, Krystal and Lucy want to know how he is doing; he has become one of their family too. They are with me through endless tests, through each halting step toward Rob's diagnosis. I share the details of the day our phone rang and we know it is the lab with preliminary blood test results, how I watch him as he holds the phone to his ear, nodding, face unreadable.

The room has that electrical charge. Below our window, life goes on in tiny Marble Hill Cemetery, pigeons flying through, the whole flock taking off from the roof of LaSalle School, and then wheeling over the bare tulip trees, making sure their feathers do not freeze.

"What did they say?" I ask when he hangs up.

Enzymes, proteins, numbers to compare; albumin, bilirubin, new words to look up—all amounting to the onset of liver failure, in a man who hasn't consumed a six-pack over the course of his lifetime.

&

What is an autoimmune condition? The self attacking the self, which lies at the core of many people's identity. The metaphor at the root of many of our psyches.

&

Rob spends five days in Bellevue Hospital. Eventually accepted into the low-income program, he is referred to a specialist, subjected to test after test, and finally placed on the liver transplant list.

"Oh, and where are you going to get the liver?" Rob asks. "The A&P?"

&

Rob's wisecracks under the worst of circumstances resonate with Krystal and Lucy. Both have an instinctive understanding of his iconoclastic way of being in the world; both have devoured his poetry collection and shared it with many of their inmate friends. They both support me in ways that help me support him through the crisis, the search for treatments, through years of prednisone, until we finally settle on the strict dietary regime that helps him avoid a liver transplant.

When the wave hits, when life turns you upside down, you cling to the most important people in your life.

Krystal and Lucy, my friends, know this better than most.

&

"Hey, Lucy, wake up," Krystal calls out.

She knows her bunkie has had a rough night. It looks like she's still dreaming. The lights are so bright they burst from the ceiling.

"Welcome to Tuesday."

The grim present in Maximum Compound.

&

Lucy brushes away the ceiling light. She's at cheerleading practice, throwing her pompoms in the air and following that with a cartwheel. Upside down or standing on her head, everything makes sense. No one catches the streamers like she does, or flings themselves into a cheer.

She runs out of the high school to the parking lot, where her older boyfriend idles his Firebird. He's been waiting, and after she hops in, he pulls a strand of wet hair that's caught in the corner of her mouth. They're on their way to his place, where he's made a surprise for her. A man's bathroom with stringy wet towels hanging from towel racks and crusty wash rags. Two long-stemmed roses float on the water. The three candles pitch their flames into her breasts and buttocks, like the prongs of Neptune's fork.

Lucy and her Firebird man sink into the tub, the cool water soft with bath oil. He has created a world where even the angels have sex, eat spinach tortellini, and take Ecstasy with two lines of cocaine. This time she'll stick with cheerleading; this time she'll stay away from the raves.

"Lucy, wake up," Krystal says, cupping her hands to Lucy's ear and whispering.

Noise that never truly douses itself is ramping up, inmates are shouting to friends to get the fuck up, fights erupt over who gets first dibs on the sink and, more important, the toilets. It's weird that in the midst of a high-decimal noise-fest, you can hear a whisper the loudest.

"What? What?" Lucy cries out, sitting up. "What's going on?"

Her thick dark hair has come out of its barrette and Krystal smooths it off her friend's forehead.

"Is it still there?" Krystal asks. "The lump?"

&

Yesterday, the lump arrived. Lucy was soaping under her arm in the shower when she found it. The shock of the thing, the it. What wasn't there before now is, like a bird's egg or an avocado's seed, planted, incubating. All night in her bunk, her headphones on, the lump drew her fingers to it, testing and teasing her. Will it be gone tomorrow? Will it be smaller? Who could stop touching such a thing? It meant nothing life-threatening. A blocked pore, a cyst; besides, a lump rarely meant cancer. Right? She falls asleep.

"Maybe it's gone," Krystal says, hopefully. Lucy now dares her hand to explore her underarm. Perhaps the lump will be gone.

But her fingers find it. If it is serious, God help her. The Medical Unit practices neglect that can't be considered benign.

When Lucy tells her it's still there, she wants to touch it. Okay. Lucy lifts her arm and guides Krystal's fingers to the lump. A hillock. Yes, Krystal feels it like a ball of cookie dough, and when she presses her thumb against the dough-like thing, it moves, then pushes back.

"We have to put in a Medical Request," Krystal says. "I'm worried."

Lucy agrees, but only if Krystal puts in one too for her episodes.

"They won't believe me. They'll think it's all in my head. Take a shower, Lucy. Warm water will help."

198

&

Today the shower is cold, the water burbles, raises goosebumps, then switches to hot— someone has started the water on fire. The angry water is scalding her, burning her. Prison. The water droplets hitting Lucy's skin are massive yellow stones. Lumps.

It's hurting me. Water droplets, how large you are.

&

The afternoon of the lump, the two felons sit at the table in the common area off the Yard. They're munching on no-name Commissary-brand Doritos and filling out the Health Services Request Form.

Lucy traces her pen over the lengthy numbered points elaborating the charges to the inmate for medical services. "The meat of this shitty sandwich is all about how much the inmate has to eat of the bill."

For free-world citizens the monies mentioned are absurdly small, but for prisoners surviving on a monthly budget of $30, the threat of having their account charged a medical visit fee discourages them from seeking treatment. If the fee isn't discouraging enough, there is the Infirmary itself. You'd think a medical facility might be cleaner, that the smudged glass would be wiped of fingerprints, that you might not smell the mouths of others. Like homelessness and socks worn for three weeks.

"This form is idiotic," Krystal says, sinking a tortilla chip in a hot red-salsa pond. "There's two stupid skinny lines to explain the reason for the request. "What am I supposed to say? 'Episodes'?"

They laugh and talk about the get-highs in their shared past.

Krystal and I had a dark time when we each indulged in drugs.
Krystal stopped a little later than me but she did stop."
—Lucy Weems, Inmate #922870C

The "get-highs" in Maximum Compound flow from the Medical Unit in the form of prescription drugs. Inmates research what medication produces a high or a sleepy effect, at what dosages, and what the meds are used to treat so they can present themselves to the Medical Unit with the appropriate symptoms. Which drugs make you feel like praying in a stone, which make you disappear into the beautiful ditch of your own mouth, which pills turn the walls soft, which bathe you in the sex of a tangerine. Neurontin, Catapres, Wellbutrin, H-80s, anything, anything that allows you to escape the dinginess. Inmates prescribed the dreamboat pills stock up on their meds in order to get the effects, or sell them at $1 to $5 a pill. Medication is swallowed in front of an officer and yet inmates still manage to cheek them.

&

Freelancing prescriptions turns into a Russian roulette with side effects, drug interactions, cardiac arrests, addiction, and overdoses. Mornings after, the music turns off and you're impaled, your throat and gut fill with sticks, and some inmates are carried out on stretchers. Your stricken lips no longer seep the tango but dry heaves.

Krystal chuckles, in her low-throated way. It makes Lucy happy every time she hears her friend's deep laughter. "Remember when we split seven Mucinex between us?" Krystal asks. "You said if we'd taken all seven at once, we'd hallucinate."

"It made us very drunk and crazy. We both threw up and pooped until the sun went down, but it seemed like a good time," Lucy says, a silly laugh tittering through her.

"I have such a good time with you, Lucy, I sometimes forget where I am. That's why I call you my life partner."

"Life partner." Lucy squeezes Krystal's hand. "Now back to my damn lump and your episodes, which I think are seizures."

&

The night of the lump Lucy can't sleep. Krystal climbs out of her bunk and pulls down her own sheet. She rolls Lucy on one side and then the other, tucking her feet in, crossing her arms over her chest, swaddling her in a sheet.

The walls have been painted beige but cracks zigzag

through the plaster, thickening and thinning like scar tissue.

"You're safe, Lucy," Krystal says, "I won't let anything happen to you. Tell me one of your weird family stories. They always make us laugh."

Lucy reaches for Krystal's hand and talks. About her family, the bikers and bookies and accountants, the ones who refused to grow up.

"I wish I had family like that," Krystal says, sitting cross-legged on the floor.

"Krystal, you were a star on the basketball court. A jock of all things."

"A basketball doesn't love you." Krystal's head rests on Lucy's bunk.

"Krystal, I think I'm bleeding again. It's not time for my period and I'm lying in blood. Oh, God, it's your sheet. I'm sorry, I'll wash it," Lucy says. "What's going on?"

&

Lucy moves the broom across the scuffed tiles of the library, no bigger than two school buses parked side-by-side. One school bus maintains the paperbacks and dog-eared hardbacks; every inked-up unappetizing book has been donated from somewhere. The legal library possesses the other school bus; which no one uses. The library floor may be the cleanest in Max. She's wearing a tampon and a sanitary napkin and still the bleeding is breaking through. She stops, leans the broom against the wall, and feels for the lump.

It's bigger. The dough thing is still there, and bigger. Her hands curl into fists. Damn, she misses her smiling grandmother who belonged to her, even stopping by her elementary school classrooms to take her for cookies and milk. The teachers would let poor motherless Lucy go.

Oh well, I have a real cookie inside me. She hears someone coming and reaches for the broom.

&

The lump is growing, becoming tender. Lucy knows it's some-

201

thing. She fills out the Medical Request Form and asks the officers to take her to the Medical Unit as soon as possible, not three weeks hence.

They ignore her, tell her to fill out the form that she's already submitted. Baring her underarm, she shows them the lump. No response. They're bored. The growth invades her sleep, absorbing her psyche.

Nights of strange fish somersaulting, killifish mutating in toxic water. Asleep, it's her first day and she's clutching her bedroll and parading naked into Reception. The way some of the inmate women gaze at her makes the breath catch in her throat. Lucy marches one molecule at a time. The piranhas circle.

&

Another week goes by and she still hasn't been seen. Lucy funnels her Medical Request up the officer hierarchy and shows off her lump to lieutenants and sergeants. She tells them she's bleeding and she just had her period. It's a flood. Whoa, we don't need to see that.

Her father calls EMCF and demands medical attention for his daughter. It goes on and on, the show-and-tell, the officers ignoring her. At last, sick of hearing the grumblings, they escort Lucy to the Medical Unit.

The nurse examines her and then the doctor passes judgment. She'll need an MRI and a biopsy at St. Francis Hospital. Lucy's scheduled for tests, although inmates are never told when their appointments will be, in the event they're planning an escape. Like praying for a glacier in the rain forest.

If you leave EMCF for the hospital or any doctor's appointment, even if you are lacking a heartbeat you will be shackled and handcuffed.
—Lucy Weems, Inmate #922870C

Lucy rides in the doggie wagon, head bowed, the 52-minute ride from Clinton to Trenton through the hardwood stands of hackberry and honey locust, the picture-perfect landscape, which she can hardly see. Trenton rises. New Jersey's colorless capital, a church steeple, the interstate's exhaust grime. Government buildings, squat courthouses, traffic floating by.

St. Francis Hospital. Prisoners are walked in the front door. The officer accompanying them orders them not to look at the bystanders. "Keep your eyes straight ahead. Stop."

Every head in the lobby turns as Lucy shuffles into the waiting room in shackles and handcuffs. A mother pulls her daughter out of Lucy's path and actually covers her child's eyes with her hands. *What am I?* People staring as if the sight of her soils them. *Does my skin glisten and smell goaty?*

Shame sinking her into the earth. The lump is biopsied. Cancer. Her profuse bleeding is the result of uterine fibroids. More waiting. The surgery will be performed at another hospital.

&

This time the doggie wagon pulls up to the front entrance of Robert Wood Johnson Medical Center in New Brunswick. Shuffling in her shackles and handcuffs down the beige halls, she smiles at the red carpet welcome mat. *Welcome*, what a beautiful word. It glows.

This hospital is more relaxed than St. Francis, and it's likely that some of the staff have friends or relatives in prison. She's treated as if she's human. Pre-op, they don't mention the shackle on one ankle. The cancerous cells are cut out and a hysterectomy performed on the 37-year-old. Post-surgery, she lies on clean sheets, and for a beautiful week she sleeps as long as she wants to.

When she turns over for injections, she thinks of her love affair with heroin, and wonders if the allure will always be there. One weekend night in Newark, when business was slow and police sirens kept scaring her dates away, she bought a supply of heroin and rented a hotel room. Her lighter cooked the spoon and her mouth went wet as the powder liquefied. Tie off, tap, eject the air. She balled her fist, drew out a thread of blood. The sink, the towel rack softened. In the mirror she appeared to be smiling—mocha cream in the mind.

&

Were the heroin days that glamorous?

She harks back to her apartment paid for by a lover, a man important in the recovery movement, once an addict and now a real estate big shot. She'd been shooting heroin and cocaine all night and passed through the pleasure dome into paranoia.

Sure someone was about to break in, she began hiding her valuables. Her long-haired cat, a Persian Blue, looked on. The neighbors were watching. Hurry, hide everything, hurry, ticking in her brain. The house key sheathed from her car keys. Credit cards, driver's license, she secreted away. Mice materialized, they flicked their tails before disappearing under the refrigerator. As she finished hiding her things she listened to the mice singing.

In the morning or whenever it was the night ended, she woke to an upside down world. Eerily silent. Airless. Everything gone. She dropped to her knees and started to wrench up the carpet. The floor smelled of wet crate. Her hands searching the dust bunnies and splinters found nothing. The Persian Blue's pupils appeared pinpointed. Had her beautiful cat done her heroin? Luckily she discovered her next fix under the litter box in a glassine envelope.

The satanic white lady. The hyena. The keys, the cards, her license the singing mice had eaten. Trapdoors kept opening, she'd think she'd hit rock bottom, but there were more bottoms. More freak sex. Aberrant green rot.

&

Upon her return "home" she's given her bedroll to carry across the compound. The Medical Unit refuses her request for a pain killer—not even a Motrin. Still hurting, Lucy returns to the Yard, where inmates congregate.

She meets Krystal, who has been worried about her best friend. The hysterectomy is only a week and a day old and no one in Medical warns her about her bladder dropping and urine

204

leakage. Lucy sits among 30 other women in their beige uniforms and she's afraid to get up because pee is trickling down her
thighs.

"To hell with the Medical Unit," Krystal says. "I'm going
to pee, too. You're not going to be alone."

Krystal pees on herself, and the two friends stand up and
walk hand in hand inside.

MOTHER'S DAY
ECMF Clinton, New Jersey

A week before Mother's Day, an inmate commits suicide in her bunk. She's saved enough pills from her daily medication regime to cause cardiac arrest. Lucy is the one to discover her body, and is devastated.

One pill, then two, then four at once, more, the pills swallowing themselves going down. Perhaps she thinks she hears crumbs of clapping. Laughter. Yes, they want her gone. More pills. How free jumping into nothingness, no longer having a body, no one to tell her what to do. This rule, that rule. She feels rain, trees, and the soft. Out in the world she's left behind five *kids*.

No one in Maximum Compound has children, they all have kids. She's given fair warning that she wants to die, but no one tries to stop her, no one listens, so she keeps to the task of saving her pills.

Inmates will dream about the dead woman who is no longer an inmate; her psyche freed to wander, the woman who killed herself with five kids out in the world. Her warm brown face cooled to blue. Her mouth stays open, yet she's counting, one, then two, four at once. She's looking for the weeds. Weeds can't talk. You have to let them cover you. If she swallows more pills, she'll find the weeds. Inmates swear they hear her counting.

I am sick to my stomach and my heart hurts. Not only did my kids basically reject me but they never sent me a Mother's Day card, not for the past three years. I have been crying, nauseated, and seeing spots. They ripped my heart out.
—Lucy Weems, Inmate #922870C

Lucy lives on the cusp of freedom; soon she'll be going to a halfway house. She wants more than anything to regain the trust of her daughters, especially that of her older daughter, Hope. In the seven years she's been imprisoned she's missed much of her children's lives.

Since Lucy's incarceration, Hope has grown from a preschooler to the coltishness of an adolescent; her oldest daughter, her heart of hearts, has said she doesn't want to live with her mother when she gets out.

While Lucy's been incarcerated, her younger daughter, Faith, has been moved to a halfway house for the autistic.

Since she's been incarcerated, her stepmother has died, and now her father will remarry, but he asks her to disguise the EMCF address on her letters, where her name is tag-teamed with her inmate identification number.

While Lucy's been incarcerated she's gained weight and lost weight, she's discovered the body of an inmate on her wing who committed suicide, she's grown close to many women, has fallen in love, has become best friends with Krystal Riordan.

She's seen the drift of prison seasons—snow falling innocently into the exercise yard, the cold-white shackled and on-camera; she's seen summers, the sun fisted above the guard towers, the razor-wire glinting as if a silvery necklace or a noose, the heat in Maximum Compound heavy, like walking in molasses. She recollects the heroin itch, raking her fingernails over her skin, the green movements of insects, feelers brushing her nose. Back in the free world, Lucy hopes to establish some sort of regular life with her daughters. Likely she won't be able to use her BS in Accounting, but it would be easy to underestimate her. Although she had an arrest record from age 18 for dealing large quantities of LSD and spent 11 months in a Connecticut prison before earning her degree, she approached job interviews with confidence. "If I go to 20 interviews, there will be one or two employers so impressed by my self-assurance and lowballing my salary expectation, they won't bother running a background check," says Lucy.

In her auditing phase, she verged on being a workaholic at the Italian Clothing Customs Brokerage House in New Jersey, where she was employed as lead accountant. She oversaw the bookkeepers, performed internal auditing to find missing money, and she loved the detective-like number sleuthing. During tax season she moonlighted, filling out returns for her personal clients. After long work days, she says, "I lived for coming home when my little Hope was still awake to run into my arms and yell, Mommy, I love you."

But then depression seeped into her soul and the workaholic mania imploded. She no longer woke in paradise but in hell. *What if I don't wake up and on goes the world?*

Heroin beckons. Find the vein and it's like a visit to Egypt. Sometimes the raisins and dates and Turkish coffee as strong as black liquor and the streets fermented in antiquities.

Mommy, I love you.

&

At a certain age there's so much living you've done; some of your choices make you proud and others shame you—but Lucy's nature doesn't indulge in guilt. Although her 12-year-old has lived with her paternal aunt and uncle since she was four years old, Lucy intends to forge a loving relationship with her when she gets out.

Reconnecting with her family and her kids, remaking her way in the world, Lucy doesn't expect it to be easy. But she's done it before. There's a divide between hard money and soft money, and on the street as a prostitute the same money could be both.

I made a painting on canvas for Hope's room. I will be sending it out on Monday when the package house here can mail it. I can't be sure her aunt will hang it up. I know that she doesn't like to open up my mail.
—Lucy Weems, Inmate #922870C

The dreaded day arrives when Hope googles her name, and finds in the digital universe the details of her mother's arrest.

Mugshots, some showing Lucy with her hair half in a towering upsweep, half-loose and tangling, her eyes hardly open; others show Lucy in EMCF's beige uniform.

"Mom," Hope says. "I'm ashamed."

I had a phone call with my daughters yesterday that set a tone for a horrible Mother's Day. My sister-in-law told me that they are go-ing to try to permanently move my children to Florida and even worse was the fact that I had to hear my daughter tell me that she doesn't want to live with me when I am out. I think that they are brainwashing them.
—Lucy Weems, Inmate #922870C

Lucy's father arrives to visit her, but as he approaches the metal detector, the officer on duty stops him.

He's wearing a red t-shirt. He doesn't know that red and blue clothing signifies gang allegiance between the Bloods and Crips; people wearing those colors aren't allowed in EMCF. Hav-ing traveled from Connecticut to see his daughter, he is annoyed and calls the officer a prick.

"Do you know your daughter has a girlfriend here?" the officer asks.

"So what?" Lucy's father answers. "Are you trying to turn me against my daughter? Because that will never happen."

My daughter has been adopted by a good family and I don't have any contact with her. It's painful for me.
—Krystal Riordan, Inmate #661387

A jailhouse lawyer tells Krystal that even in a closed adoption case she has a right to see her daughter's photograph and a health update, as well as a scholastic report card, once a year.

The last picture she has is creased and taped together. The attorney who had handled the original adoption could request a recent photo. But Krystal isn't allowed to reach out directly to her daughter, though, ever.

&

"I know my daughter will find me, like I found my mother," Krystal says.

After she had finally located her birth mother, Krystal invited Eva to visit. There were a few moments of awkward conversation, then Eva asked her daughter to go out and buy her some beer. Alone in her daughter's room, she riffled through until she found the money's hiding spots.

Krystal pictured her mother folding the rumpled bills, a slow smile on her lips, as a black-purplish hair shadow fell over her face. She pocketed the money Krystal earned getting into strangers' cars, walking into rooms where she was paid for what felt like rape. Animals know their mother's smell. Eva's smell lingers in Krystal's nostrils.

The mother she hungered for all her life had never existed.

When she's older she'll look for me like I looked for my mother. Krystal seems not to comprehend the shattering force such knowledge could have on a child.

Yet she's not one of those inmates who gets angry when she sees someone else's happiness; Krystal always asks after her friends' kids.

&

On Visiting Day, the photographer is busy capturing the transitory togetherness of children and mothers. Family members have traveled in crowded buses or a grandmother's car. They've driven for hours on the ice, to be greeted by the bleak parking lot and razor wire-shrouded buildings.

The first flakes of snow sifting down are scrawny feathers from the overcast sky. The snow falls on toddlers and teenagers, even babies. Rosettes spawned in a hot season that has turned cold.

There are some children with silence curdling inside, some who come with great-aunts and half-sisters to visit their

210

mother. Perhaps some children keep her being in this place a
secret and none of their peers know. Or else it's common knowledge, and no one cares.

&

Some children wish their mothers would leave them alone. *If
she really wants to love me then she should just leave me alone.*
Some have been living dangerously in foster care for years, and
for some, it was their father their mother shot.

To one little boy, the air tastes like metal and shame is
making his lips and throat tingle. He needs this woman, his
mother, and wishes he didn't. Someday he'll be a basketball star.

One little girl gives up her pink-beaded purse with pen-
tagon-shaped sunglasses inside. Someday she'll be a designer, a
fashionista.

"Do you have anything in your hand?" the officer asks
her. "What's that in your hair?"

Rainbow glitter from a birthday party yesterday at school.
Her mother makes the best cheesecake, she tells him, and can
Tiberius, their black Labrador who is waiting in the car, come in
too?

All join the long line of people genuflecting before the
god of metal detectors. Wire baskets wait like mouths, where
you must empty your pockets and leave your bags, everything
removable.

What will each child say to the prison mother?

&

One man becomes a 5-year-old boy again. He belongs to the
soft-spoken mother who stabbed his father 41 times. A judge ordered his grandma to take him to the prison to visit her. He still
hates court orders and exchanges. Hates talk of parental rights.

The man chews on a cuticle as the electronic doors open
and he walks into a brown blob of a room with tables and nothing on them. His mother has served 19 years, with one more to
go.

He loves her.

&

Some inmates have strong support systems and unlimited monies put into their phone cards. Those mothers with DYFS intervention, i.e., social services, in their families, even women whose crime involved children, seem to receive fairer treatment than others.

Lucy tells me about Anna, the inmate who slept with her 14-year-old daughter's 14-year-old boyfriend and became pregnant by him. While Anna apologized to the boy in front of the judge, saying how ashamed and full of regret she was, to inmate friends she explained how his boy fingers seemed so knowing that she'd forgotten his age or whom they belonged to.

She pushed him into the closet, her hands moving inside his shirt and touching the hairs that sprinkled his belly. They both got crazy.

Anna received five years for her crime. After she gives birth, a social worker comes each week on Visiting Day, bringing the baby and her 15-year-old daughter to visit. She gets along beautifully with the foster parents.

Her long-eyelashed boy-man kept saying how pretty she was, and who can resist that?

&

Some children almost draw their first breath behind prison walls. The infirmary is their would-be manger, as it was Gabriella's son's, hours away from being born in Maximum Compound. Gabriella is pretty and of Portuguese descent. Her long-ringleted hair curtains her oval face and high cheekbones. When she lifts her chin, her fine features freeze until her face looks chiseled from stone. Pride. Wearing a modest blue dress and a cross around her neck, she sobs for forty minutes on the stand; she's the only witness in her defense.

Her life, all eighteen years, comes down to one night. Pregnant, she is walking the street on her way home, passing the neighbor's house, where a group of celebrating teenagers have gathered. A warm June evening in Newark, the clouds of 2008 drifting across the moon like fraying head rags, high school graduation night. A special night for Jadzia Colón, Gabriella's next-door neighbor and the first in her extended family to graduate from high school; now she's to enroll in community college.

"Hey, trick," the girls snicker at Gabriella, a high school dropout, whose young body already shows the belly where a son is growing. Trick. Prostitute. Gabriella feels her face flush, redness spreading until her whole head is hot. Shame. All of the girls laughing at her. Humiliation. Her blood rises.

"I'll be back," she warns. Her face looks as tight as her jeans. Her boyfriend has given her a gun; just last night he brought her the black gift. Gift beyond compare—a revolver in a paper bag.

The moon floats from behind its clouds as she marches out of her house holding the handgun. Strong now, no longer alone.

"It looked funny," she says at trial, where she pleads not guilty to murder. "Like it was broken."

She does not expect it to go off, but the gun is already cocked and when she swings it up to hit her former classmate, the gun fires; the bullet passes through Jadzia's neck and into the collarbone of another girl. Gabriella flees. She's on the run, hiding at a friend's, in the closet eating cold nachos.

The gun is a black car; you get in thinking you're safe, and then rocks jut up and the steering wheel's no longer attached. Holes gape under the dashboard, and the death that leapt from one movement of your finger boomerangs and comes for you. Sirens. Police cars. Gabriella gives herself up to the family priest.

Her sentence for aggravated manslaughter is 20 years; she gives birth while a prisoner.

&

A security guard follows her into the hospital; gurney carrying Gabriella, who is in labor. He unlocks her belly chain and frees her arms.

"Nurse, can you call my mother? Please, can't she be here with me?"

The nurse shakes her head. "Sorry, baby, but only the security guards and the doctor and nurses are allowed. Raised by her mother, her 9-year-old loves soccer and science.

&

Gabriella, doing her time in Max, doesn't like to talk about her crime, but it's always there, ready to ambush her. She touches the silver cross around her neck. Lights out at 10 p.m., but it's midnight before the noise begins to fade out.

She buries her face in her pillow and still can't stop the nightmares. The dead girl Jadzia nears her bunk and Gabriella swings her hand up. There's blood in the air. The gun explodes. Jadzia's eyes leave their sockets, liquefying over her chin. Gabriella sits up in her bunk. She is holding her hand over her nose to hide the sound of her breathing.

&

The law does not recognize consensual sex among the incarcerated; an inmate can't consent to touching of any kind, and trysts with a corrections officer constitute rape.

Brittany, with her cicada eyes and dimples, believes she has no choice but to give in to the flirtations of the sole officer on duty. He corners her in her area, this beefy, round-faced male corrections officer who seduces her with his beard, his ardor, and blandishments. *You're gorgeous, those dimples, I see man-hunger in your eyes, what a shame. Think of those favors to come, babe.*

They have sex for months in the closets and off-camera corners. Her corrections officer gives off the air of being streetwise and the weight of the uniform, the write-up pad, the walkie-talkie are all meant to impress. He promises her that one day he'll shower her in presents, take her out for the famous Brazilian X-Tudo Sandwich—"Cheese Plus Everything"—grilled chicken, mayo, cheese, ham, potato sticks, bacon, and fried egg.

It is not yet that day when his photograph, along with his brother officers, stares out from the front page of The *Star-Ledger*, as one of five male officers arrested for having sexually assaulted an inmate.

The promised gifts never materialize, unless you count some fried chicken wings and a few cigarettes. Her officer must feel invincible, the power of the Maximum Compound lawman, all these toothsome women at his beck and call. Such a man wears no condom; such a man must spread his invincible seed.

Brittany misses her period and keeps missing her bloody moons, and when she starts to show, she hides it in the baggy T-shirts and sweats. She lets her officer know and he shrugs it off, telling her not to mention his name. They keep having sex. The hurried sex that can never be called lovemaking, the looking out over your shoulder.

When officers finally notice her belly, Brittany's taken into protective custody. *Don't tell them about me. Don't tell them that you're still frightened by a dark stairwell.*

She gives birth in St. Francis to a biracial daughter. She prefers not to think of her as a Rape Baby.

&

Some of the women don't talk about their children unless they have to fill out forms. Are they denying their bodies ever incubated life? Or do these mothers consider their kids as accidents, or does their crime involve their offspring?

Most of the inmate mothers gladly share photos of their children, telling each other about happy or sad phone calls. On children's birthdays, the tradition is for a group of inmates to make cupcakes and sing HAPPY BIRTHDAY to them on the phone, and if they can't phone, they sing to each other.

&

For the women with no ties to the outside, with no family visitors, for whom no mail ever comes, there are the prison clans, intergenerational mothers, daughters, sisters, cousins. The majority of the women who call out Mom, Kid, Sister, Grandma, and Cousin are not related by DNA, but claim kinship. Mom might be black with a white daughter among her black children. Mom might be white with black daughters. The family claims their own space in the Yard. They share stories.

One daughter speaks of shooing her repentant birth mother away like a fly, swatting at her attempts to reconnect, and wanting to take her stepfather between her fingernails like the blood-gorged flea he is and hear him crack. The mother who sat on her thumbs doing nothing when her husband molested her 12-year-old daughter and gifted her with herpes. Heart hardened, frozen inside while his fingers stroked the outer beauty of her body.

Prison Mom does the microwave cooking, while the daughters procure the food from the mess hall or Commissary; one daughter washes the dishes. Tonight it's spring rolls with the coleslaw (free) saved from the mess hall lunch, shredded chicken (free) from Sunday dinner. The whole family pitches in with slaw and chicken, sugar packets (free), syrup (free) saved from pancake day, hot and spicy packs (50 ¢) from ramen noodles, tortilla wraps ($1.50). Mom microwaves the coleslaw for two minutes, while the daughters mix the chicken, sugar, and spice.

They talk about the first food they're going to eat when they're released. French bread and batter-fried jumbo shrimp. Salami, turkey, ham, dill pickle. A week of meats.

Mom says grace, and after the Amen they dig in. When they're free, whoever gets out first, they're going to mess that bastard up.

Amen, again.

RELEASE
Clinton, New Jersey

No one's allowed to talk during Count. Lucy hadn't known on that first day when the officer held a clipboard and reeled off the inmate numbers. "#922870C!" he'd shouted out.

"Here!" Lucy answered, and then turned and talked to the girl beside her.

The officer looked. "Who said that?"

Lucy calculated the number of times she'd answer "Here!" at three counts per day multiplied by seven years. Like a dress with a thousand pearl buttons, you had to do and undo them each day. Now 2,190 days and 6,570 Counts later, Lucy's about to be moved from Maximum Compound to a pre-release halfway house.

&

The last few nights in Max, the same noise from LIGHTS OUT to LIGHTS ON. The inmate women argue and laugh while insomnia is raking Lucy's head against the pillow. Soon she'll be gone and this will end; the chatter she no longer needs to see or understand.

On her last full day in Max, an inmate, a hard-faced girl with a sloppy neck tattoo who has hooked up with one of Lucy's ex-lovers, is staring bloodily at her. The girl takes a swing, punches Lucy in the face. Lucy doesn't fight back. Her nose is spouting blood and she bites her tongue. It happens at 2 p.m., and by 3 p.m., Krystal, on the other side of the Compound, finds out.

By not fighting back, Lucy keeps her privileges and her progress toward release.

This is another one of those deals where you're handcuffed and shackled. You've already been thoroughly Bend, Squat, and Cough-searched. You're not allowed to have any jewelry on you.

All that has to be shipped back to Columbus House separately.
You're allowed to take this one small brown bag with your simple
toiletries.
—Lucy Weems, parolee

The day arrives and she's prodded awake at 4 a.m. and told to
dress and stow her toiletries in a brown bag. You're allowed one
bar of soap, one towel, one washcloth, one shampoo, and one
conditioner. She makes her way past the officers, but none of
them give her encouragement or a smile to congratulate her for
having made it to release. Rather, a few tell her they're not saying
farewell as they're sure to see her again when she violates parole
or reoffends. Not even an hour later, a shackled and cuffed Lucy
walks to the waiting van and climbs in back. The sun has not
risen.

&

Lucy faces the window and, as the barbed wire and watchtowers of EMCF disappear, she feels oddly nostalgic. Seven years.
Goodbye, Krystal, my friend, I liked it best when we lived right
next to each other. I knew everything about you, a 5'9" girl having sexual fantasies about midgets, as in a threesome.

Goodbye to your pooping ritual, Krystal. How you'd take
off your clothes, stretch out your legs, and cross your ankles, your
arms over your breasts. Goodbye to you sitting on the throne and
me, Lucy, the wiseacre, opening the bathroom curtain for everyone to see you in your special form. Goodbye to gathering up the
roommates to walk by and the two of us laughing crazily.

&

Goodbye to the Lucy Weems who tied up her drug dealer and
held a gun to his head.

Goodbye to the idiots who stole the microwave and tried
to hide it in their room under a sheet, to no ketchup on hot dog
day, no chicken bits in the casserole on chicken casserole day; to
½ cup boiled carrots for dessert and one hot dog bun; goodbye to
mail at the mercy of the officers, fingering your letters and tast-

218

ing your hand-painted cards; good riddance to spot inspections when you're changing a Tampax; to door-less poops behind a shower curtain, to eleven women sharing a sink, to five minutes in the kiosk to send an email; goodbye to Lock and the cage; to toothaches and thankless extractions; to thin, hardly-there mattresses and black mold; goodbye to bleeding for four days and begging to be checked out; goodbye to Bend Over, Squat, and Cough; goodbye to doggie wagons and dildos made from sanitary napkins and plastic forks. Goodbye to the marked, the mugshot, the hands that curl into fists and meaty arms that trellis with dragons and tweety birds.

At Columbus House we're strip-searched one more time before we actually and finally can choose regular clothes to wear, which are donated. They're pretty cheap about the clothes because they only give you about one outfit. And they have tons of donations. The other inmates are more generous with clothes and help than the actual staff.
—Lucy Weems, parolee

An hour and a half later, an hour and a half of being jostled around like chickpeas in a tin can, the speeding doggie van pulls up in front of Trenton's Columbus House.

Lucy passes through a metal detector and then seats herself on a chair that looks for internal metal, like jewelry, blades, nails, and razors. Contraband wrapped in plastic or toilet paper can be inserted like tampons. Officers round off the exam with a pat-down and a strip search. Again Lucy is being taught what murkiness involves as she waits on the ocean's bottom for a ray of light to reach her. She selects her outfit from a paltry pile of donated goods. Here she'll stay until June, sharing a room with four other women all transitioning to fatter mattresses and civilian clothes.

In the meantime, they're monitored and must wear ID badges, they must submit to random urine tests and security checks. They attend in-house grooming seminars that remind them to shampoo their hair twice, to use deodorant, and scrub their faces. Lucy and her new friend Laura stand like chefs over the mixing bowls, a pretend stew of peroxide and hair dye, ready to apply with paintbrush and spatula.

&

The inmate residents take day trips to the dollar store, where, for the first time in seven years, Lucy pays for a bag of jelly beans with money and a cashier asks her if she would like a plastic sack. The aisles of the dollar store gleam with choice, and Lucy touches the soaps and toothpastes and shampoos, the balloons and streamers.

She pictures her birthday in Max when Krystal went all out for her—a necklace, stuffed animals, miniature cats, each with their own litter box and chocolate chip turd, a cake, lipstick, and batteries. Here are the decorations for the birthday she'll make for her daughter. Party hats, and ballet slippers dusted with fake black crystals, and tiger-striped fans. All the knock-off designer perfumes with testers; the flirty aroma of plum, rose, jasmine, and praline fill her throat.

The waves of lavish sweetness gag her.

&

Lucy's frightened and can't stop her hands from reaching out. Pink-glitter tiaras, metallic cone crowns and matching whistles, giant green and purple tissue flowers, hanging sunflower pom-poms, hot-pink enchanted castles. She has to steady herself, and rests her forehead against the cooler; the teas seem restful and brown and calming. She needs to find sunglasses and buy a pair to cut the glare of too much color.

Seven years wearing beige uniforms, seven years without much color except for her own art, or is her panic attached to something deeper? Like opening a closet and Lucy and her brother being pushed inside and the door locked for hours while the mutter of men seeps through the wood. Like a six-foot-three dealer demanding his money in a cold voice, then swinging his

220

fist into their mother's face. His fist again shooting out from his shoulder. "Tomorrow, have my money."

The door unlocks, and the children run out to comfort their mother whose nose and lip bleed. She picks up the pipe from her lap to smoke what's left in the bowl. Their beautiful mother who watches the men touching her children, her eyes big as shot glasses, all black hair and white skin.

The parole officer takes my drug test with a very large mouth swab and it looks like I'm sucking on a very long pacifier.
—Lucy Weems, parolee

The Columbus House road to parole runs through McDonald's. All the soon-to-be paroled will first work at the franchise and become earners. A portion of their earnings are deposited in the Columbus House's coffers for resident upkeep.

When Lucy walks into the upscale McDonald's, she doesn't much care that the cuisine isn't French and the clientele not monied. After seven years the crispy fries are as titillating as tanned bodies on the Riviera. Neither does she have to bristle when the manager nods at her, not with contempt but with welcome. Seven years away from the world and the franchise now offers salads and lattes. Twenty- and thirtysomethings expect more than fat calories between white-bread buns. With Lucy's good looks and her outgoing personality she is soon chosen to be a greeter. All mid-morning and into the afternoon she mingles, she welcomes, and chats. All mid-morning and into the afternoon she attracts admiring glances.

In the days and weeks that follow, customers rave about her friendliness. An older woman brings her a stuffed teddy bear, a printer repairman leaves flowers, and men ask for her phone number, which she's unable to give. One customer, a handsome fortysomething man named Greg, is so persistent in his pursuit that she agrees to eat her complementary lunch with him. One lunch leads to three. When she levels with him about Columbus

House, he tells her he's fallen in love with her. During their next lunch she's forking a leaf of lettuce and tomato chunk into her mouth, when Greg says he'd like her to have his baby.

"Sure, Greg, but I already told you my baby-making days are over. My tubes are tied."

Still he's not dissuaded, and when she's too busy to lunch with him, he comes in anyway and stares at her for an hour. He shows her on his iPhone a zoom photo of his house. Her eyes follow the bus arrow to the other side of the tracks between the backyards and fences, where the earth smells are sweet and old. It's a quaint single-family dwelling built in the 1950s. She loves the stalks of sweet corn in the yards where struggling people put their feet up.

He asks her if she'd like to live there and have his babies.

No, she doesn't think so.

&

At Columbus House there's no access to email, and it takes time to order stamps and get mail privileges. She writes Krystal to let her know she's arrived safely and she writes me to fill me in on her progress toward freedom.

&

Hardboiled Columbus House makes Lucy's re-entry into the wider world difficult. Returning from the mean streets of Mc-Donald's, she walks through a metal detector, and then waits for an officer to examine the pockets of her apron and jacket. They're sure parolees are seduced into wrongdoing by the song of skin and the song of money. Parole is a purgatory.

&

The parole board has denied a move to her father's house in Connecticut, where a bedroom and laptop await her. The board decides that the pit bull resident in the home, as well as her father's registered gun ownership, are in too dangerous proximity for an ex-felon whose crime involved a gun.

Unbelievably, Kit, her daughter's custodial aunt (Lucy's ex-sister-in-law) offers Lucy a home with them in their Mount

222

Laurel apartment. She accepts. McDonald's offers Lucy a permanent job. She refuses it. Release promises to be a messy place with mouth swabs and drug tests.

On her last night in Columbus House she dreams of Ramon, her evil dealer. *Who cares about an addict? he says, So close the door. I've brought you money and heroin. Yup, those maniac birds. They are winged bats.* He has bags of China White. There's a piano bench where junkies sit chewing gummy bears. Ramon's wavy brown hair stands up when he runs his fingers through it. He's thin and his jeans and leather jacket hang on him. She notices a raggedy hole in one of the heels.

There might be little animals living inside his socks, even a caterpillar chewing its threads.

You think you can leave us behind? Just try.

&

The air she breathes is fresher without a staff person or an officer watching, ready for her to break a rule. She walks toward the parking lot where her ex-sister-in-law Kit's car idles. Is this what air smells like when you have a whole day in front of you? The heat stands still and only the cumulus clouds drift through the blue. Leaves hang like green glass.

Her daughter gets out of the car. After years in Maximum Compound and months in Columbus House, Lucy finds herself in the arms of her 12-year-old daughter, Hope. She never wants to let go; she can smell the sun on her child's skin, and feel its warmth when she touches the strawberry-blond hair the same texture as her own.

"You're taller than me," Lucy says, proudly.

They stand shoulder to shoulder. The shape of their faces and their bone structures are so similar, no one would mistake them for anything but mother and daughter. She takes a few steps back just to drink in the sight of her. They have been apart so long her daughter has grown up—not only the prison years but the heroin years have separated them. Now the two smile playfully, mischievously.

Where will we go?

Days follow of mall strolling, Starbucks lattes, selfies and iPhone photos, thrift-store clothes shopping, a new dog, part-bulldog, named Loki, god of mischief. Gladly, Lucy spends what she has made at McDonald's on her child. They act like sisters; they giggle and have fun. She sleeps in her daughter's room. She trims her daughter's hair and tells her stories.

"How about this?" Lucy says, laughing. "Your grandfather was dating a hairdresser and Afro perms were big then. He volunteered me, my brother, and Uncle Rocco to this lady." Hours in the salon.

Voilà! Her mouth dropped open when she saw herself in the mirror. Not an Afro that might be beautiful on a long-necked black girl but a poodle perm that even a dog would run from. "We all had tight poodle kinks. Uncle Rocco and my dad could have just been at the pet groomer."

Lucy and her brother looked worse, like the bubbly spit tickling your throat landed on their heads.

&

It's hard for Lucy to trust her ex-sister-in-law, a retired teacher, whose ruddy complexion bears the ravages of alcohol. Her flushed cheeks are vodka markers, as are her eyes, blue and vacant. Her mouth full of words, wild to fly out crazily.

Something doesn't feel right when Kit leaves Lucy in charge of the apartment and takes Hope on a week-long trip to Orlando. This is the first time Lucy has been alone for almost eight years, the first night she sleeps into the next day well past noon. Sleep—succulent, like being made love to. She opens the windows wide to breathe air, free, not like the Yard's barbed-wire enclosed air.

I will be your peony, the breeze says; your rave, your green mirror, your summer.

&

She finds waitressing jobs at two Italian restaurants. They like her easy way with the customers and she keeps the waitstaff amused

224

between the grilled swordfish and zucchini medallions. If they're not busy she'll dance a jig in the back alley behind the kitchen, where they all take their smoke breaks. Starting on her right foot, striking her heels together, leaping, and laughing. Her arms straight at her side.

The bus boy snickers. "I love that. You look like a puppet." One with a mysterious slant to her eyes.

Uber wasn't around when she went in but now it's the black SUV chariot of choice. She's spending a good chunk of change to travel, and before she finds some second-hand vehicle, she needs to renew her driver's license. That means ID and test-taking and a driving test. It all piles up, the to-do list to re-establishing a foothold back in the world.

&

After her shift ends she waits for Uber beside the street. Summer's haunting aroma surrounds her. Cars float by honking, some slowing.

Men whistling, catcalling.

My parole officer is a funny guy in terms of him being a very big cornball. He attempts to come in like he's a grandiose officer, the type that should instill fear in me. He tries to act like a tough guy and he doesn't like my jokes because as you know I like to lighten the mood with some humor.
—Lucy Weems, parolee

The bane of a parolee's re-entry is often the parole officer assigned to them. It's a complicated relationship and the officer holds all the cards. Lucy's parole officer is a five-foot, eleven-inch beanpole weighing in at 160 lbs. When he calls, announcing he'll arrive in three hours at the apartment, she must get there or be in violation. Regardless of whether she's in the middle of a waitressing shift many towns away.

Once, Kit lets Lucy borrow her car in order for Lucy to keep her state-mandated therapist appointment, to not be late for work, and to meet with her parole officer. All in a day, all in different locales. Rarely does her parole officer arrive without wearing a bullet-proof vest and in the company of another officer. He sponges her mouth with a monster swab and asks what she did three days ago, expecting a veritable walk-through answer. Wanting her to peel away her skin and expose the cartilage of her wing bones. Not waiting for the three-minute test to finish, he continues his rapid-fire questions and she tries to answer through the saliva dribbling from her lips.

He requests prescription receipts, he examines the contents of the refrigerator, and riffles through the bathroom's medicine cabinet. Lucy realizes he sees himself as a hunter-gatherer on a mission, an eater of meat he slays with his bare hands.

&

After fighting with her ex-sister-in-law all through the years of her incarceration for more access to her daughter, Lucy can't help but mistrust Kit's surprising generosity. When she and her daughter return from Orlando, the two of them are arguing. An adolescent rebelling against rules. The night bares its teeth. Her sister-in-law mixes vodka, beer, and anger. Or is it the sticky whiskeys that muddle her tongue, inflame her brain, and turn her eyes colorless as salt-rimmed tequila shots?

Kit rails against her thankless niece, whom she and her estranged husband took in when her parents chose drugs and crime over their daughter. She is cursing and babbling nonsensically. The air almost hurts to breathe and Lucy's heart pounds. When Kit slaps Hope, Lucy has her iPhone filming and recording. The bitter talk spirals out of control and the police are called.

&

Unable to sleep, Lucy fights the guilt rising up, how heroin destroyed her ability to mother her firstborn daughter (to say nothing of her second-born), how her grim addiction allowed the custody of her daughter to be entrusted to this woman, a demented know-nothing. She can't get comfortable with all the space on either side of her. She closes her eyes, coasting along.

In the long night, Lucy forgives her own mother for shutting 4-year-old Lucy into a suitcase and forgetting her. She forgives her mother for leaving windows shut in summer's swelter and open in winter's cold, her heroin mother's nodding as the oars of a box fan serenaded the river of dope and alcohol through her bloodstream.

Heroin. The empty rattle of cereal boxes. Lucy's mother hardly out of her teens. Forgive.

&

Lucy thinks of her wonderful father taking on as many jobs as he could to support his family.

When she was six years old, he ran a gas station for a friend and often took her to work with him. She had a sack of juice boxes, crayons, and coloring books. "You're my special little helper," he'd tell her. "Your job is to color."

&

The sun rises white and dry as face powder. It is the day after the blowup and Lucy's parole officer marches into the apartment. Because a police report was made, the premises are no longer considered safe for a parolee.

Kit files a temporary restraining order against Lucy. She alleges that Lucy on such-and-such a date threatened and intimidated her; she accuses Lucy of taking her car without her permission and driving without a license. Her parole officer gives Lucy days to find a place to live or else she goes back to jail.

Meanwhile, her father pays for a hotel room for the weekend. Here she is looking at herself in a soap-scummy mirrored bathroom with wrappers on the water glasses. She calls Jeff, the father of her daughter, Faith; Jeff, the steady good man she gave up for heroin, who lives with Faith in a modest ranch house in Pennsylvania. She would like to see Faith, but she's unable to leave New Jersey.

Yes, he says, he will bring Faith over the weekend for a visit.

&

They are coming tonight. Her second-born daughter, Faith, still a baby when heroin took Lucy into the streets, has autism. Will she know Mommy?

Lucy paces waiting for them to arrive, listens for a car pulling up just outside the unit, tires crunching gravel, footfalls over twigs. Broken birds dropped on their way to the nest. If she still smoked, she might light a cigarette. She hears a car door, footsteps, another car door. A knock.

&

Tell me something you remember, the girl's eyes say, almost 8 years old and a baby when Mommy last held her. Lucy remembers water trickling from the faucet and the tub smelling of fruity bubbles. She washes her newborn Faith's foot, marveling at the radiance of each toe, her hands, the tiny nails, her innocence.

You're my tiny ballerina in the lacquer music box. I remember admiring your eyelashes; I'd never seen anything more beautiful.

Now her daughter wears glasses that emphasize her large blue eyes. Her cheeks glow.

As she opens her arms, Lucy struggles to keep from tearing up. Although Faith does not speak in full sentences, she seems to remember Lucy, and both are enthralled with the other. Blond with a wide gap-toothed grin, she scripts when she speaks, repeating words and phrases from things she's heard from people around her, or from books or movies. Her words are divided from their common usage, but carry meaning for her, and for her mother.

I love you. It's a magical moment. Lucy hugs her little girl. Behind their daughter stands Jeff, not too changed from when they loved each other and made Faith. A funny Irish guy, the kind she's always liked, a head and a half taller than she and still well-built, his ginger-colored hair the same, the chin scruff, new. Men seem to favor more facial hair these days.

&

They look at each other. The charge is still there.

228

&

Lucy sees what a caring father Jeff has been. Unlike her two ex-husbands, Jeff was one of the few men in her life who didn't cheat. There's something artless and beautiful about Faith's jelly smile, as if she's discovering joy in every moment. Will Faith learn the names of her teachers, which eye is right, is left, and how to read an eye chart, how to unpeel a Band-Aid and apply it to her arm?

Faith breathes in and out her own knowledge and beauty. Faith in Wonderland.

Over the weekend, Faith came down to visit with Jeff, her dad. I'm not going to lie. We got a hotel room, and he did everything under the sun to my body. All that did was make me want him more.
—Lucy Weems, parolee

Their attraction to each other rekindles, the spark ignites, and they find themselves in bed. He loves her gorgeous eyes and fabulously mussed hair. Her breasts. How nice his hands are, their graceful movements, clean hands with a sheen to their fingernails. She likes watching them touch her.

They do everything, throughout the night. His skin is warm against her. No lookout, no sheet draping the lovemaking, no officer around the corner, no strap-on necessary. He pledges his allegiance to her body. "I don't want to lose you again."

The sky goes violet, then pink with blue streaks shooting through it. The sun rises and decorates them in glistening strands of corn silk. At dawn he strokes Lucy's wrist where Krystal's name is inked.

"Your girlfriend's name?" he asks.

"My best friend, not my lover," Lucy answers. "A fantastic girl that you'll meet one day." She promises herself that tomorrow she will send that letter to Krystal. *I will not be like all the others who leave EMCF and forget their friends.*

&

229

A court date is on the calendar. Lucy shudders to realize that Kit set her up. Sending her back to prison has been her sister-in-law's intention from the start, and, in the process, to revoke the partial custody of her eldest daughter.

Lucy intends to fight all the charges. Her iPhone footage captured her ex-sister-in-law's ranting and slapping Hope—her long canine teeth showing, her tongue rough as a demented cat. On the date she accuses Lucy of menacing her, Lucy had wait-ressed; the evidence is on camera.

&

The court date arrives. After all he had been through with Lucy, after his lonely struggle to raise an autistic daughter on his own, Jeff drives in from Pennsylvania to support her attempt to re-gain custody of the daughter she had with another man. Lucy speaks in her own defense, produces her iPhone footage and work schedule.

The restraining order is thrown out and the judge repri-mands Kit for filing false charges—yet in the blowback Lucy los-es the partial custody of Hope she'd managed to retain during her years in Maximum Compound. Lucy faces additional charges for driving without a license and use of Kit's car, allegedly with-out Kit's permission. The court allows her a two-hour supervised visit every week and she's ordered by her parole officer to wear a GPS tracking monitor on her ankle.

Keeping up with court filings and Hope's custody renego-tiations adds an extra layer to Lucy's complicated new life. After a flurry of hearings and more restraining orders, Kit and her hus-band lose guardianship of their niece, and Hope's father, Jimmy, is granted custody.

At the age of 12, and in the malaise of puberty, Hope moves in with her father and his second wife.

She surely must feel vulnerable and unprotected, even though Lucy and her ex have long since buried the hatchet and want only what is best for her.

Lucy tells me about her struggle during her prison years

to be a mother to Hope, and the frustration she is experiencing outside the walls trying to mother her eldest daughter—while wearing an ankle monitor to prove that she is near her only at court-approved times.

Hope has blossomed into a beautiful girl on the cusp of womanhood. She loves her skateboard and her fashion dolls who still tell her their secrets. She loves making her face up and coloring her hair and blowing pouty kisses into the digital universe of selfies.

The ankle monitor actually proves that I'm not going near her house and violating the restraining order. So it's supposed to work in my favor, although I think the parole officer's full of crap and trying not to make me feel bad about wearing this Big Dook-ie ass-monitoring TV-size box on my ankle.
—Lucy Weems, parolee

Jeff and Lucy play waitress and customer.

"Carrots? Cucumbers? Radishes, sir?" Lucy teases.

Jeff nods to all of them.

"Sunflower seeds, croutons? Black olives and green olives?"

"Yes, ma'am."

He lies beside her and texts her poems. I'M TOUCHING YOU. MY FINGERS DIPPING INTO THE GUT-BUCKET CHURCH BETWEEN YOUR LEGS. I WANT YOU TO BE MY WIFE.

&

I am surprised when Lucy announces that Jeff has asked her to be his wife. This time he does not want to lose her. Last time they had lived together without marriage and she'd slipped through his fingers into addiction.

They have talked about her commitment to sobriety and she tells him her love affair with heroin has ended. Lucy wants to put the gangster inside her, that half-crazed woman always searching for the round prison of a syringe, to rest.

Her daughters, Hope especially, will not forgive her again if she backslides.

&

Lucy and Jeff take their vows. Their wedding day. It is November and they stand in a park. The sky is overcast and yet they shine.

Jeff wears a red-and-black-checkered wool shirt and Lucy wears a matching red-and-black-wool skirt. Faith stands between them, her lips red, holding a bouquet of roses.

There are two cherished people missing. Hope and Krystal.

&

Even after her marriage, it takes months and piles of paperwork for Lucy to get the official permissions and parole transfer required to move to Pennsylvania where her husband lives. She is there now, living in a four-bedroom, three-bathroom house with the people who love her; her husband, her younger daughter, her mother-in-law, and her brother-in-law.

Lucy calls her mother-in-law Mom, and the relationship is a warm one. In summer, Mom gardens and she promises there will be a bounty of fresh vegetables and flowers.

Lucy feels hopeful, though not quite whole. She dreams that someday, it will be all of them, including Hope, whose father has agreed, and petitioned the court, to allow shared custody of their daughter.

&

Lucy receives official permission to move to Pennsylvania a month before the Coronavirus shuts down government offices. Before restaurants are ordered closed and Lucy loses her job.

Her new parole officer is a woman and comes to inspect the house, interview its inhabitants, and take photos of the rooms. When she opens the door to Faith's room she has to smile, the walls glow pink and Christmas lights crisscross the ceiling. Sponge Bob paintings populate the walls.

Faith delights in her enchanted world of pink. The closet has cushions and Sponge Bob pillows where she retreats to calm herself and use the cell phones she sneaks from her mother and father and grandmother.

&

Covid-19 has arrived.

The governor issues shelter-in-place orders. Only grocery stores, liquor stores, and pet food stores are open. Lucy, Faith, and Jeff make an event of the pet food store almost as big as a supermarket, the splendor of cat and dog foods, the long aisles full of surprises, the kaleidoscope of textures.

&

Gone are the pimp neighborhoods, the merry-go-round of milk-skinned beauties with bruised veins. Gone the motels and backseats of cars, the ankle monitors, gone prison, the seven years' bad luck. Forget the fingers of strangers trickling down your back, the strange tropical eye of the mirror hexing you.

Forget sandwiching the front and back pieces of your life together, the good and the gangster, trying for the middle hook, forgive the wench putting on a spidery garter belt and black fishnets preparing to sell herself.

Forget, forgive, move on.

GROUNDS
EMCF   Clinton, New Jersey

Stephanie, I can't believe I'm about to be 34. Almost 15 years since I've been locked up. Only 5 1/2 more to go. Then 5 years on parole. It sounds like a long time. Well, I hope you have a Happy New Year's!
—Krystal Riordan, Inmate #661387

Lucy is gone. Krystal has experienced this so many times before—being left behind. It hurts saying goodbye to friends who have served their sentences and leave for halfway houses, and then home. Empty promises to write, to email, to never forget the one still serving time. Goodbye is goodbye.

She understands life on the outside speeds up: finding a job and pleasing your parole officer, reconnecting. She understands no one gets nostalgic for wiping your behind with a chocolate bar wrapper or eating potatoes filched from the mess hall and baked in the filthy microwave to sputter and shrivel. Lucy is gone and her leaving has clawed a hole in her. She lies on her bunk and tries to fall into a sleep deep enough that when she wakes it will be the day before the worst day of her life.

All the years since will be erased if she keeps falling, no matter if Dray is chasing her, and she's running and yelling for someone to save her. Two figures in fire with blue burning hair. Jennifer and Krystal. She's thinking about how Lucy's mother kidnapped her and once shut her into a suitcase when she was crying. Her brother saved her, like Krystal and Lucy saved each other.

&

For weeks after Lucy leaves, she hibernates; going to classes, the microwave, and her bunk, not much else. She's almost completed her two college classes.

She loves the English Lit class, which is taught by a transgender instructor. The terminology in the outside world is changing, becoming non-binary, no longer just he and she but they, and Krystal's instructor prefers they. Krystal herself is drawn to this experimentation, to gender fluidity, to the pansexual.

Krystal immerses herself in the work and quickly excels, becoming one of the high test scorers. She reads Shelley, Byron, and John Donne. She loves her teacher; she loves John Donne. She likes it that he fathered eleven children, and that he eloped and was arrested for kidnapping his own wife.

&

"You were raped because it was part of God's plan. It was His punishment."

Krystal stares at the girl, whose freckle-splashed cheeks and upturned nose make her appear friendlier than she really is. Krystal had shared her Job Corps story with her fellow inmate, who looked impossibly young to have had a child, let alone murdered it. She is speechless.

God's plan, she thinks, smells like stale cigar smoke, feels like cold air from the long-ago hotel room's A/C, and looks like the patch of strawberry chest fuzz on her rapist's chest. She shivers.

"You're cold. Come here beside me," he says again, patting the bed. When she sits, he stands up and unzips. She shakes her head, saying she only wants to hang out. Maybe he tries to coax her, maybe he calls her a tease, more likely he says nothing as he frees his penis, while his other hand grips the back of her neck and fills her mouth, deeper and deeper in, until she can't breathe.

Job Corps' vocational training program had seemed like a godsend after Krystal's four years of attack therapy at Élan. The freedom tasted delicious; lingering over her meals as long as she liked, with no one ordering her around and calling her names.

Weekends, the Job Corps kids would rent motel rooms and smoke pot. Krystal liked the girls she roomed with, and she liked Job Corps. It felt like a family of kids. A real family, where everyone got along. When her roommates had wanted privacy, it felt safe and natural to go hang out with the guys in her group.

After the choke of milky batter, the second guy comes out of the bathroom and joins them on the bed, rolling her onto her stomach and thrusting his way between her legs. Her head pressed to the bed edge, she hears dogs barking outside the window, tiny black barks, high-pitched.

Krystal can still hear them barking.

"God's plan," she murmurs.

"How old are you, anyway?" the freckled girl asks, her lip curling.

It takes everything Krystal has to keep her hands at her side and not punch her. She wants to say that when she was raped, she'd been around the same age as the pug-nosed murderer who stands there, judging her.

In accordance with God's plan, Krystal will go to the police, give her statement, and press charges. Everyone in Job Corps will fume; the girls will stop speaking to her. The two guys are well-liked, and wasn't it her fault anyway? No one invited her to their hotel room. Both rapists will flee the state.

No one could tell you how rape felt. It felt like nothing. Only cold.

No one talks about how cold it can be. How you don't unthaw, not ever.

Krystal, locked away as a 20-year-old, will return to the world twenty years later, not old or young, but as if she'd been kept in formaldehyde.

&

If she has to do more time than twenty years, something in her spirit will crumble. Nights, she wishes she could talk to Lucy, the one friend she trusted. She won't think about the hole inside her, the place where Lucy was and now isn't. The emptiness a rabbit scrambles into. I want her to tell me how she is, just give me a sign, but she gives me silence.

"I love cats," Lucy always said. Their scratchy tongues and

rose-petal ears. "And I love you."

&

She's hoping for a letter from Lucy when mail is called. The envelope the officer hands her is a surprise. The neat handwriting in script, not print, almost a girl's penmanship, she recognizes as Dray's. *Your eyes are wildflowers, the early blue violets.*

He claims he's going to write out an affidavit proving her innocence. But he hasn't done it yet, has he? Why has he waited 14 years?

It was so long ago, but the last day and night she spent with Dray are etched into her mind, remembered when she wishes she could forget. Like she has forgotten so much of her past.

&

The gypsy cab drives Krystal and Dray up the West Side Highway, past the pound where Jennifer's friend's car was towed. The heat has followed them from the room. Dray smells. There are dark rings of sweat under his arms. High-beams blinking on and off against the skyscrapers with their ice-cube windows of light cut her.

Have you ever listened to a night city after your lover has pushed a girl's raped and strangled body into a dumpster?

He has incredible physical strength, the detectives will later comment. He takes her to a Harlem hotel.

I got arrested in the hotel room in Harlem. Dray went outside as soon as we got there. I was in the room by myself. The police knocked, and before I could get dressed, they kicked the door down and had guns in my face. I was naked.
—Krystal Riordan, Inmate #661387

Harlem. Hot breathing, watchful eyes. Street vendors hawking fajitas and chicken wings. She has to do the checking in. The Jamaican guy at the front desk has a bat by the key check and tells them it's cash only.

"No ATM card bullshit," he says. He's taller than Dray but thinner and bouncing to a reggae beat. His eyes are bullwhips. Krystal keeps hers on the black-and-white tiles, walks to the water cooler, fills a paper cup, and gulps. Do Krystal and Draymond smell of fish guts? Is that what murder does? The desk clerk keeps looking at her. The muscles in Dray's face clench.

Once in the room, she rushes to the sink and splashes water over her face. She presses herself against the vents. The air conditioner works, but the TV doesn't.

She parts the blinds, caked with a silt of gray lace. Taxis honk, a racing fire truck makes a choking red sound. Dray tells her not to leave the room, not to open the door for anyone but him. He's going out to buy weed. She hurriedly undresses, throwing the salmon-colored tube top and soiled jeans skirt, the outfit she'll wear for her arrest, into a chair. In bed she pulls the sheet over her head. Trying to hang on to something from her childhood, some piece of goodness. The leftover French bread from doggie bags she saved to eat with Finnegan, the black Labrador, the girl and dog, the two of them in the backyard grass lying in the sun, their mouths full of crumbs and butter.

What is he doing, punching a girl, his fist an exploding fireball?

Two victims. Jennifer and Krystal.

Jennifer's fine straight hair brushes her shoulders and parts on the side; the part is made further to the left so the hair falls more like a sheer curtain across her right eye.

But he hasn't proclaimed her innocence yet, has he?

Hope isn't taking her medication and keeps getting fevers. Then Faith is getting into everything. I don't have a free minute. Holy crap, no one told me it was going to be such an uphill battle with girls.
—Lucy Weems

Krystal does eventually hear from Lucy but it's not the same. It can't be.

238

Finding her feet after seven years of incarceration has been a challenge even for Lucy who is resourceful, if she's anything. If only she were two people and had four arms, if only she wasn't a full-time mother, a full-time waitress, a wife, a parolee.

While incarcerated, Lucy missed her daughters terribly, and now, in the blink of an eye, she has become their nurturer, their friend, their chef, their hair stylist, and their mom. Add the pandemic and the closure of Faith's special-needs school to her already heaping plate, and Lucy finds herself without a minute to spare. Like many in the hard-hit restaurant industry, she lost her waitressing job—and having a job is a requirement of her parole.

When her unemployment checks stopped coming and the economy started to reopen, she found another waitressing job. After the Department of Motor Vehicles partially reopened, Lucy got her suspended driver's license renewed and bought a second-hand truck.

She takes her daughters blueberry picking and skateboarding; they go on long drives. There have been meltdowns, and daughters can be tough. "My husband is so supportive," she says. "I thank the unicorns for him."

&

But Lucy promised Krystal she would never forget her, and she doesn't.

They talk on the phone as often as possible. Lucy sends pictures and emails to cheer her up. Lucy admits Krystal deserves more in their friendship, but she needs to come up for air first.

As a mutual friend, I sometimes act as their go-between. "Tell Krystal I love her with all my heart," Lucy says.

One of my favorite photos is of Lucy sleeping on her stomach, covered by a comforter except for her outstretched arms and hands. Her black and white cat lies beside her, paws outstretched as well. Twins in their poses. Lucy looks like she's been dropped on the bed, fished out half-drowned from the sea of exhaustion.

I was walking back from Mess Hall and up the street. There is a little snow on the ground and the trees are bare except for the ice frozen on the branches. The snow looked like glitter and the ice on the trees shined. At the very end of the street there is this beautiful little church. The whole scene gave me a few moments of peace.
        —Krystal Riordan, Inmate #661387

Krystal learns she is being transferred to Grounds. She's earned the move with her good behavior. There's more freedom, more Yard to walk through; paths like roads, except these don't lead anywhere. Across the street there's a church and a diner in the come-and-go world. The blinking neon thrills her.

How would it feel to sit down and order a cheeseburger with grilled onions and a pyramid of French fries doused in ketchup?

The Outside has changed since 2006. It's the gig economy, and the jobs that bloomed like lilies smeared across the backhoe's bucket have disappeared. Is she thinking of her last job—prostitute? Someday she'll travel. She pictures herself swimming in Hamilton Pool or kayaking on the Little Arkansas River; the water in one is blue sapphire, the other emerald. The color of her eyes, depending on the day. Places she's seen on TV.

Her sentence is longer than those given to murderers like Becca Christie, who bludgeoned an elderly man to death with a golf club, and Allison O'Brien, who smothered her son—and their sentences have weight and duration. These are older women whom you call Mrs. O'Brien, not ZeZe, or Apples, or Tank. Bluefish, the ocean killers.

&

She understands that in the wilder days, old horses had been feasted on by wolves and mountain lions. Can't she go back to when the whole beautiful day lay before her? Grass so lush and green like a picnic basket.

She will dream of a red lip mark on the rim of a bone

china cup.

She'll dream that lunch is a bean burrito, ½ cup rice, 3 slices bread, and for dinner 1 cup macaroni and beef, ½ cup peas, 3 slices bread.

She will dream in half cups and ice-cream scoops of canned veggies.

She'll dream that her gums are bleeding from not having fresh fruit.

COVID-19 ARRIVES IN THE PRISON HOUSE
EMCF Clinton, New Jersey

I need as many people as I can to call 1 833 947 2125 and the web-site is NJSPOTLIGHT.com. Write or call on my behalf and bring up my seizures and how they are getting worse. Because of the virus they are letting people go home if they have a medical issue. It's worth a try.
—Krystal Riordan, Inmate #661387

Krystal first hears of the novel coronavirus from the TV. But it's still far away in Wuhan, China and hardly worth giving a thought to.

Soon hundreds are infected and many are dying. Dry coughing, soaring fevers, pneumonia. Wuhan is sealed off, but not before the virus escapes. Italy and Iran lose thousands. Cruise ships become floating Petri dishes of COVID-19.

A particle swathed in protein, COVID-19's spikes lend the virus a flower's beauty, the saffron-smelling Crocosmia Lucifer, as it blooms. Once the spike proteins are breathed in, they attach to the host's cells and make millions of copies. Millions of stars in the Corona Andromeda.

It is a mastermind escapee. Airport security can't stop it. Borders can't. It invades Germany, France, the UK, the United States.

Soon, the virus has Krystal and EMCF's attention. As the pandemic explodes in New York City and reaches New Jersey, officers begin calling in sick and the prison is understaffed. All staff members' temperatures are taken before they are allowed to enter the facility.

Krystal holds her breath when officers pass.

&

242

"If it gets in here, it's going to spread like crazy," Krystal says.

She hears of officers who have contracted it, and rumor has it that some inmates are in quarantine. A unit has been cleared and is being used to isolate inmates who test positive for the virus.

Her job takes her to the same building where the officers eat and stow their civilian clothes into lockers. All movement between the various units has been shut down and inmates are allowed only to go outside to the Yard. Officers who have families have been calling in sick and the ones who report to work wear masks and gloves.

&

I fear for Krystal, in an environment where she is unable to control the space around her. "Let me know what I can do, if anything," I email her. "Please keep me abreast of conditions."

When I read of how the cruise ships have become death liners as passengers sicken from the Coronavirus and some die, I think of EMCF, a relatively closed ecosystem. No port will accept them. Leper ships. The Diamond Princess quarantines at Yokahama for weeks. More cruise ships wander the seas, like the1939 voyage of the St. Louis, the liner carrying 901 Jews, refused entry and returned to Nazi Europe. Voyage of the Damned.

&

These are the days of strange dreams. These are the days of COVID-19, the Apocalypse Virus.

I wonder if prison officials have learned about asymptomatic transmission and how a person neither sneezing nor coughing can shed virus in droplets of .0002 inches. The breath of even seemingly healthy people may contain the invader. Krystal walks in a wonderland of virus flowers—the color of pumpkins and vines tangling out of the rusty soil. The giantess above her millions of corona bits.

The sun goes down. Wings brush her cheek and she strokes the soft ocher fur of a horseshoe bat. Against her feet the pangolin rubs and makes her laugh with its scaly anteater shape, cat's face, and iguana tail. When the hunters come, she fights for the anteater and the bat, she bloodies herself. Then the lights explode, officers shout the wake-up call, and they are gone.

&

Visiting hours have been abolished.

&

I tell Krystal that for weeks New York has been in lockdown and in my East Village walk-up I've been one of the lucky ones able to work from home. Only three weeks and already in the red room, once my haven, the walls are weary of my face.

I tell her the night sky is deserted of stars like the dim buildings, their people having abandoned them. In the beginning, I thought it would not touch me or my immune-challenged partner, but now we are marooned, an island of two in a city of millions. An island within an island city.

After midnight gunshots are fired close to our building. Shooting to shoot, to wake up the neighborhood, to chill the blood, as if what runs in the veins isn't frightened enough. Everything seems wiped away. Washington Square Park and Union Square and all the dazzling couples in their sleeve and hand tattoos and rag and bone finery. Now the streets see only those scurrying out for food or medicine, those workers deemed essential like the Amazon delivery people, the sanitation workers, the mail carriers, the MTA employees, the cashiers, all disproportionately persons of color.

No fire trucks, few police cars, no jack hammers and drills. All day the loudest noise is UPS ringing the front door buzzer, the melting coos of the mourning dove, and then in the blue hours, the nothing.

&

In Maximum Compound, the virus is on the move. Officers come into Krystal's unit telling her and others to pack up, tossing her one garbage bag for her things. Most of the inmates here for years have accumulated possessions, their precious stuff.

Within hours, officers rescind the order but advise Krys-

244

tal to stay packed as they intend to transfer her soon.

I want to send Krystal a mask. She may receive it, if I order a mask from Amazon and mail Krystal the invoice proving that the package comes directly from the vendor, but I soon discover it's almost impossible to get one on short notice. The available KN95 masks are reserved for medical personnel.

I order masks and gloves from Amazon but they are not in stock and the expected delivery date is more than two months away.

&

Krystal calls via Global Tel-Link, early on a Sunday evening. At 7 p.m. the nightly cheer goes up, for the medical workers and all those on the frontlines. I hold out the phone to see if Krystal can hear the cow bells and the apartment dwellers raising their windows and leaning out to cheer and clap. Tonight an electric guitar is riffing in tribute and the chords excite and connect the entire neighborhood.

The morgue trucks bring bodies to the temporary field hospitals erected in Central Park. No one knows how long the lockdown will last.

&

There are the mornings when the first thing Rob says lifting his head from the pillows—he sleeps with four propped under and around him plus the twisted comforters—"Feel my forehead. Do you think I have a fever?"

In his shelter-in-place sleep there's no quietude. He moves constantly, shifting, climbing, tossing. Rob, the river sleeper. He waits for the thing to get in, to crawl under the door.

Today, he returns from the bodega in a state of nervous agitation. On our street only the addicts and street folk are out there in great numbers, no longer camouflaged by throngs of people strolling and spilling out of restaurants and bars. They own the sidewalk. Addicts sit on the stoop outside our building, and when the light dims they shoot up. Wearing their filthy plumage, they are naked in their hopelessness. They pass a pipe and the smoke reeks not strongly of civet but of urine-on-fire. Meth's signature—yellow apples and piss.

I imagine Rob in mask and gloves hurrying into the bicycle lane to avoid two homeless men.

They miss nothing. The taller of the two shouts, "Scared, big boy? Scared I'm a zombie? I brought smallpox here, I'll bring it to you."

&

I keep from my inmate friends the LiveScience of my nightmares. The virus is an airborne horror that begins its journey in the nose, rooting itself in the rich-cell-enzymes there and traveling down the windpipe into the lungs and multiplies, savaging the heart too, and the kidneys. Thrombosis in the pulmonary arteries. Blood clots in the lower extremities. Floating water lilies of blood clots. Conquistadors in death ships.

I have had several seizures in the last 2 days. Last night I had one and walked out in the public area on third shift and sat at the table. I'm glad my wing was able to explain what was going on.
—Krystal Riordan, Inmate #661387

Krystal's seizures continue, but in pandemic-times no further tests will be performed. She is on a seizure medication, but it has had little if any effect on their occurrence. In the last two days one of those seizures occurred in the shower. In her words, she walked "ass naked" up her wing and tried to get into the public area.

Before her release, Lucy had witnessed one of her friend's seizures.

"Lucy, come quick. Krystal is acting weird. It's one of her episodes."

She found Krystal wandering in the hallway, her eyes wide, and her pupils dilated. "Where is the bathroom?" she asked in a little girl's voice.

After years in Maximum Compound, Lucy knew her

friend could find all its bathrooms with a blindfold on. The child of long ago was lost. After Lucy led her into the bathroom, Krystal turned to her.

"Do you love me, Mommy?" she whispered.

Lucy wondered where Krystal had gone. Was it an apartment of soiled carpets where sounds travelled through flimsy sheetrock? An apartment where the mother wasn't there, and the bathroom might have been the only safe place?

Krystal blinked. Her eyes scanned the ceiling. "How did I get in here?"

Sometimes she blacks out and tries to clutch others; she calls the walls by her sister's name. Sometimes she pees on herself. Krystal tells me that odors precede the episodes. Burning leaves. Her uncle's aftershave. Incest can live its whole life in the damp knots of a bed shared by three sisters.

The Apocalypse Virus
EMCF   Clinton, New Jersey

Well 2 girls died in here in the last couple of days. I knew both of them. They both died of "heart attacks."
—Krystal Riordan, Inmate #661387

Months pass in a miasma of virtual house arrest and a half-open East Village.

July arrives. New York City is no longer the epicenter of the epicenter. The city has brought its infection rate down but underground gatherings are driving new infections. Hookah parties, weed parties, lap dancing, liquor and no masks. Saturday night we hear the indoor COVID party across the courtyard.

Rob shouts out the window, "Disease spreaders. Go on and celebrate Death."

He shouts so loud that for a minute the COVID party quiets. I pull him away from the window, telling him you don't call attention to yourself in an America that has lost its mind.

There are more who have died from what I was told. One person was in the hospital for a few days before they even realized that the lady had died.
—Sofia Perez, Inmate #987652Z

News stories of how COVID is spreading through incarcerated populations haunt me. I worry about Krystal, and the other inmates I've come to consider my friends.

Knowing how Krystal hates to write letters, her friend Sofia sends me an email in response to my questions about the handling of COVID-19 at EMCF. She bears witness to seeing

248

officers who tested positive having to come to work and nurses without gloves dispensing medication. Sofia calls the inmate who died in the Medical Unit hospital "the lady," meaning she was older; otherwise, she would have been "the girl."

"From what I was told..." Is this hearsay or actual? Hard to know, but I've heard enough reports of substandard health care to believe it.

&

No one notices how still she lies, when such a short time ago she was struggling, her head spinning with COVID visions.

No wonder she couldn't breathe, her lungs had become watery sacs of gray sludge, and the soiled hospital gown clinging to her hips already reeked of fish when they stuck her into it. They are swimming over her—those silvery shoals of don't-give-a-fuck aides, techs, nurses. Hovering shapes. By the time her unmotion was noticed, glassfish had found shelter in her. By the time a sheet covered her she was cradled in plankton.

&

Sofia is sure she had COVID. Although she tested negative before her illness, her bunky tested positive, and the test is only good for that moment in time.

EMCF had been using the reception area to quarantine infected inmates and they'd run out of beds. Days later the diarrhea starts, and she loses her sense of smell and taste. For three weeks she suffers a bad cough and can't breathe, with a temperature of 99.4.

"The nurse gave me Mucinex and cough drops along with Tylenol and sent me on my way," she says.

Sofia is a Newark girl, and tough. The fatigue of her illness puts her into a sleep that's hard to wake from. COVID gets into her head and fills it with the boarded-up hardware and shoe repair, the graffiti-scarred pawn shops, the blistered turquoise bar of her old neighborhood. There's that old man walking his dog with its chain wrapped around the stump of his left arm and the dog never runs or pulls on it. He waves at her with his good arm. Perfect rhythm.

She keeps trying to think of their names while she coughs and coughs, and the man and dog keep walking. "I choked out all the mucus. I think it was the Coronavirus. My immune system beat it, though."

We all contain so many selves; some are our better angels. Sofia, still young after a decade in prison, has disavowed her former self. She's moved past the horrific crime she committed when she was 20. Perhaps she has also beaten the apocalypse virus.

Sofia is the first to alert me that "a few of us watched our friend Tiffany 'Big Baby' Mofield pass away a few weeks ago in Ad-Seg."

&

The Administrative Segregation (AdSeg) solitary confinement cells, which inmates refer to as Lock, have in the past been used as punishment cells to separate the offender from her unit, her friends, and her privileges. In the age of COVID, the punishment cells are being used to sequester those suffering from the virus or those displaying Covid-like symptoms. AdSeg or Lock is now the COVID ward.

Inmates suffering fevers, their bodies smoldering like mattresses on the burning pile, languish out of sight. Inmates experiencing shortness of breath, fatigue, a dry cough, headache, loss of taste and smell, hallucinations, rash, and a host of other maladies are treated as if they are well and strong and here to be punished, since the same rules apply to them.

In a changed world, there is no change in the rule mandating that the inmate must be handcuffed when she is taken out of her cell. That she must wear a tight belly belt when she showers, and the shower stall itself is locked and can only be opened by an officer.

Tiffany "Big Baby" Mofield died of COVID begging to be let out of a shower.
—Sofia Perez, Inmate #987652Z

250

Tiffany is serving a five-year sentence for attempted bank robbery and has one year left. Her lovely, high cheek-boned face with dark eyes and long silver eyelids is extremely photogenic, even in the pictures taken at her sentencing. In another photo, she wears a blue jean jacket, and behind her a limousine and the bejeweled lights of the Brooklyn Bridge. The nightlife glows hotly, a flaming steak.

I try to imagine what kind of pressures led her to walk into TD Bank in Salem, New Jersey, at 11:30 a.m. on a Saturday with a pair of box cutters, holding a bank employee at blade point and demanding money.

Other employees call the police and the hostage escapes Tiffany's grasp. Hiding herself in an office she panics and begins to jab at her own wrists. The bank people are laughing at her. They are outside the door. *You're not even a good thief.*

In an age of iPhone and surveillance cameras, to walk into a bank in the same small city where you live seems an impulsive and desperate act.

When the police arrive, they talk Tiffany into giving up the box cutter; they describe her as distraught and weeping. She's taken to the hospital where the wounds on her wrists are treated. Perhaps she wants to be a bird and live in a tree; instead she plea bargains and receives a five-year sentence.

&

Tiffany is already planning her homecoming party when the virus enters the prison. COVID-19 doesn't care that she's a mother of three, grandmother of four, much loved by her family, and the life of the party. She suddenly collapses with deep fatigue, her legs pulled out from under her, a pounding headache. She's taken to EMCF's Medical Unit hospital, which provides not even the bare minimum, where you can bring nothing of your own, where soap at the sinks is a rarity. One inmate describes the hospital in three words—dirty, dirty, dirty.

Tiffany is treated for a cold with over-the-counter remedies by staff who rarely respond to an inmate asking to be taken to the real hospital.

Treated and released.

&

After release from the Medical Unit, Tiffany is walked down a long gray hall past metal doors with only a square window cut into them—high up, the size of an officer's face. She is being sent to AdSeg.

An officer strip searches her, telling her to reach for the sky, peering into her armpits, and behind her ears. AdSeg is usually a noisy cacophony of inmates yelling, but it's quiet now. An asthma sufferer and overweight, Tiffany "Big Baby" Mofield is locked into her solitary confinement cell.

How long has she been sick? One day, two days? Her daughter and brand-new granddaughter just dropped in through the ceiling. Have you brought Big Baby a French donut all puffed up with real whipped cream inside? A latte from Starbucks?

Her head steams, heat scorch followed by chills, her teeth banging together.

Her worried family calls EMCF and are told Tiffany is in the hospital. They understand that to mean the real hospital.

&

The square in the metal door fills for a few seconds with an officer's face, then a rattle and the breakfast tray slides in the slot. You better be ready for it. Rubbery toast. An ice-cream scoop of greenish oatmeal.

Shower day. Big Baby's burning up, and she's working hard to breathe. Fever. It feels like she's drowning. Her flesh is smothering the air. When the officer comes to escort her to the shower, the belly chain goes tight around Tiffany's girth, and her wrists are handcuffed to the chain. She tells the female officer the belt is too tight.

"Loosen it," she pleads. "It's hard to breathe."

The officer tries to adjust it. The officer's voice and her own sound sluggish. A sentence so slow Tiffany can watch for a hundred miles and the words come no closer.

252

What the officer says is "Let's go." The mockingbirds snicker.

&

Michelle Angelina, a transgender inmate, her AdSeg door diagonally across from Tiffany's, can hear not only the officer's voice but Tiffany's.

Michelle and the other inmates housed in AdSeg stand against their doors listening. They hear Tiffany and the officer pass by, the door to the shower opening, the handcuffs unlocking, the footsteps of the officer passing by once again. Disappearing.

&

I picture the water droplets steaming over her skin, too hot, they hurt. The humidity.

Her mouth is wide open gasping. No air anywhere. She shrieks to be let out. "Let me out! I can't breathe. I can't breathe."

She is suffocating. Birds are singing in the fire poppies of her hair. The weeds sprout wildly; the ferns grow tall as trees. She screams.

"I can't breathe."

The rain is going out, the shower too. Her screams go on and on. No officers come. They are too far away to hear.

&

Michelle rejects the anonymity offered her when talking to reporters.

"She began calling out she could not breathe," she tells them. "The shower is a converted mop closet," she adds.

&

When an officer finally comes and unlocks the shower door she finds Big Baby slumping and unresponsive. The officer calls for backup and more officers quickly arrive with an automated defibrillator. They start CPR immediately, then wipe the water from Tiffany's chest and apply the electrode pads one above the right breast and the other on the left side below the armpit.

They shock her heart but breathing does not return. The inmate stretcher crew bring a wheelchair and lift Tiffany. She dies before the ambulance arrives.

Michelle, who witnesses it all, says, "She died in front of my neighbor's door."

&

Reading over the reports of Tiffany's death, I am impressed by Michelle Angelina, her articulate appraisal of what went so terribly wrong. While she doesn't blame the individual officers, she excoriates EMCF's Administrative Segregation rules, which mandate sick inmates must be handcuffed to belly chains and locked into showers.

I imagine the panic Tiffany experienced being locked inside a steamy converted broom closet and unable to breathe. Michelle believes inmates would have cared for Big Baby better than the Medical Unit hospital staff, who treated Tiffany's difficulty breathing and dry hacking cough, the signature notes of COVID-19, as a common cold.

The wild animal hunter will always be bringing his bounty into the wet markets where the cages are stacked. Badgers, ostriches, wolf puppies, salamanders, snakes. The punishment cell, the locked shower, the windowless room, the cage are the universal means of imprisoning. The air trembles with their terrified silence.

&

I think of the different ways an inmate can be hurt by the virus writing its name inside the body. Tonight I read that New Jersey legislators may pass a bill that will release prisoners who are within one year of their release date. This would mean 20% of New Jersey's prison population is likely to be freed. Murderers, but not sex offenders.

Will Krystal, who is five years from her release date, number among those freed prisoners? By the numbers, it seems not.

&

I feel guilty for complaining about the new world, the one that looks more like Krystal's realm. We want to find the lost street that leads back to normalcy.

At the beginning of the outbreak, on my last day in the office, I crossed Third Avenue to the Astor Place subway station. The construction workers had finished digging up the Cooper Union triangle, and the earth no longer had the look of gashed flesh. Asphalt covered almost everything except the tiny park where three magnificent trees thrived.

As I did every weekday, I threw seed to the flock of pigeons that roosted in the trees. They descended, like a single magnificent hundred-winged being. A month later I returned and they mobbed me. If this abandonment goes on deer will return to the park. Already the ghost deer watch from the trees near dusk.

&

There are masks hanging from every nail in our apartment; we have fresh masks in boxes. Masks have crawled into my sleep. Rob insists that when we leave the apartment we wear not only a mask but a shield. The last day of July is hot.

Rob and I walk together outside for the first time in months. Our custom has been for only one of us to leave the apartment at a time. We are heading to Fed Ex to pick up medical supplies for our cat.

Like inmates lining up for Count, we walk in single file, easier to dodge others and to keep our distance from those not wearing masks. The stakes are high, life and death.

&

The moon is so much brighter as it shines over a contagion. Last night a pink super moon rose over the megalopolis—an inflated lung, a humid marigold.

Although Krystal knows lockdown only too well, she does not feel satisfaction that the wider world is tasting a morsel of her reality. She wishes she could be one of those city dwellers leaning out of their window and cheering; she wishes she could take that humid marigold in her arms.

AFTERMATH
Weehawken, New Jersey

Krystal unlocks the door to Room 37 and pushes in. The heat thrusts back like a fat crowd of people at a discount table. There is no breeze, and her head and chest ripen with perspiration.

The unmade bed is no longer a snarl of soiled sheets. Draymond has stripped the bedding and dumped it, and only the mattress remains. She walks closer and notices the blood soaking it.

The man knocks outside. "Lisa?"

Raising the mattress and flipping it over, she sees nothing. Not Jennifer fighting, arching up. Not Jennifer's nose spouting red bubbles.

"I'm right here," she answers in her low voice, a voice deeper than the one you'd imagine coming out of her soft face, her heart-shaped mouth. Krystal's voice is older than she looks; husky, a little Lauren Bacall but more monotonous. Expressionless. If her voice was dough, it had been flattened by a rolling pin. The Coke can sweats and she lifts its cold to her forehead. The carbonation stings and she treasures the prickling, hurting swallow. A sob catches in her throat. *I'm doing this for you.*

&

On her last day as a prostitute she's 20 years old, and the lean man with the nest of wrinkles is her last sex with a man, her last day in the free world.

I love you, I love you.

&

Did you know Krystal went back to the murder room?

So the detectives claimed.

The future is already asking the question.

&

The detectives who first enter the room talk about the unspeakable filth and heat—almost ninety degrees, the air conditioner not working. The crime scene in shambles. The calendar reads July 27, Wednesday, twenty-four hours after the murder, yet it will always be a steamy July dawn becoming a reeking hot day in room 37 in the Park Avenue Hotel.

"Jennifer didn't scream," Krystal said.

Candida Moore's Victim Impact Statement states, "A while later, when Krystal entered the room after hearing Jen's screams, she witnessed him violently beating her in the face."

The story is a shape-shifter, and what happened there stays there, in a room obliterated by a wrecking ball.

&

Now, instead of the 85% rule, the law may be changing. Inmates who were sentenced to more than 20 years while under the age of 24 will serve 65% of their sentence. If the law actually changes, Krystal will be released almost five years sooner.

I look forward to a normal bed. Wearing real clothes and shoes. Eating good food. Not being told what to do all day. Peace and quiet. Learning how to drive. There is so much I want to do.
—Krystal Riordan, Inmate #661387

Even when she is released, Krystal will be marked. For some, she will always be the girl who watched, the kidnapper, the accessory after the fact. The JEN-SLAY HOOKER: the one who lives on while Jennifer Moore walks endlessly along a dark highway.

For some, Krystal can never repay the debt she incurred in that Weehawken hotel room. But my own experience with impulsiveness and bad judgment has shown me that life sometimes does give us a second chance, and that we must seize it. We cannot fully abandon our former selves, but we can go beyond them.

I cheer Lucy as she struggles with her new freedom. And I hold out much hope for when Krystal leaves EMCF for a halfway house, and then moves into the wider world. Krystal looks forward to helping women and children who have been abused or are in abusive relationships. She wants to share her story with others. As an inmate she has struggled to grow, she has undergone therapy, she's taken college classes and shone in them. She's been a friend to me and many others, and is known for her generosity.

How will she fare on the outside after spending over half of her life incarcerated? How will she navigate the unfettered world? So many wants. She wants to wear real shoes and clothes again, to eat real food, and to learn how to drive.

&

I still mourn Jennifer's terrifying death.

I mourn the four-year-old Krystal. She will always be lying in bed with her sisters and crying from hunger. The oldest sister finds them cold Spaghetti-O's and dill pickles. I mourn the day the sisters are separated. Krystal can't stop screaming while policemen carry her to a waiting car.

I mourn so many lives blighted by violence, abuse, or neglect. Sometimes, I mourn for the whole world as its inhabitants fight, shoot, kill, are caged, and fall to an immune system that attacks itself—or a terrifying virus that floods their lungs. There is a new world coming into being, born from wildfires and hurricanes, from pandemics and destruction of habitats, from a poverty of compassion.

&

During the shutdown the birds whistle and chirrup from midnight to dawn. Do they always sing?

There is irony to be found in the fact that years after I made an emotional and practical commitment to these incarcerated women, a pandemic has made virtual prisoners of me and my little household, along with much of the country.

But I'm among the lucky ones. There is order in my day world, this neutral space, this home office, where my best self must support, serve, and work. The days move along, and on my desk, the financial statements abide with me. In these pandemic days, I interact remotely with my co-workers, but even when we shared a physical space, I had a secret life that I didn't share with them.

They may have heard that I write, but few are interested. I keep my real life to myself. I don't talk about it; I nurture it by practicing my art. My focus stays on my work and on the important people in my real life—like Rob, like my friends Lucy and Krystal.

I type, in my one-handedness, the financial statements. Year in, year out. Like Krystal, I am serving my time; me in my cubicle and she in her unit. I want to keep talking about how two girls—one buried in me, and the girl in Krystal—meet in some illusory place. Maybe in that place, we can both walk free.

Disclaimer

While this is a work of creative nonfiction, other than Krystal Riordan and Lucy Weems, inmate names and identification numbers have been changed to protect their identities.

Acknowledgements

The author wishes to thank the editors of the publications in which essays from this book first appeared, sometimes in an earlier version.

Another Chicago Magazine, Columbia Journal, Exposition Review, Into the Void, Isthmus Review, Jelly Bucket, Ocotillo Review, So to Speak, Stone Canoe, and *Tarpaulin Sky.*

I owe a debt of gratitude foremost to Krystal Riordan and Lucy Weems, who shared first their friendship, and then their stories of life as incarcerated women. You, my writer-friends, I can hardly begin to name all who deserve a gift basket so I'll begin with a special thank you to Jill Hoffman and the Glass Table Workshop-- the splendid Alice Jurish, Robert Steward, Jack Herz, Dell Lemon, James Trask, Dorothy Friedman, Raquel Solomon, Kevin Arnold, and Anna Halberstadt for their encouragement. Many thanks to the Two Bridges Writers Group and the insights of Walter Cummins, Astrid Cook, Tony Gomes, Talia Carner, Henya Dressler, Susan O'Neil, Laura Weiss, Pamela Walker, and Joanna Laufer. Thanks to Rosalind Palermo Stevenson for her graciousness and unstinting support that has meant more than I can say. Thanks to Tony Burnett, my publisher at Kallisto Gaia Press, and to the brilliant editor Mary Day Long whose work helped shape the book. Rarely does life give you much more than you expect and Mary is one of those rarities. My gratitude goes out to Cynthia Anderson, Scott Perrizo, and Michael Weston, whose friendship has endured through what seems like many lifetimes. Lastly but not least I thank my partner, Rob Cook, who has listened, inspired, and motivated me in the years of my involvement.